M.O.P.S.
Price, $3.50

My Own Particular Screwball

BY AL SCHACHT
Edited by Ed Keyes

The Clown Prince of Baseball came close to never making the team at all. Al Schacht's mother was a hotheaded little Jewish lady who was determined that her son give up the game and become a rabbi. But Al stuck to it, became a fair pitcher, and eventually made the major leagues, only to have some difficulty in staying there. It is as a comedian—the greatest zany ever to eat a meal off home plate—that Al Schacht has made his mark in baseball.

A sore arm plagued Al while he was with the Giants, and it came back to let him down at crucial points throughout his playing career. Hence the clown routine. It doesn't take a very good arm to send the bleachers into fits. It just takes a triple-play sense of the ridiculous—and this Al has in abundance.

This rollicking biography is filled with marvelous stories about the Golden Age of Baseball—stories about Babe Ruth, Lou Gehrig, Tris Speaker, Hans Wagner, and all the rest. It is also an inspiring object lesson in tolerance; Al was one of the first Jewish players and took almost as much abuse in his time as Jackie Robinson did many years later. Al's recollections stretch back over four decades of baseball. And they make wonderful reading.

JACKET DESIGN BY JEROME KUHL

BOSTON PUBLIC LIBRARY

my own particular screwball

my own particular screwball

an informal autobiography by

AL SCHACHT

edited by ED KEYES

DOUBLEDAY & COMPANY, INC., garden city, N.Y., 1955

to my **Mother** and **Father**

foreword

When the rumor got around I was going to write my autobiography, some wise guy said I was too illiterate to write a book. After looking up "illiterate" in the dictionary, I decided I ought to print my diploma from P.S. 42 in the Bronx, New York, on the first page of the book. That way, the readers, if any, couldn't help but believe I was educated enough to write a book. This book, anyhow.

But I couldn't find my diploma. So I went to the president of the New York Board of Education and told him my story, hoping he might issue me a new one. But he said he couldn't just hand me a diploma. I reminded him I graduated from P.S. 42.

"Suppose you say you were graduated from Yale," he said. "Should I give you one of their diplomas?"

I told him I didn't go to Yale.

"No kidding!" he snorted at me.

Finally he gave up and asked what year I graduated. I said 1909. I pitched for P.S. 42's baseball team.

He said, "I'm not interested in your pitching."

According to my record, nobody ever was.

He said he'd have to look up my school record. Two hours later he came back and said he couldn't issue me a diploma because the records showed I'd spent four terms in 4B and had never gotten out of that class. (Which was understandable, because my teacher was stuck on me and was waiting for me to grow up.)

foreword

But I said to him: "My friend, if I never got out of 4B, how did I get in 5A?"

"You must have sneaked in," he replied.

Being very anxious to get that diploma, I next asked him point-blank what my next move was. He said I'd have to go back to P.S. 42 and finish 4B before I could get a diploma.

So, if you happen to see me pitching for Public School 42 in the Bronx next season, you'll know why, and you better be there the first inning.

my own particular screwball

chapter 1

I came into this world very homely and haven't changed a bit since.

There is talk that I am Jewish—just because my father was Jewish, my mother is Jewish, I speak Yiddish and once studied to be a rabbi and a cantor. Well, that's how rumors get started.

The fact is, I am Jewish, plenty Jewish. And I was never allowed to forget it when I was a kid. Nor sometimes later on in life. Now I see others getting slapped down because of their religion, and it makes me feel bad; it doesn't seem to happen to me so much anymore because now I am considered a "success."

There always was something blocking my way. It was either because of my religion, or because I was sickly as a kid and then ill for years afterwards; even my mother blocked my path for a long time.

All kids, by a certain age, think they know what they want to be when they grow up. Some want to be doctors, others engineers, others cops: some even want to be Good Humor men. The only thing I ever wanted to be was a big league baseball pitcher. I believe it's as honorable a profession as any other, and often more rewarding. But my mom didn't think so. According to her, anybody who had such ideas was a no-good. She was sure I would turn out to be a loafer and a bum. In a Jewish family, a young fellow was expected to work or go to business school to prepare for work.

My mother was always very religious. She still is. As I write this, she's a grand old lady of eighty-five. She's Orthodox Jewish, which means she has always strictly observed every belief of the old Hebrew faith, with an extra powerful respect for God. It's safe to say Mom ruled our family. Whatever ground rules we had, she made them.

And whenever the rules needed enforcing, she used her homemade, double-lash whip. Although she's a tiny woman, she never hesitated to whale the stuffing out of me or my three brothers, but especially me. She tried to drill into us a deep sense of love for our fellow men and just as deep a faith in the Almighty. She even hoped I would turn out to be a rabbi. When I finally wound up a professional ballplayer, with a cut of tobacco in my mouth trying to strike out Babe Ruth, it was about the only argument I ever won from her.

But I think it was my dad, God rest his soul, who taught me what has proved to be my most valuable rule of living: to keep trying in spite of any setbacks. It is strange that my father should have been the one to give me this idea because he was a mild-mannered man whose sole aim in life was to work hard at his trade and provide as well as he could for his family. He would leave the house every morning at seven and return at six in the evening. Then he'd have dinner, read his newspaper and doze in an easy chair. He loved us and he was gentle. But the discipline and the counsel, as well as the washing and cooking, he left to Mom. He didn't smoke or drink, and I doubt if he swore more than once or twice in his life. He died when I was twenty.

My father was a skilled locksmith and ironworker. An immigrant from Russia, he was only in this country for a few years when he'd gained respect as one of the most skilled craftsmen in his line. He received the highest wage of any locksmith in those days, twenty-five dollars a week.

Once, when I was small, my father let me help him in his shop for a whole week, while he sweated to perfect a mysterious, special kind of iron door. It must have been one of the toughest assignments he ever had, because he'd leave the shop discouraged in the evening, eat dinner even more quietly than usual and return to the shop at night to keep working on it. Finally, one night I went back to his shop with him, and after watching him for a while, I said, "Pop, if you're having such trouble with this idea, why do you keep working so hard at it?"

"Son," he said, "remember this: if you ever want to do something, don't go around asking people if you should do it or not. Have faith in your convictions and give your ideas a good try."

I never forgot that. Especially because it happened he was creating this special door for none other than the White House in Washington, D.C. Theodore Roosevelt was President. And when my dad did install it at last, the President was so delighted he called him in to personally congratulate him and even gave him an order to make another set of beautiful iron doors for the White House. No immigrant was ever prouder than my father.

My mother and father followed a dream. They left what in Russia were considered comfortable circumstances to come here and start from scratch. My dad, whose name was Samuel Schacht, was born in 1863, the son of a prominent farmer. Mom—Ida—came from an aristocratic family. Her father was a learned rabbi, and in their village the old man was sort of like an umpire in baseball. Any crisis that arose and a vital decision was needed, the people would go to Mom's father, my grandad, for advice. And his decisions were always final, too.

Sam and Ida were married in 1887. Right away the government tried to conscript my dad into the Army, although he wasn't up for the draft. As I said, he was a fine locksmith, and the authorities wanted to put his skill to good use in the military, saying he wouldn't really have to soldier. But Sam and Ida were too much in love just to accept this latest government oppression, so they decided they would flee Russia and head for America, where two of Dad's brothers, Barnett and Max, had already settled.

After making elaborate plans, they joined another small group of refugees and tried to sneak across the Russian border with fake visas which they'd bought from the family of a deceased neighbor. Everything went as smooth as vodka and they were just about safely out of the country when the border guards, somehow tipped off, seized my father and dragged him back into Russian territory. My mother escaped with the rest of the party.

The police threw Dad into a jail situated on the Russian side of the border. Meanwhile, my mother, frantic with worry but, as usual cool under fire, set about contacting friends of her father's. Their first move was to sneak a harmless roll to my father's cell, having bribed the guard. Inside the roll was a note telling my father to keep his chin up and his mouth shut, warning him not to admit he was married for fear the secret police would cross the border and capture Ida too. Then these friends began snuggling up to the local police authorities, and it wasn't long before some coin crossed palms and my dad blew the joint. He rejoined my mother, and they arranged passage on a boat to England.

They lived in London for fourteen months. Rather, I should say they existed, for my father couldn't find work. Unemployment was high, particularly in such a specialized trade as locksmithing, and a Russian immigrant who could barely speak English stood no chance against the many native craftsmen who also were having a hard time. So, in order to eat, my mother, who had never worked a day in her twenty years, wangled a job cleaning furs in a fur factory.

Finally, my dad, swallowing his pride, wrote to his brothers in America asking if they could forward money so that he and Ida could get on a ship and cross the Atlantic. Barnett and Max sent back only enough money for one passage, saying that was all they could afford, and suggested my father come to the States alone and send for Ida later. Dad was very bitter at this setback and found it hard to break the bad news to his wife. When he did tell her, my mom shyly said she'd managed to save some money in the year she'd worked, which she'd planned would keep them going a while when they did reach America. Joyously, with her savings and the money his brothers had sent, my father bought tickets on a crowded cattle boat.

My uncles Barnett and Max got Sam and Ida a two-room apartment on the top floor of a four-story tenement on Catharine Street in New York City. It was the best they could afford and they considered themselves lucky to get that. The house they moved into looked just like the one alongside it, and the one alongside that—row after row of gray, dirty, tired old buildings all the same height. Inside, they were damp and smelled from stale odors of food. The halls and stairs were dim and rickety and lit only by candlelight. The tenements lined block after block of the sad-looking cobblestoned streets that made up what is known as the lower East Side. This was the sort of environment I would know practically all of my young life.

By the time I was ten, my family had lived just about everywhere in the metropolitan New York area. Starting with Catharine Street, at the age of three I found myself in Brownsville, Brooklyn. When I was six, we moved back to the city, to East Ninety-fourth Street. Then, to East Ninety-second Street, out to Bayonne, New Jersey, and on to the Bronx. Next stop was Plainfield, New Jersey, which was as close to high society as I ever got. But back to the Bronx we went and finally stayed, from about 1902 on. But not in any one place. Any neighborhood you visit in the Bronx, people will tell you the Schachts lived there once. In fact, my mother and sister, Esther, still have an apartment on Walton Avenue, near the Yankee Stadium.

As for Catharine Street, let me say right away that that's where I was to be born. Anybody who has ever made any kind of success in life usually claims to have been born in the slums of New York's lower East Side, so why should I be different? I remember at least two famous personalities who came from that street: Al Smith and Jimmy Durante.

Going from east to west on Catharine Street, you'd see pushcarts selling bananas, or secondhand shoes, sweet potatoes, or hardware. On the other side, going west to east, you'd see more pushcarts, selling ladies' underwear, men's socks, marinated herring, blintzes. It was like an outdoor department store, except that in a department store you don't have cats and dogs chasing each other under and around the counters, fire engines racing up and down the aisles, cops chasing the salesmen and mothers flinging bologna sandwiches out of windows to grubby little kids.

My dad got a job as an ironworker. Mom set up housekeeping, and the Schachts had one corner of their dream nailed down.

Sam and Ida wanted children badly, as most young married people do who are so much in love. Their shabby surroundings and lack of money didn't bother them, as it does many couples today. They just trusted in God, knowing He'd take care of them and allow whatever was best for them. But, married two years, Ida still showed no sign of pregnancy, so she went to a doctor a short while after they'd settled in Catharine Street.

After examining her, the doctor grimly told my mother she would never bear children. She was stunned and bewildered and she worried for a long time.

But within months, Ida was pregnant. She was delighted and afraid at the same time, and so was my dad. They remembered what the doctor had said, and they felt something was bound to go wrong. But the thought of possibly having a child made them pray harder than ever. The doctor kept a very close watch on her and tried not to show how worried he was. For what he hadn't told her was that if she had a baby she probably would die.

In 1890, three years after their marriage, a son, Louis, was born to Sam and Ida Schacht—an American citizen. Mom had no ill effects. The doctor was amazed; but Catharine Street was as happy as if a black cloud had suddenly rained pennies from heaven. Friends streamed into the Schacht apartment. They sat around staring wide-eyed at Mom and Lou, and Mom showed off the baby from every angle.

When a second son, Alexander—that's me—came into the world on November 11, 1892, the doctor really was popeyed. This time he wasn't the only one.

chapter 2

By the age of twenty-five, my mother had had two children, and she was still fit as a fiddle. But it began to look as though the doctor's prediction about sickness and death was coming true about the second kid, me. From the time I was born, I was nothing but trouble and worry to my parents, particularly Mom. I was weak and underweight and generally sickly. There were times I would be so sick that my mother would have to take me to a doctor as often as three times in a week. I was having wicked stomach pains and cramps, but none of the doctors seemed able to figure out exactly what was wrong with me.

I never really got rid of those stomach pains. And starting when I was fifteen or so, they got worse. For years in desperation I went to countless doctors and hospitals to learn what was ripping my gut to shreds. It was not until I was thirty-six years old that one wise doctor discovered what my trouble was—but I'm getting ahead of my story.

I don't remember much about my sister's coming into the world. All I know is, she was born in Brownsville, just before we moved to East Ninety-fourth Street in the city. Actually, I didn't know what was going on in our family, if anything, because I never was in the house. I was always out playing and only came home at suppertime. Even my brother Lou and I were like strangers at times. As I've indicated, Lou was, and is, very bright, and he was not much for playing the silly games outdoors that I and most other dopey kids did. He preferred to study, especially music. He must have been born with a string instrument in his hands, because he was nuts about playing the violin. In later years, he always seemed to have either a cello, violin or bass which he played constantly; and on the side he practiced with a mandolin and banjo. My mother was sure Lou would turn out to be a great musician, and she kept after me to be more like him instead of running around throwing rocks at tin cans or playing catch with other kids.

Lou wound up a designer.

Anyway, besides our differences of interests, another reason I didn't see much of my older brother was because he had started in school at Brownsville. I didn't begin my high education (?) until we'd moved in to East Ninety-fourth Street. It began one of the roughest periods of my life.

Between East Eighty-fifth and Ninety-sixth Streets, from Lexington to First Avenue, was a rough neighborhood for Jewish families to live. Lexington and Third Avenues were where the Irish lived, and the Italian section extended east to Second and First Avenues. The Irish or Italian gangs, or both, were always roaming around looking for Jewish kids, who were scattered about in that part of town and not organized. The real Jewish ghetto was up around

106th Street, I found out a little later. So a Jewish boy had to grow up tough, and shrewd, in order to outsmart the toughies or, in case he got caught, to try to fight his way clear. I soon learned the only times we Jewish kids would get a breathing spell was when the Irish and Italians were battling each other—which was pretty often at that.

Shortly after we'd moved to Ninety-fourth Street, into a four-story tenement which was quite a bit like the one on Catharine Street, I saw which way the wind was blowing. Since I was always out on the street playing, I was a prime target for the Irish kids. After a couple of beltings around, I knew I had to think of something or else get my brains scrambled before I was seven.

Among Orthodox Jews, it is forbidden to build any kind of fire, or even light a match, on Saturday, the Sabbath. Since it got just as chilly on Saturdays as on any other day, we either had to get some Gentile to light the fires in our stoves or else freeze. I got the idea to go around and recruit the Irish kids in the neighborhood to go to Jewish families' apartments Saturday mornings and light the fires, for a fee naturally. I decided not to ask for a cut for myself. All I wanted was to get on the right side of the Irishers.

So I became East Ninety-fourth Street's official Agent for Gentile Firelighters. It took me a few weeks, but I soon gathered quite a stable of firelighters. They were making easy money, three cents a fire, and I wasn't getting beat up any more, although the Irish kids still let me know they didn't have any use for Jew boys. They didn't take me into their crowd, but they did tolerate me, which was all I wanted. And they shielded me from the Italian gangs who came looking for trouble.

I didn't make out as well when I started first grade in school. Always full of fun and not much interested in being confined to a classroom for so many good play hours, I would spend my time mimicking and making fun of my teacher from the back of the room. Of course, I was also trying to make a hit with the Gentile boys.

One day, I forgot to bring my books to school. The teacher, a woman, asked me to read and I said I left my books home. So she called me up to the front of the room and asked me what was the matter with me.

I just looked down at the class and giggled.

This must have driven the teacher off her rocker, because she spun me around and slammed me right across the mouth with her open hand, screaming:

"You damn kike!"

It hurt but I didn't cry. I just hauled off and kicked her in the shin. She yelped and started to shake me until I thought my teeth would come loose. I wrenched away and ducked behind her desk, and she ordered me home. I beat it out of there fast.

I couldn't go home and tell my folks I'd been thrown out of the first grade class. So each morning I'd make believe I was going to school, then would head for Central Park and play baseball with the other kids who were playing hooky. I got away with that for a whole week, until the teacher sent a note home asking what had happened to me. My mother hustled me back to class in a hurry, and I had to stay after school for another week. But it wasn't so bad: the kids in that school were so unruly, there seemed to be more of us staying after school than there were during the regular classes.

My scheme for keeping out of trouble didn't last as long as I'd hoped. One afternoon I came into the house with a big mouse on my eye. My mother had a fit. I'd been playing ball down in the street and another boy had come along and accused me of having stolen his rubber ball. When I denied it, he popped me in the eye. With all the rest of his gang standing around waiting for me to make a wrong move, all I could do was take it. But to make it worse, this kid called on his father, and the old man came up and slapped my face. Mom was half crying and half shaking with anger; she told me to tell my dad when he came home from work.

When I told Pop what had happened, he didn't say a word. He just took my arm, and we marched downstairs and along the street. When we got to the corner candy store, I spotted the kid's father inside and said to my dad:

"There's his old man, in the candy store."

My father walked into the shop without saying anything. The

other man was about the same size as Pop, who was a six-footer, but heavier. Dad tapped him on the shoulder, and when the man turned, wham! smack on the nose. The guy staggered back against the counter, his eyes popping and blood spurting out of his kisser. Just then I saw the kid who'd accused me running out of the store. I grabbed his sleeve and belted him. My dad strode calmly out of the store—I ran like hell myself.

From then on, my duties as agent for the Irish kids were suspended. And I had to fight my way to and from school each day, like the other Jews in the vicinity. As time went on, I won my share of fights—in fact, I can truthfully say that while I didn't always *win* a street fight, I only really got licked once.

That one defeat was actually a one-punch job; it happened because of my brother Lou and because I'd got too cocky. As I've said, Lou rarely got into any scrapes because he was always in the house studying or practicing on his violin. He attended the same school I did, two grades ahead of me. Going to school, and music lessons after school, were the only times he would be seen outdoors. One day he came home from a music lesson with a gorgeous black eye and his violin smashed. Right away, I jumped up and went to defend his honor. As older brother Lou brushed me off.

But I did some investigating in the neighborhood and learned that a tough, oversized kid in my own class was the one who had roughed up Lou. So I went to work on him. Every day for a week, as we stood on line waiting to go into school, I'd sneak up and give this tough guy a small poke for exercise, and promise I was going to get him for my brother. He was bewildered, not understanding how a midget like me had the nerve to threaten him. Meanwhile, I was taking great pride in wearing him down, figuring I'd soon have him rattled. Fortunately, I never told Lou what I was doing until long after.

Came the day I finally decided to let him have it. My strategy backfired. I waited for him after school, then ran up and cried:

"Okay, wise guy. Now you're gonna get it."

I never saw the punch. It exploded square in my face, and the next thing I knew I was galloping toward home with a puffed, black eye and minus a tooth. So, the way it turned out, the dentist got more satisfaction out of the whole thing than anybody.

None of this, of course, increased my respect for music; nor, for a while, my brother Lou. On my sprees to Central Park, I'd developed an interest in baseball, and as the months passed I came to love the game more and more. Instead of just roaming around playing aimlessly in the streets and back alleys of the slums, I patched up an old glove and spent nearly all my time playing catch in the street or "one o' cat" in the vacant lots nearby. In my enthusiasm, I'd often ask Lou to come out and play catch with me. But his inventive mind was always hungry for study, and he'd just sneer at me. I found I resented him sometimes, partly because of his lack of interest in kids' games and probably partly because I was a little envious of his brains.

My mother didn't help to build up admiration in me for Lou, either. She was always comparing us.

I'd come straggling home day after day with torn clothes and cuts and bruises, and she'd shout at me in Yiddish:

"Why can't you be more like your brother Lou? He's always studying and practicing his violin. All you do is stay out and fight and play with the bums!"

Finally, one night Mom was more boiled up than usual and was stomping about the apartment wailing about how I was turning out to be a no-good because I was always out in the streets. Dad put his arms around her and said:

"But Mama, he doesn't steal, does he?"

That's what my pop cared about. And because I respected him so, I don't believe I ever could have gone really wrong.

But Mom kept trying to make me the way she wanted me to be. She was deeply religious, and she made us kids go to synagogue every Saturday. But I was always looking to sneak out of the synagogue to play ball; so particularly on holy days, she would escort us inside and take a seat in the first row where she could keep a sharp eye on *me* in the children's section. But, accepting the challenge, even then sometimes I'd manage to get away.

Then, she got smarter and had a rabbi come to the house twice a week to give me Hebrew lessons, still convinced she would make me be a rabbi myself some day. I remember one day he asked me to recite what I'd learned about *Avrom*, which is how the Hebrew sounds for *Abraham*, the great Jewish prophet. I was tired of studying, so like a clown I asked him with a straight face: "Abraham who? Abraham Lincoln?" Mom belted me across the kisser. But you know something?—the rabbi asked me who Abraham Lincoln was.

It was many years before Mom saw how useless all these efforts were. But even then she refused to give in completely, and made me sing Jewish hymns to her before I could go out and play. It wasn't that I didn't believe in the Jewish religion. I just couldn't understand my mother's strictness, and so I guess I rebelled. I told my dad once how I felt, that I didn't like going to services so much and taking extra instruction. Dad didn't attend synagogue as often as Mom wanted either, but he had a quiet, devout faith in God.

I said, "Who could possibly be as religious as Mom wants me to be?"

"When a person is religious," Dad said, "he's got to believe in God and live by His word."

It was years before I understood what he meant.

I began to hang out in the Jewish section around East 106th Street, and we were constantly at war with the Irish and Italian gangs. Most of the battles were fought at no-man's land, between 106th and Ninety-sixth Streets.

There was one big free-for-all that I remember, which was so violent it put an end to the war for a while. It was brought about by a professional prize fight at the Lenox Athletic Club, 106th Street and Madison Avenue, between Leach Cross, a Jewish boy, and One-Round Hogan, an Irishman. There was a large, mixed crowd there, and neighborhood interest was high. Adults and even children stood out in the street waiting to hear who won. Cross kayoed Hogan. And as the crowd poured out and broke the news, an Irish kid socked a Jewish boy.

That started it. The Jews banded together and headed for the old Ruppert's brewery at Ninety-fourth Street. Most of the guys were bigger than me, but I tagged along to watch the fun. A bunch of Micks were waiting in front of the brewery. With about fifteen on each side, they went at it. (I'd like to point out here that in those days respectable gangs used only fists, not knives or zip guns like the little gangsters do today.) It was a lulu of a brawl. It lasted maybe twenty minutes, and when they were all worn out, they broke it up and staggered home. That ended the all-out warfare for a time.

But there were always individual fights. Any time of the day or night you could see someone slugging somebody else in the street. There were muggings, and window-breaking and shouting in the streets at all hours. Women didn't go out at night; neither did kids, of course. Except one evening my dad sent me down to the bakery in the next block, and coming back I got into trouble.

Running along, I saw a man lying in the cobblestone gutter a few doors from our house. I went over to him cautiously and smelled the liquor fumes ten feet away. There was blood all over his face. Evidently, he had tripped and fallen off the sidewalk. He was moaning, so I tried to help him up. Since I was only seven and pretty light even for that age, I was struggling when a young fellow about twelve came from nowhere and pushed me.

"What are you doing to this man, you?" he barked.

"He's hurt," I said. "I was trying to help him."

He came over and shoved me again. "Trying to rob him is more like it," the boy said.

Then three others about his age came around the corner and he called to them, holding me by the arm.

"This little Jew bastard was trying to heist the drunk," he said. They looked puzzled, so he turned and swatted me across the ear with his fist. That woke them up. One of the newcomers let go with a right to my belly and the others piled on.

They gave me a real going-over. When I limped upstairs, my clothes were torn and dirty and I was cuts and bumps from head to foot. My mother took one look at me and held on to the door or she would have fainted. Then she cried to my father:

"Look, he can't even go to the store for five minutes without getting killed." Even Dad seemed mad at me this time, although I showed him I still had the rolls from the bakery.

By a strange coincidence—and it really was coincidence—the very next day we moved out of that block to Ninety-second Street, near Second Avenue. That was the Italian section. Out of the frying pan into the oven.

chapter 3

Soon after we settled in a four-room apartment in another four-story tenement in Ninety-second Street—every house was the same to me—my mother presented us with twin brothers, Mike and Herman. It was a tough spot for kids to be born in, although that never stopped any of the families in the neighborhood from multiplying. Kids swarmed all over the streets and tenement stoops. We all looked alike, with raggedy clothes that featured torn stockings and worn-out knees on our knickers, like badges of honor. Any kid who came around looking neat was a sissy and due for a rough time. Everybody was poor, and nobody was supposed to try to make it look any different.

The kids were even wilder in Ninety-second Street than in Ninety-fourth Street. There was more stealing, for one thing. They had a pet trick of charging the herring wagon and swiping as many herring as they could. The poor Italian man who drove the wagon wouldn't know which of them to chase, and he'd get all flustered and red-faced and scream at them in Italian as they dashed off. They'd pull the same stunt with the bread wagon; and when a load of fresh vegetables arrived at the grocery store, they'd steal pocketfuls of potatoes. With all this loot, the gang would retire to an empty lot in another neighborhood and cook themselves a feast. Actually, they couldn't have been badhearted boys, because if they had any food left over, they'd head for the stables on our block and feed bread or potatoes to the horses. The kids would also steal sugar from the counters when they went shopping with their mothers, and save it for the horses.

As usual, because I was "a Jew boy," I wasn't admitted to the gang. So I had to stay honest, whether I liked it or not. It was just as well, because many of the kids got in trouble with the police; or else, the cops would often grab a bad kid and drag him home to his old man where he'd get a beating. It seemed in that block all you'd ever see was boys scattering in all directions. When a cop even looked like he was heading our way, the stampede would start, and in twenty seconds the street would be cleared, just like in a Western movie when the hero and villain are getting ready to shoot it out on the main street. Or if it wasn't the police, it was the mothers tearing around trying to catch their problem children. Although the neighborhood was mostly Italian, there were several different nationalities living there, and it certainly was a strange sight and a strange noise when a posse of mothers charged through the streets shouting their different lingoes all at once.

As for me, I took to playing ball with an Italian boy named Tony, who was my age. Tony had a ten-cent catcher's mitt of his own and we used to play by ourselves almost every day. Tony never seemed interested in stealing or fighting like his friends.

One afternoon, I was playing catch as usual with Tony in front of our house. It was the first day, I recall, that we got the idea to make believe we were a big league pitcher and catcher. He had the mitt, so he was catcher. It was the first time I ever thought of being a pitcher, and when I saw how good I could throw a ball, I knew what I wanted to be when I grew up.

Tony and I had just had an argument. He was calling balls and strikes, and he called one a ball which I thought was a perfect pitch. We got very excited and started raising our voices. We were nose to nose, shouting at the top of our lungs, when Tony let loose with a string of Italian. I didn't understand the language, but I knew damn well he was giving me hell. So I stepped back and let him have it: *Fa brond zoldst du weren*, which is Yiddish for "I hope you burn up." (Of course Yiddish really can't be spelled out like that; it has its own characters. But that's the way you'd say it.) That stopped him cold.

Just then the elderly Italian woman who ran the grocery store near our house and who lived across the hall from us came out on the front stoop and called to me to go in the house, my mother wanted me. I made believe I didn't hear her, thinking my mother wanted to bawl me out for playing ball again. But the old lady insisted, and after a while I figured if I didn't go in Mom would only come after me with her strap. So I went inside.

We lived on the ground floor in the rear. As the Italian woman and I went towards the apartment, she said:

"Your mother was crying."

I didn't know what she meant. But when I got inside I saw my mother sitting alongside one of the twins' cribs, weeping. Lou was standing near her with a kind of dumb expression. I looked to the Italian lady, and she said:

"Your little brother Herman is gone."

I walked over to the crib and peeked in. Herman was lying there very quiet. Mom put her arm around me, and hearing her sobbing I felt tears in my own eyes. It was my first experience with any tragedy, and I was dazed by it. I found out later what I should have known all along. Herman was sickly—Mike was all right—and finally the doctors had given up hope of pulling Herman through. In those days, a baby's first year was its most critical one. I wasn't too sure what dying meant, but I somehow knew that Herman wouldn't be there any more.

Mom sent a message to Dad at the iron shop, and he got home an hour or so later. He didn't cry. He stared down at the crib for a long time; then he took Mom in his arms. Mom hadn't said much all afternoon, just gazed at the crib misty-eyed. When Dad held her close to him, she said in a low voice:

"Anyway, he's with God, Sam."

I went up to my father and tugged at his sleeve, asking what would happen to Herman. Dad squeezed my hand and only said, "Go outside, son." When he spoke in that deep voice, I knew he meant it and walked away.

Next day, according to Jewish custom, little Herman was buried. The short service was held right in the apartment. A little later Tony knocked at the door and asked me to play catch with him.

Very sorrowful, I told him I couldn't because of a death in the family. He went away. The next time I saw him, he apologized for having cursed me in Italian.

It didn't figure that we'd stay on Ninety-second Street much longer after Herman's death. It had become a sad memory for the Schachts, especially for my mother. So, within a month or so, we packed up and moved to Bayonne, New Jersey.

We got a three-room apartment over a hardware store, in a house where a cousin of my mother's lived, named Blumenthal.

There were Mom and Dad; Lou, me, Esther and Mike.

We lived on a kind of quiet street, with trees and old private houses and stores. A block away was an enclosed baseball park, the first one I had ever seen, where the Bayonne A.C. team played every Sunday. People flocked from all over Bayonne and other parts of Jersey on Sundays to watch the games, which were semi-professional. And it was there that I saw my first organized ball game and was convinced my aim in life was to become a star pitcher.

I got to know some of the neighborhood boys by playing ball. They weren't as rough as the crowds back on New York's East Side, but they were pretty hard guys and managed to get into plenty of scrapes. So I felt at home. A mob of maybe fifty kids used to stand outside the Bayonne ball park on Sunday during the game. We couldn't afford to pay our way inside, so we'd wait for a foul ball or home run to be hit over the fence. There'd be a wild scramble, and the one who came up with the ball and returned it to the gatekeeper got in to see the game for free. After a few Sundays of getting nothing but lumps for my trouble, I figured out an angle.

Getting three other guys together, we sneaked down to the ball park one Saturday night. While one boy kept an eye out for the watchman, the rest of us dug a big hole underneath the board fence at the rear of the park. Then we covered up the hole with some boards we'd found, so the watchman wouldn't notice the hole on his rounds.

Next day, we went down just about game time and hung around behind the park. Since I was the leader in the plot, I waited until last to crawl through the hole. The others had made it inside and

I was halfway in when suddenly somebody grabbed my legs. My head and chest were in and my legs and fanny out. Finally, the watchman gave a terrific yank, and pulled me outside. But the jagged bottom of the fence gashed the back of my head. I knew he must be steaming mad, and I waited for a licking.

But the watchman stared at me and cried: "Your head! What happened to your head?"

When I saw blood on my hand where I'd touched my head, and seeing he was frightened all of a sudden, I played it for all it was worth. Flopping over on the ground, I groaned and made horrible faces.

He picked me up and hurried to his office, where he washed off my wound and sent a boy to get tape and bandages from the players' bench inside the park. He cut my hair around the gash and bandaged it. I was still playing weak, hoping he'd feel sorry for me and let me into the game for free. But instead he sent me home.

My mother yelled at me when I told her what had happened. Again she called me a no-good, and said it "serves you right," adding sternly:

"I don't want you ever to hang around watching those bums play again."

It wasn't so much that I was a disobedient boy that I disobeyed her the very next Sunday—baseball just had gotten into my blood and it seemed there was nothing I could do about it.

Besides that, I couldn't stand the thought of having been outsmarted by the watchman.

The following Saturday night, we dug another hole at a different point under the fence. And the next day I made it—I went first. The watchman spotted us again just as the last kid slipped through. He searched for us all during the game and we kept moving around through the crowd. But I didn't mind this inconvenience, because I was seeing my first big ball game and I was thrilled.

In fact, I was so carried away that as soon as the game was over, I dashed out onto the field, grabbed the home team's bats and helped the team mascot, who was smaller than me, to carry the equipment into the clubhouse. The "clubhouse" was the rear of a saloon next to the ball park. I stood around with stars in my eyes watching the players undressing and listening to them bull about the game. But I did receive a minor disappointment: my heroes all guzzled what seemed like barrels of beer, and most of them had beer bellies.

Anyway, I hung around so much after that and was so eager to please, that pretty soon they made me official, full-time mascot. I don't remember what happened to the other poor kid whom I'd pushed out of a job.

My biggest thrill was being allowed to shag fly balls with the players in practice. And I got paid ten cents a game, plus a brand new baseball (slightly used).

It wasn't long before one of those baseballs got me into another jam. Getting a kid to "warm me up" one day, I pitched a few, then wound up and let go with my fast ball, just as I'd seen the Bayonne pitcher do. It sailed high and away and smashed the big plate glass window of the corner saloon. Who comes roaring outside but the watchman from the ball park, who happened to be the saloonkeeper's brother. This time he didn't let me fake him out—he dragged me home and made my dad shell out five bucks for the damage.

Right then and there, Mom put her foot down—down my throat. I was forbidden ever to play baseball again, or even think about it. I thought my career was ruined. And I didn't even get my ball back. Although the incident did disprove the unkind things said about my pitching when I finally did get into professional baseball—that Schacht couldn't throw a ball hard enough to break a pane of glass.

After a while, I worked up enough nerve to ask my dad for fifteen cents for another ball. I told him I wouldn't play with it, but just wanted to have it, period. He stroked his chin, then handed me the fifteen cents.

"But don't tell Mama," he said.

I couldn't stop thinking about baseball. I found an old bathing suit of my father's, a gray one with long legs which looked from a distance just like a baseball uniform. So, on Sundays I'd sneak into it, with a pair of Dad's socks, and with my ten-cent glove and fifteen-cent ball would sit up on our second-floor porch nonchalantly flipping the ball. When the fans streamed out of the ball park after the game, they'd see me, and I got a kick imagining they thought I was one of the players.

I'd forgotten about baseball, almost—when a great calamity struck Bayonne. The oil tanks caught fire. One by one the big tanks spouted flames, and try as they might, the firemen couldn't seem to stop the huge blaze. Even citizens pitched in to help, but the fire got worse and worse. It began to look as though the whole city would go up in flames.

The third day of the fire, my father came home from work early and announced we were getting out of Bayonne. He said other families were already leaving the town and that he'd rented an apartment in New York, in the Bronx. That night we traveled to our new home at Third Avenue near Wendover Avenue, at about 170th Street.

Mothers forget. Mom didn't even know it when, shortly after we moved to the Bronx, I organized a baseball team. It was my first real team, and naturally I made myself the pitcher. In those days, there was always some place to play ball in the Bronx, some parts of which were still wide open spaces. But we picked nearby Claremont Park because in one corner of the field was a big boulder about ten feet high which was a perfect backstop for the catcher. I was so eager about playing, I laid out the diamond myself, going by measurements in a beat-up old rule book I'd bought. We used flat rocks for bases, and the field was so near the street that the center fielder had to play out in the middle of Webster Avenue. But we loved it. We played there so often we wore out the grass, and after a while you'd have thought that field had been originally designed just for baseball.

It was while playing ball that I found my first real friend, Banty Halberstadt. He was a little, stocky, bandy-legged guy who looked like he'd have to press his pants over a barrel. He was not only comical looking—he's the only one I ever met who had a bigger nose than me—but he had an hysterical laugh that used to break me up. No matter what I'd say, he'd laugh. And he'd encourage me to clown. Maybe it was Banty who really got me started in that direction. Anyway, we got along perfectly, even though the rumor was that Banty's family had more money than anyone else in the neighborhood. It seems he owned the biggest sled around; and the Halberstadts lived in a fancy apartment house—they had brass railings on the front stoop of their tenement. Banty and I were in the same class at P.S. 2. We found we both were crazy about baseball, and when he said he was a catcher, that was the clincher for me. From then on, Schacht and Halberstadt was the battery for the neighborhood sandlot team.

I began to eat and breathe baseball, even reading the newspapers, which I'd never had time for before, to follow the scores and standings of the big league clubs. The Giants were my favorites.

Because I'd taken to hanging around the newsstand on our corner every evening to catch the late scores in the final editions, the newsdealer asked me if I'd like to distribute the *Sports Bulletin* for him. The *Sports Bulletin* was a cardboard about the size of a newspaper page which was printed in a local shop every day about 5:30 P.M. and contained all the baseball scores and late racing results. Kids like myself would distribute them to all the saloons, where they would be displayed behind the bar.

I got paid fifty cents a week. My route was only a few blocks, from Wendover Avenue to 149th Street along Third Avenue, but it usually took me a good two hours. There was a bar on every corner and some in between. And as I'd go from one saloon to the next, I'd grab a handful of smoked herring off the free lunch counter.

When I'd finally get home, I'd be too full to eat dinner. All I could do was drink quarts of water, I was so thirsty from that herring.

That was one of the things my mother always brought up when she yelled at me for not gaining any weight. I was growing taller but was still skinny. At the ages of nine and ten I weighed the same as I did at seven. My folks had forgotten that first sickly year of my life and never considered there might still be something wrong with me. But every now and then since I'd been five I had been getting sharp cramps in my stomach; they'd last only for a few minutes at a time, then were followed by diarrhea. But I was too busy playing to think of this as any worse than an inconvenience.

Meanwhile, I also first suspected I was partially deaf. At school, my seat was in the back of the room, and I had to tell the teachers I didn't hear them when they asked me questions. But they just thought I was lying on top of everything else.

About this time, my mother, who, as I've said, had decided I should be a rabbi, realized I had a pretty good singing voice. You'd never know it today, but then I was an alto. So she took me to audition for Cantor Cooperstein's Jewish choir, which specialized in singing at services on Hebrew holy days like Rosh Hashana and Yom Kippur. I sang a popular song of the day, "Oh, Bedelia," for the cantor at his home, and he liked me and signed me for his choir.

If the word "signed" sounds commercial, that's just what it was. I was to receive five dollars for singing on three holy days. At first, we'd agreed on four dollars, but he let me have a solo, so the ante was upped to five dollars.

I didn't think too highly of the cantor because I thought his voice was not as good as it was cracked up to be. So, even before my first appearance with the choir, I got bored and began sneaking off to play in the streets with my gang. We were rehearsing for the Rosh Hashana services at the time, which would be my debut, and the cantor had to complain to my mother that I was skipping rehearsals. I tried to explain to Mom that I didn't like the cantor, but her mind was made up that I was going to sing. On Rosh Hashana, she marched me to the synagogue personally and sat in the first row with her eagle eye on me.

By now, Dad had gone into equal partnership with Uncles Max and Barnett in their iron shop, and we started doing a little better financially. Then, a relative of ours who lived in Plainfield, New Jersey, persuaded Dad to buy a house there, away from the crowded city. That was what Dad had always wanted, so he bought an old two-family frame house in Plainfield for twelve hundred dollars, with five hundred dollars down, and we packed up and were off again. Banty Halberstadt and I were practically in tears when we said good-by.

Many society people, Wall Street executives, lived in Plainfield then, on beautiful, fashionable estates. But our house was in the poor section, the other side of the tracks you might say. Still, no matter how poor people were, every family seemed to own their own home. There were very few apartment buildings. Our house was on a quiet, tree-lined street; we had a big back yard with wild cherry trees and room for a vegetable garden, and to me, from New York's slums, this layout looked like a big farm.

School in Plainfield seemed strange after the rough-and-tumble of the New York public schools. In P.S. 2, for example, we used to whoop it up in class. But in my new school, the kids were all quiet and polite. And instead of departmental teachers, we had one old hag about fifty who was tough. Her favorite punishment was rapping our knuckles with the edge of a long ruler. During exams, she walked up and down the aisles trying to catch somebody cheating.

I always felt she hated children. One thing was sure, she hated me. Almost from the first day I joined the class, she rode me. Right away she began popping questions at me, and if I didn't have the answers—which I usually didn't—she'd haul me up to the front of the room and embarrass me.

"Really, I don't know what's the matter with you, Schacht," she'd say. "You don't study, you don't pay attention; you're stupid. You'll never amount to anything. . ."

I suppose she might have had some reason to dislike me. While I was never a mean sort, I tried to get acquainted by pulling pranks on some of my classmates, just for laughs. But they never appreciated my sense of humor and would tell the teacher on me.

Once I found a field mouse in our back yard. Trapping him, I tied string to his tail and brought him to school the next day. On my way in, I planted a piece of cheese near the teacher's desk. I sat on the aisle, so during the class, I took the mouse out of my pocket and let him go. He made a beeline for her desk. She jumped up on her chair with a shriek. He kept running around her desk, and three times she jumped up on that chair, raising her skirts and yelling. When I saw how scared she was, I let go of the string and the mouse scooted out of the room.

But somebody squealed on me, and the teacher chased me out of school, suspending me for a week. When I returned, I really went to work on her. For three days I drove her nuts by rolling a wooden matchstick under my shoe, making an annoying rumbling noise.

Then, I trapped another mouse, and one morning I slipped it into teacher's desk drawer. When she opened it, out he jumped. Boy, was there a stampede! Girls screamed and boys raced all over the place trying to catch that mouse. When things settled down, teacher knew who to blame—I was the only one doubled up laughing.

So, she kept me after school and made me write, "I am a bad boy," a thousand times. By the time I finished, I almost believed it. Even today, people compliment me on my excellent penmanship, and I think "I am a bad boy" is the reason why. But my one consolation at the time was that that crabby teacher had to wait around until I finished writing.

One thing I did like about Plainfield was a job I got making deliveries on Saturday night for a big grocery store, Mann & Co. They let me drive a wagon pulled by a tired old brewery horse, my pay being a bag of my favorite cookies, ginger snaps. Later I talked them into letting me help behind the counter when deliveries were slow. But they made the mistake of letting me weigh the ginger snaps for customers. I bet I ate more than I sold.

One day, my dad was repairing our front fence and sent me for a bag of nails at the hardware store. I got on my bike and was passing through a colored neighborhood when I noticed a bunch of Negro boys standing on a corner. They blocked my path and I had to stop.

"What are you, wise guys?" I bluffed.

"That's a nice by-cycle y'all got, sonny," one of them said. There were about six of them grinning at me. Then the kid who spoke grabbed the handle bars of my bike and threw me off onto the ground. He started to get on it and ride away, but I jumped up and sent him flying into the gutter. The rest of them piled on me. We all went down, me on top of the bike and them on top of me. I kicked and punched and bit one kid on the wrist. Everybody was shouting.

Just then my sister Esther, who was learning to go shopping alone for my mother, came out of a store and saw the brawl. She ran back inside the store screaming for someone to "help a poor boy who's getting hurt." When she ran out again and saw I was the "poor boy," she started to cry and jumped on the colored boys, scratching and kicking them. A couple of shopkeepers and passersby finally broke it up and chased the gang.

I made sure Esther was safely on her way home, then got on my battered bike and continued to the hardware store. I was supposed to buy fifteen cents' worth of nails—instead, I got five cents' worth and spent a dime for a heavy ax handle. I rode through the colored neighborhood with the bag of nails hanging off the handle bar and holding the club in one hand. When I got home, Dad bawled me out for getting only a nickel's worth of nails and sent me back with my ax handle for the other ten cents' worth of nails he wanted. I didn't tell him what had happened. Returning this time without a weapon, I rode far around that neighborhood.

What with unpleasantness at school and things like that, I was glad when Mom and Dad agreed it was too tough for him to commute so far every day. As for myself, I now knew I wasn't for this country living—I was just a gutter rat at heart. Anyway, they sold the house, at a loss, and we moved back to the Bronx.

chapter 4

Brook Avenue where we lived next was only a few blocks or so from the place we had when we first moved to the Bronx. The first thing I did when we got back was look up Banty Halberstadt. The old battery had a grand reunion.

I'd returned to P.S. 2, and even though I had to drop back another year to the fifth grade—from one thing or another, my development was being retarded—I was as happy as a pig in goo. We were living in the same old tenement type house as before, without a big back yard and sunflowers; and Mom was still after me to study my Hebrew and stop playing ball with "the bums." But it was good to get back to my own kind of people.

Came the spring, I was back playing baseball more than ever. When the star pitcher of the local team came down with appendicitis, I volunteered for the job and it wasn't long before the sick kid found himself permanently off the team. I was so serious about baseball by this time, and had developed into such a good pitcher, that when it came to baseball the other kids all were beginning to look to me as leader.

When the team sort of dissolved, Banty and I organized a new outfit called the Tigers. And to make sure the team stuck together, we immediately joined the local league of teams from the various neighborhoods in the area. All but our team were named after streets—the Mixdales, the Bathgate A.C., Fulton A.C., the Websters, Washington A.C. and the Tigers.

Naturally, I was captain of the Tigers as well as ace pitcher. And the thing I wanted most was uniforms for the players. None of the other teams had uniforms. The trouble was, uniforms cost two dollars apiece; with nine kids, we needed eighteen dollars, which might as well have been eighteen thousand.

But we tried. Whipping up a minstrel show in the basement of one of the tenements, we drew up our own signs and advertised it all over Brook Avenue. We charged five cents. It was all in blackface. I was interlocutor and also featured soloist. My biggest laugh was supposed to come from this:

"Why did the chicken cross the street?"

"To get over."

The show didn't cause a smash—not so much because it wasn't funny, but because hardly anyone showed up. After five minutes, we called it off because of threatening attendance. Later we found out the price had been too high.

A week later, on a Sunday morning, the Tigers all chipped in to challenge the Mixdales to a ball game at three dollars a team. (Actually, the chipping in was a bit unbalanced: one of the kids, Nate Adler, who was considered the block's richest child because Mr. Adler was in the diamond business, talked his dad into putting up two-fifty of the Tigers' three dollars.) The teams gave the six dollars to a neutral bystander to hold and then went at it.

This is where an old nemesis of mine named Rough Rider came

back into my life. I had known him when I lived in the Bronx before and had engineered a beating he took from a boy named Joe Jeanette. Now Rough Rider was the manager of the Mixdales ball team and although we won the game, nobody could find the guy holding the money.

Not afraid of Rough Rider anymore, I marched right up to him and spouted:

"I think you guys stole our money!"

With a shout he takes a swing at me. I duck, but before I can straighten up, Banty is all over Rough Rider. Then it starts. Both teams got into a terrific brawl. When we all staggered off the field, we had plenty of lumps but no six dollars.

Realizing we'd never get the loot if I didn't think of something, I went to Rough Rider at school the next day and said:

"I'll pitch for your team next Sunday against the Bathgate A.C. for nothing if you'll get back our six dollars."

The Bathgate team was run by a guy named Brud, a real toughie, who was Rough Rider's most hated rival. He'd do anything to show up Brud, and, knowing I was a good pitcher even though we didn't get along personally, Rough Rider said:

"Okay. Tell you what. I'll give you five dollars now out of my own pocket"—the bum had our six dollars all right. He'd never have had five bucks of his own—"and the other one after the game Sunday. I want to make sure you show up."

I didn't show up. Hell, five dollars was almost as good as six. Sunday night, after dark, Rough Rider and his gang came to our house and threw stones at our second-floor windows, trying to make me come outside. I didn't budge. They would have beaten my ears off. Even though I explained to the family that the guys were just kidding around, I didn't fool my mother. She ranted at me for being a hoodlum and slapped me. Even my dad looked at me strangely. He would have defended me in any trouble, but I think that night he wondered what I was up to.

Next day, on my way to school, I saw Rough Rider and four or five guys hanging around outside, waiting for me. I grabbed a rock. When I approached, I said:

"Any of you guys come near me, I'll let you have it in the face."

Just then, a real tough guy passed by: the brother of big Brud, Rough Rider's rival. This guy was known as the best fighter around. He saw what was about to happen, so he ran over to me.

"You come with me, kid," he said, spitting toward the gang. "They're not gonna touch you." And we walked right through them.

The Tigers finally got their uniforms, but in a strange way. Lou Sugarman was a basketball player with the famous Henry Street Settlement team downtown, where many top players started out, including Nat Holman of the original Celtics and later C.C.N.Y. coach. Lou also played baseball and booked games for a team called the Swathmore A.C. from the lower East Side. He contacted me one day and asked me if I'd like to pitch for his team at Van Cortlandt Park, far up in the wilds of the north Bronx. He promised if Swathmore won behind my pitching, he'd not only give me a twelve-dollar guarantee but would put up the remaining dollar the Tigers needed for uniforms (we already had the five dollars I took from Rough Rider).

That was some team Sugarman fielded. They were a bunch of hard guys, some of them thugs. Especially the shortstop and first baseman—Lefty Louie and Gyp the Blood. Those two were executed for their part in the famous Rosenthal gambling murder about ten years later.

Anyway, I saw I had to pitch like never before or I might be a very sorry boy. We won. But in the excitement after the game, I got separated from the other players and found myself lost in the north Bronx, which was all country then. So, without money, I hiked for a couple of hours until I found civilization and walked the five miles back to Brook Avenue.

Sugarman made good on his promise. A few days later, he himself went to the Halperin Sporting Goods Company and ordered nine uniforms, with "Tigers" across the fronts. We were so excited when we got them that some of us wore them to school for a week.

Although my mother was dead set against my baseball playing, I felt I might be able to swing my father to my side. At least, he never said anything about it. He'd never even seen a ball game. So, one Sunday I persuaded him to come with me to Crotona Park to watch the older fellows play. It was the Suburbans. The Suburbans first baseman was John (Jafsie) Condon, who afterwards was a public school principal and baseball coach and later became famous as the go-between in the Lindbergh case who was to have delivered the ransom to the kidnapers but never got a chance to. He was a fine ballplayer at this time, but he had a horrible temper. Every few innings he would explode and start loud arguments with the umpire.

My dad didn't say much the first few innings. The only question he asked was: "Sonny, who is that player who everybody shouts at?" I said that wasn't a player but the umpire.

After another of Condon's outbursts, Dad said: "Is the loud one the boss of the two teams?" I told him Jafsie just had a lot of spirit.

"Somebody ought to chase him away from the game," Pop said.

Finally in the eighth inning the umpire had enough Jafsie and did boot him out of the game. So what does Dad do? He sticks up for Condon.

He says: "You told me that fellow was not a player. How can he chase the poor man from the game?"

Dad never did get straightened out about baseball. I guess I didn't do a very good selling job, for he never saw another game.

Meanwhile, Mom still was struggling with her own dreams for me, as with the other kids. Another boy, Larry, had been born to add to her work.

I was still singing in Cantor Cooperstein's choir, but Mom was getting dissatisfied. In those days, there weren't enough synagogues to handle all the Jews who turned out on the big holy days, so cantors would hire a hall and hold services there. They'd sell tickets to the services to get money to rent the hall, and have billboards printed with pictures of the choir for display outside, almost like a theater. That's the way Cantor Cooperstein had always operated. But now Mom was getting ambitious for me to sing in a real synagogue.

She heard of a synagogue choir that needed a singer and applied for the job for me. Synagogues paid much more than cantors who used halls, and there was great competition. When Cooperstein heard about this, he immediately raised my salary from five to seven dollars. When Cooperstein's boy soprano heard I would be making more money than he was making, he quit and got the synagogue job my mother had heard about. And he wound up making more than I did with Cantor Cooperstein.

The holy season in 1905 was the last time I ever sang well. I ruined my voice singing at a party celebrating Nat Golden's birthday, which lasted all day and half the night. Harry Ruby, who was to become a top songwriter, was there and played the piano, and I sang for hours. Suddenly toward the end of the evening, my voice cracked in the middle of a song. The next morning I was very hoarse. I never got rid of the frog in my throat and still have it.

I thought my mother would never forgive me. In fact, she refused to believe my voice was gone. When I dropped out of Cantor Cooperstein's group, she kept scheming and found me another singing spot. Her plan was real cute, because it also served to prevent me from playing ball on Saturdays, the Jewish Sabbath.

She arranged for me to sing every Saturday at services far downtown. As I wasn't permitted to ride the trains after sundown Fridays, I'd have to leave the Bronx after school Friday, take the El downtown and report to an uncle who ran a laundry on Henry Street on the lower East Side. I'd spend what was left of Friday delivering packages for him, to pay for my lodging and meals overnight. His home was to the rear of the laundry, but I slept on a cot in the back of the store. Saturday morning, I'd go to sing at services in a nearby synagogue. Then I'd have to return to the laundry and just twiddle my thumbs until nightfall. Orthodox Jews aren't allowed to ride trains between sundown Friday and sundown Saturday.

It took me a while, but I began to suspect there was more to this than just forcing me to continue singing. Mom was definitely keeping me off the sandlots on Saturdays. It didn't work for long, though, because the cantor downtown soon saw my voice was shot for good and he respectfully requested my mom to take me the hell out of there.

So I got to playing ball again on Saturdays. There didn't seem to be anything else Mom could do to stop me, short of chaining me to a bedpost. But one Saturday, when I came home all dirty and sweaty and my clothes torn, she got so mad and was so frustrated, she beat me until I was blue. I remember backing into a corner and saying:

"If you keep hitting me, I'll die."

"Maybe it would be better, you bum," she said in Yiddish.

And I said, "If I die, I want to be buried with a baseball and glove on my chest."

Dad turned to her and said in Yiddish: "I don't think you'll ever stop him from playing baseball."

I was working part-time pretty steadily now. My next job was Sundays during the winter racking up balls in The Gimp's pool parlor in the basement of a house at Park and Wendover avenues, under one of the Bronx's first Nickelettes. The Gimp was a punk who, along with big Brud and a guy named Nig, ran the neighborhood. I had long arms, and used them to line up the balls instead of racking them. The Gimp hired me because he got a kick out of watching me rack up this way. I earned twenty-five cents each Sunday.

Spending so much time in the poolroom, I got to play pretty good myself. So, just before closing, The Gimp would challenge anybody to play me for fifty cents a game; he'd back me up, then bet on me. One night, The Gimp took me aside.

"Listen, when you play later," he whispered, "you're gonna blow a lot of shots the first time around."

"Yeah? How come?" I asked.

"There was a mugg around here before bragging what a great player he is. I want you to get into him for some cash. He's coming back, see? I'll give you the sign, and when he sees you missing he'll be anxious to play you."

"Then . . . ?"

"Then you let him have it, understand? We'll take him good."

I played a game with one of the regulars in the poolroom who was really good. The guy beat me bad, 50–36. In the middle of the game, The Gimp gives me the high sign that our pigeon has arrived. And when I lose, I can see The Gimp looks pleased because he thinks I'd been faking as we planned. But I hadn't been. The Gimp builds me up big for this guy.

And he bets heavily on me when the "sucker" challenges me to a game. I got murdered, 50–21. The Gimp lost all his dough, and I lost my job and was even barred from the parlor indefinitely.

Next I got a job after school working as a scene shifter at the Crystal Film Company, which had one of the first movie studios in this country. It happened to be located, by the way, right across the street from The Gimp's poolroom. I saw a sign outside the studio saying, "BOY WANTED," so I went in and got myself hired for five dollars a week. This was the big money.

After a time, I wangled a bit in a silent picture as a newsboy. It was *East Side, West Side*. When the film was finished I didn't get a chance to see it at the studio preview, so I had to search for it all over the Bronx. Finally I caught up with it at a Nickelette, Jacobs Moving Picture House. A Nickelette was nothing but a few rows of camp chairs lined up in the rear of a store, say a grocery store, in front of a screen. A projector would shoot the silent films onto the screen. There was usually a piano for mood music during the picture and between reels. It was called a Nickelette because admission was five cents.

I sat through three showings of *East Side, West Side* and never saw my scene. When I stormed back to the studio to ask what happened, the director told me they'd had to cut my bit out. So I quit. There's no business like show business.

I figured I got revenge by landing another scene-shifter's job at the Biograph Studios at 174th Street and Crotona Avenue. That was where the great Mary Pickford got her start. I remember watching fascinated as Mary and her leading man, whose last name was Johnson, rehearsed romantic scenes. The motion picture business was interesting, and I hoped like mad to get a part in one of Biograph's pictures. I'm still hoping. As a matter of fact, the closest I ever came again to a movie role was in a picture very close to my heart, about thirty-five years later. I was rejected at the last minute, and that time it really did break my heart. But I'll tell you about that later.

I was now about thirteen and, like many kids, I had all sorts of schemes for making money. Among other things, I learned to make my own baseballs, since we rarely could afford new ones; and soon I learned I could make money selling them. In case you ever want to go into the homemade baseball business, here's my secret: you take a small ball of gum and carefully wind wool around it until it's packed hard and just about the size of a regulation ball. Then you can use some cheap leather for a cover and box-stitch it on. That's where my baseballs were distinctive—I was an expert box-stitcher. I sold them for fifteen cents apiece.

I also took to making and selling my own lemonade before games I was to pitch and during games when I wasn't playing myself. My favorite stand was Claremont Park, because most of the spectators there knew me as a promising pitcher. On hot summer days, other kids would try to sell their lemonade, too.

Claremont Park's main baseball diamond was on top of a hill; and I noticed that the other lemonade peddlers made their stuff at the bottom of the hill where the water fountains were and then lugged it up to the field. By the time they'd get to the top of the hill, the sun would have melted the ice and they'd have warm lemonade.

So I got the idea of making mine under the bleachers, on the hilltop. I'd lug my ice up before the game and keep a thick towel over it to keep out the sun. This way, I was the only kid selling real cold lemonade. I charged three cents a glass.

I transferred during the sixth grade from P.S. 2 to P.S. 4, our family having moved from Brook Avenue to Wendover Avenue, around the corner from the house on Third Avenue where we'd first lived in the Bronx. I never thought about it at the time, but now that I recall how often we moved, I wonder if the fact you got a month's rent free every time you moved to another apartment house had had any influence on my parents.

Quite a few celebrities have come out of Wendover Avenue: songwriter Harry Ruby, Harry Cohn, now big shot of Columbia Pictures, and Bert Gordon, known to many as "The Mad Russian," to name a few. Most of the kids in the block hung out at Barney Ginsberg's candy store, where we'd buy—or swipe—candy before and after school, and play with—and usually break a few—toys.

Suddenly I was a musician.

It began when I came home from school one day and found a piano in our front room.

"You're not gonna try to make me take piano lessons now, are you?" I protested to my mother. She said the piano was for Esther. Mom had bought it on the installment plan, with no down payment and two dollars a month probably for life. Esther began taking lessons and proved a natural. When Lou and Esther took to playing certain classical pieces together, I couldn't help but get interested.

So I bought a drum, secondhand for two dollars.

As with everything I get excited about, I couldn't get enough of it. I played the drum everywhere, in the street, at home—I damn near drove poor Lou and Esther crazy. Finally I even pounded the drum at school. P.S. 4 wanted two kids to play the drum and piano to march the students to and from assembly. All I knew how to play was a roll, but I'd try to follow the piano played by Harry Ruby. We had those kids hopping.

Meantime, Lou, who'd graduated from P.S. 4 and was attending Morris High School, was forming a small dance band with two other fellows who played piano and cornet. I asked him if I could make it a quartet with my drum.

We practiced for a week at home. Then, every Sunday, we'd take the El downtown to the lower East Side and search for weddings or big affairs. We played for a good many parties and got paid off usually with marinated herring.

That summer, we kids got our first chance for a vacation in the country. A relative who had a farm in Napanoch, New York, in the Catskill Mountains, invited my folks to come up for the summer and bring the family. They also said it would be all right if Lou brought along a couple of friends, but that they'd have to sleep in the barn. Lou figured we might get some business for our band up there, so he invited the piano player and cornet player.

My dad stayed home. He had an important job to take care of. He'd made quite a reputation for himself, and his precision ironwork was used by such people as Admiral Dewey, the rich Gould family, Secretary of State Hayes, and the great architect Stanford White. He'd just begun work on the job for President Roosevelt, which I mentioned earlier.

The farm at Napanoch was more run-down than most of the tenements we'd lived in. The farmer grew very few crops and the only animal he had was a broken-down horse that limped. Lou and I joined the other two musicians in the barn with the horse.

The first day we got there, we made plans to throw a dance to introduce our band and make a name for ourselves. So we all chipped in, hired a hall in town, which was about five miles from the farm, and had circulars printed to advertise the dance on Saturday night. We made Esther cashier.

Esther didn't have a thing to do. We didn't sell one ticket; nobody showed up. We were busted.

A few days later, Lou answered a newspaper want ad for a band to play at a dance at a resort hotel some miles away. They hired us sight unseen. To get there, we hitched the limping horse to a hay wagon. On the way, I lost a drumstick, and we stopped the wagon while I climbed a tree and broke off a thin branch to use as a stick.

When we began playing at the dance, I left a tuft of leaves on the end of the "drumstick." When I heard the crowd laugh, I clowned for all I was worth. At intermission I even told a few jokes.

After the dance, the manager came to me and said:

"Kid, you're a lousy drummer. But you ought to stick to clowning. You're pretty funny."

But in spite of that evening, that summer on the farm was a bust. The band wasn't making any money, and I was getting tired of it after the first kick had worn off. Nights on the farm were deadly, so black and still. Besides, I missed playing ball on the lots back in the Bronx. I began to feel I was wasting the summer in the Catskills.

So I said to my mother one day: "I feel sorry for Pop."

"So?" she said.

"Well, he's all alone down in the hot city while we're all enjoying ourselves up here."

She thought about it for a moment. Then I dropped my bombshell.

"Ma, I think I'd like to go back and keep Dad company. It's not right he should be so lonely."

In a while I had her talked into it. Not only did she think it was a good idea, but a sparkle in her eyes told me she was proud I was so concerned about my father. Her hope for me was renewed.

After just three weeks on the farm, I boarded a train and went home alone. It was wonderful. All I had to do all day was play. When it got too hot, the apartment was always cool and empty. And when Dad came home from work, I would have supper waiting for him. He and I had a swell stag time.

I got a job in the Nickelette that opened in the neighborhood. Harry Ruby and Harry Cohn, now president of Columbia Pictures, were working as song pluggers then, and they played the piano at this Nickelette. This place had something new: while reels were being changed, they'd show slides on the screen with words of popular songs of the day. Ruby got me the job of leading the customers in singing.

That summer, I made my first entry into a big league ball park. Banty and I used to hang around the Polo Grounds trying to sneak in; but it was no soap. Or we'd try to get a job selling pop and peanuts inside, but we could never get to talk to the right people. But getting to see a game itself wasn't tough. The ball park was surrounded with trees, so we'd climb a tree and have a box seat.

One day, I was up in a tree that overlooked the bleachers in left field. It was a tight game, and when Cy Seymour of the Giants belted a long hit, I got so excited, I forgot where I was. A second later, I landed in the bleachers. A park attendant started after me, but I ran underneath the stands and found the office of the concessionaire, Harry Stevens, father of the Stevens family that now operates the concessions in most sports arenas.

"Mr. Stevens," I panted, "you gotta give me a job selling peanuts or pop."

He was startled, but then he grinned and said, "Well, you look okay to me." He said to report to work the next day, and handed me a badge.

From then on I sold scorecards. Also I began to go to the Polo Grounds in the morning and practice with the players, whom I was getting to know. I shagged fly balls in the outfield. One day the great Christy Mathewson took me aside and showed me how he threw his famous "fadeaway" pitch, now known as the screwball. Mathewson always had been one of my favorite players, along with Roger Bresnahan, Dummy Taylor, Mike (Turkey) Donlin and Hooks Wiltse. I even cleaned the players' shoes in the clubhouse before the games. I was in my glory.

In those days, Giant manager John McGraw was in the habit of going back to his apartment to rest after the team's morning practice. After he'd gone, the players would start a crap game under the grandstand. I took to watching them, and one day second baseman Billy Gilbert, who'd been losing heavily, said to me in desperation:

"Hey, kid. Pick up those dice and see what you can do for me."

With trembling fingers I rolled them. It was the first time I ever shot crap. I made six straight passes, and Gilbert broke even. Some of the others seemed to resent this, so they made me leave the game, assigning me as lookout to watch for McGraw.

I worked harder than ever to develop as a pitcher. I was building a good reputation around the Bronx as a pitcher, and teams started to compete for my services, even teams from downtown who came up to play at Crotona Park. I would pitch on Sundays for any team that would pay me a dollar.

In September of that summer, 1906, after my mother had brought the kids home from the farm, we moved again to another house on Wendover Avenue. It was one of twin red brick apartment houses side by side. Our apartment was on the third floor front. One night about seven a man came to the apartment with a subpoena for me. I wasn't home, so the man went away.

When I got home Mom was fidgety and worried.

"So, what is this soo-peeny?" she asked me. I wasn't sure myself, but I knew it had something to do with law and the courts. But I couldn't imagine why they'd be delivering one to me. I wasn't in any trouble.

The next evening, the man came again, this time with a lawyer. I was home, and they handed me the subpoena. It stated they wanted me as a witness for the defense of a guy named Hymie.

Hymie was a bum and a slickster who'd previously been suspected of a series of robberies in the neighborhood. He never played ball himself, but he acted as agent for a downtown club that wanted money games in the Bronx. I'd pitched for him a couple of times that summer, the last time just the Sunday before.

It seems a cop caught Hymie fiddling with the door of the janitor's ground floor apartment in the house next to ours. He alibied he was looking for me, and, not knowing which of the two houses I lived in, was going to ask the janitor. A strange thing was, Hymie usually hung out in a poolroom in the basement of our house. Anyway, the cops claimed he'd been trying to jimmy the janitor's door. They were out to get him and put him away. His lawyer wanted me to testify for his good intent.

So I went to court the following week. Before I left home, Mom said:

"Just remember, whatever happens, you tell the truth."

I sat in the small witness room at the Center Street Tombs downtown with Hymie's sister and brother and big Nig, the tough guy from the neighborhood, who was a pal of Hymie's. Then I was called into the courtroom. I was shaking.

The prosecuting attorney was Travis Jerome, who later gained fame in the trial of Harry K. Thaw, who'd murdered Stanford White, the architect, on the roof of the old Madison Square Garden over the affections of a show girl, Evelyn Nesbit. Mr. Jerome first asked me what I did for a living.

I said I was in the sixth grade. He said:

"The defendant claims he has hired you to play baseball for money. Aren't you supposed to be an amateur?"

I said I didn't know the rules on that, but it was true I had pitched for Hymie's team.

A little later, the judge, named O'Sullivan, who had only one arm and one eye and squinted with his good eye, said:

"Young man, turn around to me."

I had calmed down by then because I knew I was telling the truth. The only thing that bothered me was that I'd have to ask Mr. Jerome to repeat a few questions because I hadn't heard them clearly. My ears again.

In a loud voice, Judge O'Sullivan said:

"I want to ask you some questions myself, and I want only one answer to each of them—yes or no. First, has the defendant ever escorted you to your home?"

"No, sir."

"Has he ever rung your bell to call for you?"

"No, sir, not that I know of."

"Did he ever stand down in the street and talk to you or anyone in your family up in your window? Or did he ever see you come out of your house?"

I thought for a second. "If he did, Judge," I said, "he'd know where I lived."

That killed the case. Hymie was acquitted. But not for long. Several years later, when I was with the Giants, we played an exhibition game at Sing Sing prison. Sitting in the stands was Hymie.

chapter 5

Even before they transferred us from run-down old P.S. 4 to shiny new P.S. 42 in the seventh grade, I knew I wanted to go to the High School of Commerce in Manhattan when I graduated. By now, all the kids who played ball with me had their sights on the High School of Commerce because that school had a reputation for baseball around New York like Notre Dame has in football. It seemed all the best sandlot players in the city were drifting to Commerce, and even players already enrolled at other high schools were switching. With my ambition to be a big league pitcher, and feeling I was pretty good, I figured I'd go to Commerce and find a stepping-stone to professional ball.

I damn near didn't make it to high school at all.

My troubles began—I have to admit, I brought them on myself—the very day we piled out of P.S. 4 and hundreds of boys and girls marched to P.S. 42. It was my first parade, and I played the drum and another kid tooted the cornet. The new school had been built to relieve the crowded conditions at P.S. 4, which was only about eight blocks away. We were all feeling gay, and it went to my head. I handed my drum to another kid and, wrapping my handkerchief around my head, played my drumstick as if it was a flute. *The Spirit of '76*. The teacher leading the parade must have had bunions—he stopped the parade and bawled me out in front of everybody for making a mockery of *The Spirit of '76*.

P.S. 42 was different from the other public schools. Everything was new, and the teachers were tough. In P.S. 4 we'd had pretty much our own way, in class and otherwise. But here, because kids had been transferred from a number of crowded schools to 42, the teachers cracked down, apparently realizing that with all the mixed groups the school would soon turn into a shambles if the kids were allowed to run wild.

Early in 1908, I was so anxious for the baseball season to get started, I got together a group of guys to hold preseason workouts. Our baseball coach was a Mr. Brown, also our history teacher, and we had a fine ball club.

Mr. Brown had other troubles, though, in history class. Namely, me. While they wouldn't have had to burn down the school exactly to get me out of it, I was not really much of a student; not in history anyway. I just couldn't stay interested in things that happened hundreds of years before, although I did know what happened in 1492—the rumor was the country had been discovered about then, and I believed it. But actually, all I wanted to know at this stage of my life was who was pitching for the Giants that day.

So, I was not surprised when Mr. Brown took me aside about a week before final exams and said: "Al, you have a clean record in this class. You haven't answered one question all term.

"Your daily history marks are very low," he went on. "And I must warn you that if you fail your final examination next week, you will not graduate."

It was something to worry about. Besides the embarrassment of being left back, which had never happened to me, the most important thing to me was the possibility of being retarded in my baseball plans for a year. I was counting on going to the High

School of Commerce—and I shuddered at the thought of pitching again the following season for P.S. 42 and having people gossip that I was too dumb to get out of public school. My mother would kill me.

I studied like a beaver for the next week, but I just couldn't seem to bone up fast enough. Fortunately for me, I got a break.

At that time, night classes were being held at 42 for "greenhorns" who'd just come over from Europe and settled in the Bronx and wanted to learn English. The school principal, knowing I was a linguist—I could speak English and Yiddish—had asked me if I would act as "interpreter" at these night classes, which I'd done for several months.

My job was to direct the greenhorns as they stood on line each night, getting their names and addresses in Yiddish and pointing out which classrooms they were assigned to. We had *Litvaks*, who came from one part of Russia, and *Galitzianas* from another sector, and they all spoke different dialects. Although I was getting a great kick out of being an interpreter, it was rough, because every night there were mixups and confusion—they didn't know anything about our strange customs, and they couldn't understand English and I was having a hell of a time understanding their Yiddish. But it was remarkable how fast they picked up enough English to get by.

Anyway, one night, while strolling through the darkened history room—just sightseeing—I happened to open the teacher's right-hand desk drawer, and there was the history exam. It was a big moment for me: should I copy the questions, or take my chances on passing legitimately?

After a terrible struggle, I sold myself that it would be better both for the school and myself if I graduated from 42. So I copied down all fifteen questions and went home and studied them.

The test was a few days later. Mr. Brown turned around to start writing the questions on the blackboard, and I had the third answer down on my paper before he finished the first question. He'd walk up and down the aisles between questions, and once when he passed my seat, I already had the fourth answered, although there were only two questions on the board. I'd have been dead if he'd noticed. I could have wound up with a flat 100 on that exam but was too smart for that. I answered two questions wrong on purpose, knowing damn well Mr. Brown knew how lousy I was in history. As it was, I got a 96, the highest mark in the examination, and was able to graduate. Mr. Brown looked at me kind of funny when he announced it.

I know now what a silly trick that was. God knows how much better off I might be now if I had studied. Anyone who cheats, either in school or elsewhere in life, is only kidding himself.

My folks wanted me to go to Morris High School in the Bronx, where Lou was. But I made a big sales pitch for Commerce, playing up how fine a school it was for business courses, and this appealed to them. One of their objections was that it would cost twenty cents a day to send me to Commerce, which was downtown at West Sixty-fifth Street off Broadway—a nickel carfare each way and ten cents for a hearty lunch. I never did tell them why I really wanted to go to Commerce.

When I entered high school I lost my pal, Banty. Having got out of P.S. 42, he had no ambition to continue to high school. His father, who was a diamond cutter, had wanted him to follow in his footsteps, but Banty decided to work his way up in the dress manufacturing business with his older brother. So, he forged far ahead of me financially. But the important thing was Banty never caught for me after that, and we sort of lost track of each other.

I managed to get a lot of mileage out of that twenty cents my mother would give me. Four or five of us would get together at lunchtime and meander to one of the local saloons, ordering a five-cent sarsaparilla—none of us drank beer yet, which was also a nickel then. Then we'd casually wander past the free lunch counter in single file and each load up on what today might be two dollars' worth of food. I'm sure many readers remember those old free lunch counters and the great variety of foods they had. Every tavern had a sign in the window with a picture of a schooner of beer, and underneath, "BEER, 5¢," and underneath that in bigger letters, "FREE LUNCH."

After three or four visits to one saloon, the bartender usually got wise to us. So we'd pick out another every few days. At that rate, even though there seemed to be a bar on every corner, we gradually ran out of free lunches. But for a long time I managed to sock away a nickel of my lunch money every day.

I tried out for the great Commerce ball club that spring, 1909. Right away my troubles began, the same which would plague me later on wherever I went as pitcher. The first day of practice, the coach took one look at me and asked:

"How much do you weigh, son?"

"About 125," I said.

"And you're a pitcher? I think you ought to try out for some other position, say second base."

You show me a second baseman who can't hit, can't field and can't run, and I'll show you a bum second baseman. That was me, in spades. Of course, knowing damn well I was a pitcher, I didn't go all out to make the team as an infielder, but pestered the coach into keeping me on the squad as an extra pitcher. Actually, he needed only one pitcher, since games were once a week, on Saturdays. So, that whole season I never got to pitch once—in fact, I didn't even get into a single game.

For a number of reasons, that June, after Commerce finished its baseball season, I quit school. First, naturally, I was very disappointed at not having gotten a chance to play for the high school I'd dreamed so long about. Also, I was such a terrible student I felt it was silly for me to keep fighting my books.

I was also disturbed about the increasing trouble I'd had with my hearing in school. It had been several years since I realized I didn't hear as well as I should, and it seemed to be getting worse. For the first time, I mentioned it to my mom and dad, and they immediately sent me downtown to a free clinic that specialized in eyes, ears, noses and throats. As with any free clinic, I'd have to stand on line sometimes for hours. And when the doctors finally did get around to me, there was nothing they could tell me. They'd peer into my ears and blow tubes into them, which only tickled me, but they couldn't find out what was wrong. I was almost deaf many years later, when a wonderful doctor performed an operation on my ears that cleared up my trouble to a great extent.

That summer, I took a job during the week at the Cohen & Rosenberger jewelry store downtown on Spring Street as a stock and delivery boy. I also played semi-pro ball for various clubs on Sunday afternoons.

To get to play semi-pro regularly around New York you had to be "in" with a guy named Jack McGrath, a cutie who'd thought up a sweet racket for himself. Jack, who worked in the Douglas shoe store on 125th Street, was a great ball fan. Seeing so many semi-pro players drifting around scratching for games, he set himself up as a baseball booking agent, maybe the first in history. McGrath got together a set of nine uniforms, and having booked a game he'd round up nine players. He had a set of letters of the alphabet, and each week his teams were supposed to represent different upstate towns like Schenectady, Poughkeepsie, etc., which made a team more attractive to the gate in New York. All he'd do was pin the first letter of that week's town on the front of the shirts. I doubt if any of McGrath's players ever saw the towns they were supposed to be from.

So, you'd go to McGrath and ask, "Where do I play Sunday?" and he'd have a game lined up somewhere, with a guarantee all set. No matter how much you wanted for playing, he'd try to get you for five dollars less. But he did pay as high as fifteen dollars a game for a pitcher. Even so, Jack weaseled a percentage of whatever you made.

Before he knew it, McGrath had eight teams coming and going each week. It was a profitable business, and soon other sharpies came along to cash in on the baseball fever around New York. McGrath's biggest rival was Nat Strong. Strong later became the number one booker, dominating semi-pro and independent baseball in the area from his office in the old World Building on Park Row. Anyhow, Strong moved in so quickly and powerfully that a war developed between him and McGrath. If McGrath booked you to play, you were automatically blackballed from playing on any of Strong's teams and vice versa.

Finally, McGrath forced a showdown. Picking the best players under his control, he challenged Strong's most popular Brooklyn team, the Bushwicks, to an all-star semi-pro game. I pitched for McGrath's New Yorkers.

We had them beat 4-0, in the ninth inning, when my left fielder walked out on me. With two out, the Bushwicks sent up a pinch hitter named Bailey, who was a left-handed batter. Dick Mahoney in left field, seeing me break a big curve over the plate on the first pitch, figured Bailey didn't have a chance to punch the ball to left, for he knew my style of pitching and also that when a right-handed pitcher throws curves that snap in toward a left batter, it's almost impossible for the batter to hit anywhere but to right. So he walked off the field and watched me strike out Bailey from the clubhouse. I never knew he was gone. It was one of the few times in baseball history that a team finished and won a game with only eight men in the field.

I kept working for Cohen & Rosenberger right through the beginning of 1910, then quit and returned to Commerce in the February term. The ambition to play on that school's great nine still burned inside me, and I was bound to correct the error in judgement I felt the coach had made the previous season. Besides, I'd heard during the winter that Commerce's star pitcher had left school.

This time I made the team as its pitcher. And going back to high school turned out to be the smartest move I'd made yet, because I was fortunate to make such a good name for myself that it led directly to my dream, pro ball.

By the time Commerce had won three straight, the local newspapers were praising us as the greatest collection of schoolboy players ever put together. Our team was so good, we could lick many top college teams of the day. I'll never forget a game we played at Fordham College field in the Bronx against Fordham Prep—at at least, we started out playing the Prep.

By the fifth inning, with the score tied, Jack Coffey, the former Suburbans shortstop who was then coaching both the Fordham College varsity and the Prep team, had sneaked in his entire college nine against us. Even so, it was 1-1 going into the ninth.

Back then at Fordham, they had a big clock in the tower of one of the dormitories, and this clock had a loud bell which rang every day at the dot of 5 P.M., at which point all activity on the campus was to cease. Even if a guy was running for a touchdown in a big football game and that bell rang before he crossed the goal line, his score didn't count.

I came to bat in the top of the ninth with runners on first and second, and nobody out. I remember noticing the clock read exactly *ten to five*. I laid down a neat sacrifice bunt along the first base line, trying to move the runners up a base each. Fordham's pitcher, O'Rourke, fielded the ball and, in a hurry to get me at first, whirled and fired without looking. The ball conked me square on the noggin and went bouncing off into the outfield.

I saw stars and fell into a swoon. But as I'm falling, I'm smiling, because I can picture both our base runners scooting home to score on the wild throw. But just as I pass out, what do I hear?

"Dong! dong!" The bell.

I woke up later in the dormitory, and a priest was holding my hand.

"Are you a rabbi?" was the first thing I said.

He told me the game had been called, 1–1, in the ninth. Fordham had been saved by the bell. Jack Coffey still coaches baseball at Fordham, and I always kid him about being one of the best bell ringers I ever heard.

Commerce went on to knock over all opposition that season, and we came down to the championship high school game against Stuyvesant. It was to be the big game of the year, and the newspapers really played it up. Every high school kid in the city looked forward to a pitcher's battle between two unbeaten chuckers, me and Fred Banker of Stuyvesant.

Banker and I often played opposite one another in a Sunday semi-pro league. Most of the Commerce players were picking up pocket money on week ends, playing as a unit for the Emerald Club. To cover with the high school authorities, we used phony names. I was "Alberts."

The day before the big game, a Friday afternoon, the whole Commerce team was called to appear at the Board of Education for what we figured would be a pep talk. When we arrived downtown, Fred Banker and his Stuyvesant catcher were there, too. Six officers of the Board were sitting around a table. The president stood up and addressed us.

"You are all charged with playing professional baseball," he said for a starter. And he called out every player's right name and alias. We were trapped.

"Now," he went on, "the Board must take action in this case. But before we decide a verdict, has anyone anything to say?"

Me being the pop-off guy, I appointed myself attorney for the defense.

"I think I can talk for the rest of the guys," I said. "My folks haven't got a lot of money, and they really can't afford to send me through high school. I figured the only way I could really get an education was to earn some money on the side. It's been done before. In fact, right today there are college teams which play in the summer for pay, and I don't see why we should be martyrs."

From the Board members' cold expressions, you'd have thought I hadn't said a word, and they got up and went out of the room to decide our fate. Fred Banker, who was chewing a big wad of tobacco, was so sore he took the wad from his mouth and fired it up against the ceiling. It was a white ceiling. The tobacco juice splattered all over it. I knew that would be the clincher if they ever spotted it, so I moved my chair closer to the door for a fast getaway if necessary.

When the jury returned, the president was very dramatic.

He said, "Gentlemen"—which was a promotion right there—"you are supposed to be amateur athletes of good example to future students. But you've thrown away the trust put in you, for a few measly pennies. So the Board must declare you boys"—no more gentlemen—"ineligible to participate in any further scholastic athletics." We were dismissed.

The meeting was partly a success. They never did notice the tobacco juice on the ceiling.

I quit school for good shortly after this, feeling there was nothing left for me at high school if I couldn't play baseball, which was all I wanted anyway.

Unknown to me, while I'd pitched for Commerce, I'd been scouted by, of all people, a public school principal named Abe Goldberg, who also was manager of an independent semi-pro team at Walton, New York. One day after leaving school, Goldberg approached me at Bronx Oval, where I was pitching, and asked if I was interested in pro ball as a career. He offered a pitching job at Walton for four dollars a week and board.

"Big-league scouts," he added, "are crawling like ants around Walton and the other towns in our league are looking for talent. I think you have the stuff, and this would be the perfect spot to show it off."

I accepted.

Very solemn, because I would be leaving home for the first time, I announced my plans to Mom and Dad. They took it without any arguments. Mom had lost some of her old opposition to my baseball because from the first time I'd made any money playing I'd given her every penny. I think she felt I might not turn out to be a bum after all but possibly an asset to the family financially.

chapter 6

Walton was in a league composed of small towns like Oneonta, Stamford, Norwich, Liberty, Norris, Roscoe, Sidney, Delhi and others. Most of the clubs were represented by college players from such places as Brown, Cornell, Syracuse and other schools in the East. But for Walton, Goldberg recruited semi-pros, independents and what-have-you from the metropolitan New York area, and we nicknamed ourselves "the Riffraffs."

Each team in the league was financed by local merchants of the town. What it amounted to was, whoever bought twenty-five dollars' worth of stock in the club became a director and automatically a baseball mastermind. That meant, for example, that a farmer who milked cows all week was supposed to be able to judge if a player was good enough to make the team. When I arrived at Walton, I went straight to the ramshackle old ball park, which had all open bleachers, got into uniform, and walked out on the field, ready to dazzle everybody with my stuff. There was a group of men sitting together behind first base, and when they saw me warming up, they started chattering. They turned out to be the club directors, thirty-five of them. And they were deciding right then and there I wouldn't do.

After the workout, the directors called Goldberg over to them and said he should send me back to New York, that I was too young and too light. (And I'd thought I was getting strong—my weight was up to 129.) Besides, I learned later, they liked a local boy named Adams who was also trying out as a pitcher, and since I was the fourth pitching candidate and the club could only use three, they figured to dispose of me.

But Goldy stood up for me. "I saw this kid pitch," he said, "and I brought him up here knowing he could make the team. If you gentlemen don't like the way I run this club, maybe you ought to get a new manager. I'll go over to Delhi" (which was Walton's biggest rival, only eighteen miles away) "and take the whole team with me!"

So I stayed. I even got to pitch the opening game on July 4 against Oneonta, which was represented by almost the entire Brown University team. I never will forget that game—it was my first organized pro game and I won, 2–1. Also, during the game we got the flash that heavyweight champ Jack Johnson had kayoed Jim Jeffries, who'd come out of retirement, in the fifteenth round at Reno, Nevada.

It was then the practice of the Walton townspeople to present the winning pitcher, or the hero of a game, with a three-dollar meal ticket from Evans Dining Car and a ten-cent ice cream soda at McLean's Drug Store, free. But after I beat Oneonta that day, I didn't get either. The directors must have figured I'd been lucky. I won my second game, and my third and fourth—I won thirteen straight before they admitted I might have something, and then they broke down and gave me one meal ticket and free soda. After that, they came through regularly.

The meal tickets came in handier than I expected. By the time the season was nearly over, I was the hero of Walton. I recall one of my big thrills was standing in front of McLean's on Main Street one Saturday night, with the street crowded with farmers shopping or going out on the town, and seeing a wagon pass by with a fellow on the back clanging a bell. A big sign on the side of the wagon read, AL SCHACHT WILL PITCH TUESDAY. That wagon went up and down the street five times, and you can be sure I didn't miss it once.

But still I was lonely. Everybody on the ball club seemed to have a girl friend in town but me. But in the middle of my winning streak, flowers started to be delivered to me at Peck's boardinghouse where we roomed, after each game. There was never any card, but they had to be from a girl, and that scared me a bit because I'd never been out with a girl in my life. And after my tenth straight victory, a delicious cake was delivered to me, also without any message. The guys, who all knew I never bothered with girls, mostly because I was too shy, ribbed the hell out of me.

Well, one night after another win, the town threw a victory dance at the local armory. I got spiffed up and went with the rest of the team, but as I didn't know how to dance, I stood around and watched. Finally one of the fellows told me that Margaret Guild wanted to see me.

Margaret was the town belle. She was a beautiful brunette whom every player on the team would have given a day's base hits to get in good with. I looked over at her sitting along the wall and she was smiling at me.

"Hello," I mumbled brilliantly, and stood there fumbling with a button on my jacket.

"Would you dance with me, Al?" she smiled.

"I'm sorry, I can't dance," I said and backed away in a hurry.

She danced with a lot of guys, but I noticed she looked over at me now and then. Finally, near the end of the dance, Margaret strolled over to me and said sweetly:

"Al, it's raining out. Would you like to get an umbrella and take me home?"

My face was burning, but I scrounged an umbrella and Margaret and I walked home together in the rain. She talked to me but I didn't know what to say except "yes" and "no."

When we got to her house, I said quickly:

"Well, I have to pitch tomorrow, so I guess I'll get right home and go to bed."

But she said, "Oh, Al, it's so early. Come sit on the porch with me for a while." And she took my hand, which was trembling, and led me to a hammock on the porch. I didn't even know how to sit in a hammock, as I'd never lived in neighborhoods in New York where people had such things.

So we sat there. The rain had stopped and the moon came out. And she was sure pretty. I wanted to get out of there.

"I hope you win tomorrow," she said after a while.

"Yeah," I said. Suddenly I remembered the flowers I'd been getting, and the cake, and turned to her with a puzzled look.

She must have known just what I was thinking, for she smiled and said:

"I've been sending you flowers after the games. Did you like them?"

I began to stammer my thanks, and she started to move closer to me on the hammock. Instinctively I edged away, but she was a lot faster than I was in a hammock. Before I knew it we were both at one end—and crash! down it came throwing Margaret and me flat on our backs.

She began to laugh and I was trying to help her up when the front door was thrown open and a loud voice cried:

"My God! What's going on out here?"

It was her mother, and she was boiling. That did it. I took one look, dropped poor Margaret like a sack of potatoes and ran like hell. I was out the gate and down the block before either of them could say a word. And that was the end of my romance.

When I returned to New York early in September, I was feeling very independent, having saved all of twelve dollars over the season —I'd sent two dollars home each week and usually squandered the other two, but even so I'd managed to save twelve. I proudly presented this extra loot to my parents, and while Mom didn't exactly turn handsprings, because she was still just a little uncertain about baseball as a career, I could tell she was pleased. Dad also looked happy, and I guess he saw a twinkle in Mom's eye, because he hugged her and smiled, "See, he's not in such a bad business, eh, Mama?"

Apparently my fame had preceded me to New York, because right away I was approached to pitch for a big semi-pro team managed by Joe Judge, who later would be a teammate of mine with the Washington Senators and become one of the all-time great first basemen. Joe offered me five dollars, plus dinner at his home. I held out for six bucks and got it. We played on a bumpy field underneath the Fifty-ninth Street Bridge in Manhattan (which spans the East River to Queens).

That winter, I got a job in a razor blade factory in downtown New York, sharpening blades on an electric machine for six dollars a week. After I quit the blade factory, I got a better job with an exporting firm, where a cousin of mine was general manager. For twelve dollars a week, I sorted Levy & Company merchandise to be shipped to Europe. This plainly was much headier work than sharpening razor blades.

The next baseball season, 1911, I returned to Walton. They'd offered me a raise from four dollars a week to ten dollars, with board, plus the freedom to travel to New York every Sunday if I wanted, to pitch semi-pro ball, where I could make as much as twenty-five dollars in one day. I went back and forth to New York quite often, and felt I was moving up fast in the financial world. Soon it was no longer the question of money that bothered me, but how long my arm could hold out pitching so much.

It was at Walton, by the way, that I first tried professional clowning. I had always enjoyed mimicking or impersonating people, and my big chance came shortly after the season opened, when the town announced a social, honoring the ball club. They got local talent to entertain, and I was asked to put on a one-man act. I did this in pantomime, first impersonating a famous actor of the silent films, and then giving my impression of a baseball pitcher who is getting slammed all over the lot but refuses to leave the ball game. As a matter of fact, we had such a pitcher on our club, so my act went over good.

They laughed so hard, it occurred to me I might have something in the way of a comedy routine, although I'll admit I didn't think about it too seriously that first time. After that, every time the town had a social function, they asked me to perform. I was getting a big kick out of it. And I gradually came to be known around the league as a clown pitcher.

That season we played an important game against the Cuban Stars, a team from Cuba which was touring the United States playing independent clubs like ours. Their ace pitcher was a Negro named Mendez, who was so good he had shut out the American League champion Detroit club in three straight exhibition games in Cuba. The day before the game, I was told a scout for the Cincinnati club of the National League, a Mike Kehoe, was going to watch me against the Stars.

Realizing my 132 pounds and slight build would never impress anyone at first sight, I decided to add some weight immediately. So I appeared wearing two thick sweatshirts, two pairs of stockings, bulky sliding pads and anything I could find that would blow me up to look 150 at least. I don't think my own teammates recognized me as I went out to warm up.

It was brutally hot that day, but I never worked so hard. Picture a baseball-crazy kid whose one ambition is to get to the big leagues, knowing he has two strikes on him because of his size and youth, sweating away and stealing looks at that scout in the stands, with every pitch imagining himself in the Polo Grounds against the Giants. This could be it, I told myself over and over.

I pitched quite a ball game that day and beat the great Mendez, 2–0. It was the only game he lost in two years.

Kehoe never spoke to me. For two weeks I moped around, thoroughly disheartened. Then a wire arrived, from Clark Griffith, then manager of the Cincinnati club. It read, PLEASE REPORT CINCINNATI TEAM AT WASHINGTON PARK BROOKLYN EARLIEST DATE.

The train couldn't get me to Brooklyn fast enough. I grabbed a trolley to Washington Park, then the home of the Brooklyn Superbas, now the Dodgers, and dashed into Cincinnati's dressing room.

"Mr. Griffith," I grinned, breathless, "I'm Schacht."

He looked me up and down. "Oh, yes. Well, when is your brother going to report?"

"*I'm* Schacht . . . the pitcher," I murmured.

He did a double take.

"Kehoe said you weighed about 160," he said gruffly.

"I usually weigh 140," I lied, "but I lose a lot when I pitch, and I just pitched yesterday. It'll come back."

I could see he was disappointed, but finally he told the clubhouse boy to give me a uniform. I was so excited, it wasn't until after I had the uniform on that I saw two of me could have gotten into it and maybe sneaked my brother in too.

I never got to play. After about a week of pitching batting practice and warming the bench, Mr. Griffith called me to his office and said he wanted to farm me out to the Fort Wayne, Indiana, club for "seasoning." I didn't blame him, as I knew I needed not only seasoning but lots of steak to go with it. But I couldn't see going to Fort Wayne when I could make more money pitching semi-pro ball the rest of the season. So I thanked Mr. Griffith and went back home.

I was not in the least discouraged, strange to say, because I realized how young I was and that this had been only my first stab at the big leagues. I had long since made up my mind that one day I would be a big league pitcher. Period.

chapter 7

The next winter I again worked for Levy & Company, and was promoted to shipping clerk, with a three-dollar-a-week raise. I also fell in love.

Esther Levine was a beautiful, dark-haired Jewish girl I'd seen around the neighborhood, and when we were introduced formally at a party one night, we seemed to like each other right away. So I got up my nerve and asked her if she'd like to go to a vaudeville show.

To make it a big deal—it was my first real date—I also took Esther to dinner at a restaurant downtown before the theater. Sitting there waiting for our order, I was so nervous I lost my appetite. It was the first time she'd ever been taken to dinner too, so she was as nervous as me; we didn't say anything, but stared at the tablecloth and smiled shyly at each other occasionally. I don't know which of us was the bigger busher.

Not remembering how much money I had, I excused myself and went to the men's room to count it and see if I could cover the check. I had eight dollars, and that was plenty, because our dinner for two cost only $1.60 altogether. That's right—in those days, even a steak with all the trimmings cost only thirty-five cents.

After that, I saw Esther practically every night without realizing that we were going steady. It was something for me to be going out with a girl at all, much less start worrying about what comes next.

One day I ran into Billy Gilbert, the former New York Giants second baseman, who was then managing the Erie club in the Class C Ohio-Pennsylvania League. He said he'd watched me pitch several Sundays the previous season and asked if I'd care to try out for his team that spring.

I figured, What the hell! it's a step up from Walton, and said, "Sure!" on the spot.

"There's one thing though, Al," Gilbert said. "You're pretty light."

I told him, "Billy, you don't have to remind me. That was my trouble at Cincinnati. I can't seem to put any weight on."

"Well," he said, "there's one idea that always works pretty well. Try drinking a couple of bottles of Guinness stout every day. If you keep that up between now and the spring, you ought to add a few pounds."

My mother should have heard this: she'd have had a stroke. Though I was nineteen, I'd never had even a glass of beer before, so I'll never forget my first run-in with Guinness stout. I strolled into a restaurant at 149th Street and Third Avenue and guzzled two whole pints of stout in a hurry. Sitting peacefully in the El train on my way home, I suddenly couldn't stop myself from giggling. For ten minutes I snickered and chuckled out loud, and everybody in the car was staring at me like I was nuts. I giggled at people and at the advertisements on the walls of the car. After a while, they all were laughing with me, although they had no idea what we were laughing at, and neither did I. That must have been the happiest bunch of subway riders in history. When I reeled home, I went right to bed without letting my mother get a look at me—or a whiff of me—and slept in my clothes for four solid hours. From then on, I cut down to one pint of stout per day.

When I reported to Gilbert's Erie club a couple of months later, I weighed 133, exactly one pound more than when I'd started on Guinness stout. And to think I'd almost gone broke belting that stuff down.

The Erie team was made up of a number of ex-big leaguers who were slipping slowly back down the ladder. They were hard old-timers, and paid absolutely no attention to a skinny young punk like me.

The season opened and ten days passed, and all I was doing was reviving those old calluses on my fanny. Not only did I not pitch, but the club even added a new pitcher, named Reis, who had been sent down by the St. Louis Cardinals of the National League. Finally, on a Sunday morning, Gilbert took me aside in the hotel lobby and said:

"Al, I have to tell you I don't know what to do with you. You seem to have the stuff, but you're so small, I'm almost afraid to take a chance on you. Tell you what. I'll pitch Reis this afternoon against Akron. He's lost twice already since joining us, and if he gets knocked out again today I'll get rid of him and give you a start."

That day, for the first and only time in my life, I sat on the bench and pulled against one of my own teammates. Evidently I didn't have enough pull, because Reis pitched a beautiful two-hit shutout to win. After the game, Gilbert handed me my notice.

After packing, I decided to sit around the hotel lobby and try to figure out what to do next. It got to be eleven o'clock, and the place was getting empty, when Gilbert came in and sat down next to me.

"Boy, I'm glad you're still here," he said. "I've been looking for you."

"You mean you want me to stay?"

"No, but I think I got a good tip for you," he said. "There's a guy named Jack O'Connor who used to manage the St. Louis club in the American League and now is managing Cleveland in the new United States League. He contacted me this evening, wanting to know if I had a pitcher I could recommend."

"And . . . ?"

"And I recommended you. Of course, the United States League is an outlaw league . . ."

"Billy, how can I ever thank you?" I grinned.

"Never mind that," he said. "You go to bed, because I told O'Connor you'd be in Cleveland tomorrow evening. The club is leaving tomorrow night for Chicago for the opening game."

Unfortunately I overslept and missed my train the next morning. Having to get to Cleveland before 6:30 P.M., I took the only way out, boarding an interurban trolley for the longest trolley ride of my life. We must have clattered through every town in Ohio. After bouncing all day, I arrived in Cleveland at 5 o'clock and went straight to the Gilsey House and found O'Connor, sitting in a corner of the lobby.

"I'm Al Schacht," I said.

It was just like with Clark Griffith the year before. O'Connor stared at me for a long second, then that same sour expression pinched his Irish puss.

"You're pretty young, and light, ain't you?" he said wearily.

Disgusted, I said, "No, I just didn't eat lunch today."

He thought for a minute, then rose and put his hand on my shoulder. "Tell you what I'll do, kid. We open in Chicago tomorrow, and we'll be back here in ten days. You be here, and I'll take a look at you then."

I had to do something fast. Remembering the $120 in my pocket, having been paid off at Erie, and deciding I wasn't too hungry yet, I looked him square in the eye and said:

"Mr. O'Connor, I rode a trolley all day to get here. And I'm willing to ride all night on a train. I'll even pay my own carfare to Chicago—if you'll let me pitch tomorrow. Just give me this chance."

A different kind of expression spread over his face, and he grinned.

"Kid," he said, "I think I will take you—on your guts alone."

Most of you never having gone through the experience of a young ballplayer joining a new club for his first really big chance, it would be hard for you to appreciate how lonely a fellow can be, particularly on a quiet train late at night. You sit listening to the wheels clacking away, knowing that train is taking you to your showdown—when you get where you're going, and you get the chance you've been battling for, either you make something of it or you flub it. No matter how cocky you may have been up to then, you can't help wondering if you've got the stuff to go on.

I sat up alone most of the night, jittery and a little frightened, and homesick, and staring out the window at the blackness, picturing myself standing on the pitching mound with eighty million fans yelling down my neck. Then a wonderful guy sat down beside me.

It was Howard Wakefield, an experienced catcher who'd played in the big leagues and had joined the United States League. He was cheerful and friendly, and we hit it off good. Howard talked to me about baseball almost until dawn. He calmed my fears and told me not to get discouraged, no matter what might happen. It's impossible to say how much good he did for me in those few hours. When I finally got to sleep, I wasn't scared any more. (Howard, incidentally, was the father of the celebrated Dick Wakefield, the "bonus baby" who was such a sensation with the Detroit Tigers in the early 1940s and then sadly petered out, never living up to his great promise.)

Next day was the big opening of the U.S. League season, at Gunther Field in Chicago. Cleveland and Chicago were in the western division of the League, along with Pittsburgh and Cincin-

my own particular screwball 67

nati; in the east were Reading, Pennsylvania, Richmond, Virginia, Washington and the Bronx. The U.S. League, like the Federal League a few years later, was trying to form what amounted to a third major league, the idea being to break the two big leagues' monopoly. The major league bigwigs and their backers called it an "outlaw" league.

A pitcher named Moyer, formerly of the Washington Senators of the American League, started the game for us. I had pitched a few balls in batting practice when O'Connor, after watching me a while, told me to quit because he might want to call on me in the game.

In the third inning, O'Connor sent me down to the bullpen to loosen up just in case, for Moyer looked a bit shaky. In the fifth, Chicago started a fuss, and before we knew it they'd scored a bunch of runs and had the bases full and none out. O'Connor waved from the bench for me to come in and relieve Moyer. It was no easy spot for anybody, not to mention a rookie, and my hand shook when I walked in and took the ball away from Moyer. But I gritted my teeth and pitched.

I struck out the next three batters on nine pitched balls. The big crowd sort of gasped. In the sixth inning, I struck out the side on nine more pitches, and the crowd was roaring. In the seventh, when I fanned the first two hitters to make it eight straight strikeouts, I thought they'd tear the roof down. The stadium stayed intact for a while, though, because I walked the next batter and he scored after a couple of errors by our side. In our eighth, we slammed across ten big runs to take back the lead and put the game on ice. And I managed to strike out three more Chicago hitters in the eighth and ninth innings, for a grand total of eleven strikeouts out of fifteen outs in the five innings I'd worked.

Tom Murphy, owner of the Cleveland club, was so elated that at a victory party at the Sherman Hotel that evening, he presented me with his own beautiful gold watch and chain as a token of his appreciation. Believe it or not, the next morning after breakfast, while proudly wearing the watch on my vest, I was leaning out the window of my room on the seventh floor of the hotel, idly watching traffic below, when the chain slipped loose and the watch fell out. It was smashed to a million pieces on the sidewalk. And I felt that my heart had gone with it.

I didn't pitch again during that road trip, but back in Cleveland, at Luna Park, I made my first start and won. We went on the road again, and I won two more at Pittsburgh and Cincinnati. Then, back to Cleveland, where I won my fifth straight.

It had been the story all along that the U.S. League was in trouble financially because of weakness among the eastern division teams. Anyway, the club was making its first eastern swing, with the first game scheduled against the Bronx club at Bronx Oval. Naturally, I was especially excited about playing there with a chance to strut my stuff before the home folks. We were already at the Oval, dressing, when word came the league had folded and the teams were being disbanded immediately.

I felt I was right back where I started, and in the Bronx no less. But as I was shuffling out of the Oval, a big fellow named Joe Wall stopped me. We talked about what had happened, and he went on to say he'd seen me pitch and thought highly of me. Joe thought himself a baseball brain because he'd had a brief trial with the New York Giants once.

"I got a pretty good semi-pro outfit that plays on Sundays," he said, "but I need a pitcher. You pitch for me next Sunday, and if you win I'll personally see that you get a job with the Boston Braves."

"And how will you go about that?" I asked, a little doubtful.

"The manager, Harry Smith, is a special friend of mine," he winked.

So I pitched for Joe Wall's team, on which he was first baseman in addition to manager. We won the game, but when I looked for him after, he had gone. The following Saturday I was pitching for another club at Bronx Oval and noticed Wall standing on the sideline. I cornered him and said:

"Well, how about the Boston Braves?"

He looked around him, then said, "I'll see you after the game in the saloon across the street."

Dolly Stark, a friend who wound up as a top big-league umpire, waited outside the saloon with my bag when I went in to see Wall later. Wall was at the bar, chatting with a group of men, and I took a seat at a table. I waited almost an hour but he never noticed me. Finally, he downed a drink and turned to leave, and I caught his sleeve and said again:

"How about the Boston Braves?"

"I'll tell you, kid," he said, placing his hand on my shoulder, "the Braves first baseman just got hurt, and I'm sending myself up to Boston instead. Sorry." And he walked out.

When I got outside, my tail really dragging, there was Dolly Stark curled up with my bag on the curb, sound asleep.

That Joe Wall was a fabulous character. He was about thirty then and built solid, and always wore a dirty old New York Giants uniform. When he was managing semi-pro teams, he used to send the box score to the New York *Press*, which each Monday morning carried all the box scores of Sunday's semi-pro games. According to the *Press*, Wall batted about .950. Every time he reported a game, he listed himself as hitting 4-for-5 or 5-for-5. The funny part was, we found out later, Joe couldn't read or write, but dictated his reports to his brother.

After the U.S. League folded, I got an offer to pitch for the great Metropolitan club on Sundays.

Sunday baseball—that is, charging admission to ball games on Sunday—was prohibited in New York at that time. So the big league teams had Sundays off, and the fans therefore flocked to see the Metropolitans. How did the Metropolitans get away with it? We sold scorecards. We had red ones for fifty cents and green ones for twenty-five cents, with the holders of red scorecards getting the best seats. In other words, the scorecards were the admissions. It must have been illegal, but the police were very co-operative. At the start of each game, the local precinct captain would hand our manager, Jack McGrath, a summons, but would let the game go on. I suspect there might have been a little politics involved, because the next day, McGrath would go to court, plead guilty and pay a ten-dollar fine. The same routine every Sunday and every Monday. For only ten dollars a week, the Metropolitans were able to play ball all season and the money was rolling in. I made thirty-five dollars a game.

70 my own particular screwball

We had some fine ballplayers on that Metropolitan club, many of whom could have made the big leagues if they'd wanted to take the rap in minor-league ball first. Joe Judge, the first baseman, and I were about the only ones who were crazy enough to want baseball as a career. We played against some rough competition. The major leagues having Sundays off, they'd get teams together and play us often, and we regularly licked them. One of my biggest thrills ever was pitching against the great Cy Young that season at Lenox Oval. He was about forty-four then, having retired from the Boston Red Sox after winning more big league ball games in his career than any other pitcher. When he lost that day, he quit for good and never pitched another game.

I also got a job with the New York Edison Company, pitching for its independent ball club on Saturdays and working as an "inspector" during the week (I didn't know a gas light from a candle). Edison's baseball manager was Albert Goldman, who later became postmaster of New York. With my ball playing and inspecting, I earned $17.50 a week. Add to this, fifteen dollars I received every Thursday playing at Riverhead, Long Island, and seventy-five dollars every Sunday with the Metropolitans—by now I was pitching doubleheaders, morning and afternoon, for the Mets—and I was getting rich, making $107.50 a week. No taxes, either. Not bad, considering I'd only gotten fifty dollars a week with Cleveland of the U.S. League. I turned all the money in at home, asking for some back only when I needed it. By this time, my mother was convinced baseball was okay. She was even bragging about me to the neighbors.

I held my Edison Company job after the baseball season ended. My job as an inspector was to investigate all applications for electric service. When I got to the apartment of someone making a claim, I had to count the number of lights required and make out a report on whether or not there was a meter installed yet. A very heady job, as you can see. Even so, I was usually in hot water with my boss. During the summer, while making an inspection, when the noon whistle blew I'd quit work, no matter where I was at the moment, and head for baseball practice. At other times, when an applicant would beg me to get him electricity fast I'd call the office and make up stories about my cousin needing lights badly and please, please turn them on right away.

After several such cases, Mike Donovan, manager of lighting applications and our shortstop during the season, said to me, "Schacht, if all your cousins had come to see you pitch, we'd have filled the ball park every Saturday." Considering the job I was doing, it's remarkable the Edison Company progressed as far as it did.

That winter, my first real romantic crisis came up. I'd been going with Esther Levine steadily for a year with, as I said, no serious thoughts. I hadn't even kissed her. Then, one evening when we didn't have a date, I spotted her with another guy from the neighborhood, Jack Greenberg, and was I jealous. The next time we met, I bawled her out for going out with somebody else, and she had that look in her eyes. So, for the first time, I was asked up to her home.

Her mother was very polite, asking me questions about my education and business background. Finally Mrs. Levine took me into another room and, very serious, asked:

"Alexander, what are your intentions toward Esther?"

"I don't get you," I said.

"Well, frankly," she said, "I can't say I'm in favor of Esther marrying a . . . a ballplayer."

Whoa! I said to myself, the old lady is way ahead of me. While I now knew I loved Esther, I had no idea about marriage yet. Because I felt that if I got married, I'd have to give up baseball and get a steady job, which I wasn't ready to do. There was no question in my mind that I could some day reach the top in baseball, but I knew what a tough climb it would be, and it wouldn't be fair either to a wife or myself to get weighted down with such responsibilities before I made good.

I fumbled and stalled, finally excused myself and ran home. Esther's mother had rattled me with that marriage talk, and I started not coming around so much after that. I wanted to see Esther all right, but I was afraid of getting hooked, not so much by her but her mother. The next thing I knew she was going out regularly with Jack Greenberg and I was finished. They were married early in 1913.

Every so often during that winter of 1912–13, I'd gotten into the habit of dropping into the Mott Haven Athletic Club in the Bronx, a gym where prize fighters trained. Becoming acquainted with such great boxers as Benny Leonard, Soldier Kearns and others, I got the idea I might like to try boxing myself, not for a living but to keep in shape for the next baseball season. Since I clowned at it, naturally everybody at the gym rode me—and they soon kidded me into believing I'd become a pretty good judge of fighters.

So, I got excited the day I received a letter from a cousin in Boston who told about a fighter named Joe White. My cousin said this young fellow, who came from South Boston, showed great promise, and, having heard through family channels that I was now interested in boxing, he suggested that if I'd take the kid in tow as his manager I might have a welterweight champion on my hands one day. It seems White was having tough luck and was broke, and the idea was for me to pay his carfare to New York and arrange to get him a room. I sent White twenty-five dollars the next day—I'd borrowed it from Billy Gibson, sometime manager of Gene Tunney and Benny Leonard, who owned the bar at 149th Street and Third Avenue where I'd gotten looped on Guinness stout. White got to New York just before Christmas, 1912, and I started supporting him, first getting him a room in a boardinghouse near the Polo Grounds in upper Manhattan. He was a swell kid, kind of tough, about my own age.

After a couple of weeks I went to Gibson, who also operated the Fairmont A.C. at 138th Street and Third Avenue, and told him to get me a fight right away and he'd get his twenty-five dollars back.

"Whattya mean, 'Get me a fight right away'?" he growled.

"I got a boy who's ready," I said. "I am his manager."

"The hell with that," he said.

"You want your twenty-five bucks, don't you?"

That rang a bell, and after questioning me about White, Gibson arranged a meeting with his matchmaker, Tom McArdle, and a bout was set between White and Arthur Donovan. This is the same Donovan who later became a great referee.

It was a good brawl. I'm really not sure who won, but I remember Donovan was no pushover and my fighter also made a good showing. Our take was a hundred dollars. I was a bona fide fight manager.

Two weeks later I got White matched against Kid Graves, one of the country's top welters. White won the decision. Now the boys at the Mott Haven A.C. were really talking. And I was getting so interested I actually trained with White. He didn't drink or play around with women, but it took a derrick to get him out of bed. To make sure he kept in shape, I'd meet him at his boardinghouse mornings, drag him out of the sack and lead him by the nose to an open stretch called the Speedway, behind the Polo Grounds, to do our road work. In the evenings after work I'd box with him. It got so I wasn't sure which of us might be champ some day.

White won a couple more fights, and we were riding high. Then came a great break for me. At the Mott Haven A.C. one day, a man I'd come to know named Bob O'Donnell, then treasurer of the Bronx Vaudeville House, said to me:

"Al, I hear you're a pretty good pitcher."

I modestly told him I thought so.

"I've never seen you play, myself," he went on, "but my boss, the manager of the theater, is friendly with the president of the Newark club, George Solomon. Maybe we can work it so you get a tryout this spring." This Solomon, he said, was really a shirt manufacturer and not much of a student of baseball.

What a backdoor deal! Here's a guy who never saw me pitch, who gets to know me through boxing, recommending me to the manager of a vaudeville theater who also never saw me pitch, and in turn is supposed to recommend me to a shirtmaker president of a ball club, who doesn't know buttons about baseball! But it was important to me because Newark was then a farm club of the Brooklyn National League organization and was just one step below the big leagues.

So, suddenly, I was not only manager of a near-champion boxer, but also a Class AAA baseball pitcher, almost.

One afternoon in February 1913, I came home from the gymnasium and noticed my mother's eyes were red. She said:

"Papa is very sick. He has bad pains in his chest."

Dad was lying in bed, pale and breathing heavily. Mom looked worried.

"Maybe we ought to rub his chest with alcohol," I said.

In a few minutes, the doctor came. After examining Dad alone, he came out and had a conference with Mom, as the other kids and I watched. Then he called me over.

"Your father has pneumonia, Al. It's serious. I want you to get to the nearest drugstore fast and get me a portable oxygen tank. That's the only thing that can save him."

I raced the block to the drugstore in nothing flat. Charging inside, I breathlessly asked the clerk for a small oxygen tank, explaining the situation.

"You'll have to leave a five-dollar deposit," he said.

"I don't have five dollars now," I cried. "I'll come back with it. Give me the tank. It means my father's life."

"I'm sorry," he insisted, "it's a rule. We must have a five-dollar deposit."

I was desperate. Suddenly, shoving him out of the way, I vaulted over the counter, grabbed the tank and scrambled out of the door. He was so surprised, he didn't even come after me. Even if he had, there wasn't a cop in New York who would have stopped me.

When I got back to the apartment, my sister Esther had her arms around Mom, who was taking it hard. The doctor took the tank and went into Dad's room, closing the door. We fidgeted for a while, then somebody suggested we all ought to go to the synagogue and pray for Dad. We were in the synagogue, praying, when a friend came and told us Pop was dead.

Dad had only gotten ill that day. But the doctor found he must have been walking around for maybe three days with that bug inside him and had refused to give in to it, until it was too late. He was buried the next day.

All Dad left was a thousand-dollar insurance policy. Of the family of six, only two of us were working, Lou and I. Lou had a decent job, but he wasn't making enough to support everybody. Because I was beginning to make good money at baseball, I knew the larger burden was on me. Now I *had* to make good as a pitcher.

chapter 8

Ten days after the death of my father, I received a notice to report for a tryout with the Newark club of the International League. Meeting several of the Newark players from the New York area, we took a boat from New York to Savannah, Georgia, where the team trained. Fortunately, I had the presence of mind to put my fighter, Joe White, in the hands of a friend who would look after my interests while I was away.

For the first few days in Savannah I was unhappy and spiritless. I couldn't even get excited about baseball. At the end of a week, Harry Smith, the manager—remember, he was Joe Wall's "special friend" who managed the Boston Braves—spotted me mooning around and spoke to me.

"Boy, I had the same misfortune you've just had when I was about your age," he said kindly. "The only thing to do is try hard to forget. It works two ways: if you're serious about baseball, you've got to forget your sorrow; and if you really want to forget, bear down on your baseball." Harry straightened me out, just like my father would have, and I immediately acquired a healthy respect for my new manager.

Harry Smith was one of the most comical and best-liked men I ever met in baseball. He was not only a smart baseball student and a real good catcher, but was able to keep his teams relaxed by his continual clowning and practical jokes. And I, as the youngest rookie in camp, soon became the number one butt of his gags. Now that I think back, I can see he picked on me right off the bat just to get me smiling again.

One morning, after we'd been at Savannah about three weeks, Harry said to me:

"There's a new pitcher arriving today. I want you to room with him."

"Sure, Harry," I said.

"There's just one thing—he just got out of a lunatic asylum."

My eyes must have popped.

"Oh, the doctors say he's all right now," Harry said. "You joke around with him, Al, make him feel at home . . . and sort of keep an eye on him. You know."

The guy arrived a bit later, and Harry introduced him as Beanie Hall. He didn't seem like a bad fellow, so I figured it would turn out okay. That night, about ten-thirty, I went up to my room on the fourth floor of the De Soto Hotel, intending to turn in early. When I opened the door and flipped the light switch, the lights didn't go on. The room was dark, but from the hall light I could make out objects in the room. I thought I saw a form on the bed.

"Hey, Beanie," I called. No answer. When I got closer, I saw it—my new roommate was sprawled across the bed on his back, wearing his complete game uniform, and there was blood all over his chest and face!

I stood there for a moment, paralyzed, remembering what Harry Smith had said that morning. Then I tore out of the room and ran downstairs. Finding Harry in the lobby, I cried:

"Harry! that guy *is* crazy! I think he killed himself. The lights are out, and he's lying on the bed in uniform with blood all over him. He's even got his spikes on!"

"What?" Harry roared. "I'll take care of that. Let's go up."

When we got to the room, Harry said, "You wait out here," and went inside. I watched him stomp over to the bed, pick up Hall's body, lug it to the open window and dump it out. Four stories! I felt faint. Harry just walked by me, brushing himself off, and went downstairs. I raced to the window and stared out, and there was the body on the ground below. I almost fell out myself.

When I stumbled down a few minutes later, the lobby was full of players laughing. I could have dropped dead when Harry Smith and Beanie Hall walked up to me. With tears in his eyes from laughing, Harry explained how he'd rigged up the dummy.

Whether because of Harry Smith or in spite of him, I was making pretty fair progress during spring training. But I knew it would be tough for me to make the team, because there were a number of veteran pitchers who'd played the previous season, plus three former Brooklyn pitchers, George Bell, Sy Barger and Rollie Atchison. There was room for only one young pitcher. Eight rookies were trying out, including myself. Just before we got back to Newark to play a final exhibition game with our parent club, the Brooklyn Superbas, the competition between the rookies seemed to have come down to Beanie Hall, a guy named Prince Gaskel, and me.

I walked into the Newark clubhouse at Wiedmeyer Park the day of the Brooklyn game and found a pink slip in my locker. It read:

"You are hereby notified that you are optioned to the Richmond club of the Virginia League. Report there without delay."

With this was a letter from Charles Ebbets, owner of the Brooklyn organization, in which he said that while I hadn't looked bad, they didn't intend to carry any young pitchers that season. He added it would be to my advantage to get another year's experience in organized ball.

When Harry Smith read the notice and letter, he said thoughtfully:

"Hell, I'd like to keep you, kid. Maybe there's a way. If you want to pitch against Brooklyn today, I'll pitch you. If you win, I don't see how they can let you go."

When I was announced as the Newark pitcher, a hum of surprise rolled through the stands. For Brooklyn and Newark were great rivals and played all out against each other. In those days if a player had two good weeks with Newark, the parent Brooklyn club would call him up. Two bad weeks with Brooklyn, and back to Newark. They wore out the Hudson Tubes shuttling players back and forth between New York and New Jersey.

Brooklyn was loaded with stars, including Jake Daubert, Zack Wheat and Casey Stengel. But you're hearing from a guy who went out that day and licked them, 3-1, allowing only five hits. So the club sent the "lunatic," Beanie Hall, to Richmond.

Casey Stengel struck out twice that game. And to this day, I kid the now great manager of the New York Yankees about him being my "breathing spell" in the game and that it was him who kept me in the International League.

The Newark club decided to keep both Prince Gaskel and me, and that led to trouble. In fact, when the season began, the whole team was being ripped by dissension problems. What it amounted to was a revival of the Civil War—about half the players were Southerners and the other half from the North. In spring training, a few arguments had broken out which didn't seem too important at the time. But the tension increased to a point where guys were fighting in the clubhouse, and everybody on the squad was snapping at one another. It even got under one fellow's skin so deep that he pulled one of the rottenest tricks I ever heard about. It so happened I was the victim.

We had a catcher named Higgins, a southern boy, who was related some way to my rival, Gaskel, also a Southerner. The Prince and I were struggling hard to stay with the club, not really fighting each other but just giving it everything when either of us got a chance to pitch. But after a few weeks, Gaskel was not making too good an impression, having been rapped hard a couple of times. And Higgins, who was clearly rooting for Gaskel, got more surly than ever with me whenever I was pitching. I began to think the whole thing must be preying on my mind, because I was straining and wheezing and having a tougher time getting opposing batters out, even on days I thought I had good stuff.

One afternoon, while I was warming up to pitch against Buffalo, an umpire named Bierhalter walked over and asked in a low voice:

"Who's catching you today?"

"Higgins, I guess," I replied.

"Kid," he said, "don't mention I told you, but you don't have a chance with that guy catching you."

"What do you mean," I asked, startled.

"Remember last Sunday in Jersey City when you got knocked out? If you recall, I was umpiring behind the plate—Higgins was telling each batter what kind of pitch you were about to throw."

I couldn't believe my ears. It ate at me all the while I warmed up, and finally, just before the game, I went to Harry Smith and said:

"Harry, I wish you'd catch me today."

He stared at me. "Why?"

"Well," I hesitated, "I don't know, I don't seem to have any luck with Higgins..."

"Hmmm," Harry mumbled. "You two guys having trouble?"

"No. I just wish you'd catch me instead of him."

So my manager caught for me, and I won. I never said a word to Higgins.

In my battle to stay with the Newark club, I was assigned mostly to relief work and got very few starting chances. Even with the dissension, the club was in the thick of a tough pennant fight with Rochester, and it figured that Smith would rather rely on veteran pitchers than rookies. But after a series in Montreal, one of the experienced pitchers, Rollie Atchison, got into a brawl in a saloon and disappeared. He hadn't reported back to the team after nearly two weeks, and we were going into Rochester for an important four-game series. So I went to Smith and all but got down on my knees for a chance to start one of the games.

He hemmed and hawed, but finally agreed not only to give me a starting shot, but to let me open the series. And I pitched a near-perfect ball game! Until two were out in the last half of the ninth inning, not one Rochester player reached first base. Then I allowed two hits but we still won 1–0.

That night Prince Gaskel was released. I had made the team.

That victory put Newark in a tie with Rochester for the league lead. Even so, I didn't get another start for some three weeks. This bothered me more and more as the days dragged past, and I began to suspect that although Harry Smith liked me, he was being pressured by other members of the team to freeze me out.

It was partly the North vs. South split on the club—but I finally came to see what I hadn't recognized clearly before, that some of them resented me because I was a Jew.

I was one of the first Jewish boys to get into professional baseball. In those days, Jews had almost as rough a time breaking in as Negroes in recent years. I heard of several Jewish players getting kicked around in baseball, but it never worried me much because I'd been brought up on the streets of New York.

I'd thought I was getting along okay despite a certain amount of riding which I had learned to take, but midway through that 1913 season, the problem came to a head.

I was pitching against Rochester again, and we led 3–2 in their half of the seventh inning. Leading off for Rochester was Hack Simmons, and as he stepped up to hit, our first baseman, big Harry Swacina, suddenly shouted to me, "Walk him! Walk him!" Everybody in the ball park heard this, which must have sounded ridiculous to the fans because we were just starting the inning and there was no call to put Simmons on base intentionally. But it happened that Swacina and Simmons were then battling each other for the league batting leadership, and Swacina knew, as I did, that I was Simmons' "cousin"—he could probably get a hit off me in the dark with his eyes closed. In fact, he already had two hits that day.

Naturally, I paid no attention to Swacina, and sure enough, Simmons smacked my first pitch for a double down the left field line. Swacina was boiling. At the top of his lungs he yelled:

"That's the way to pitch, old boy!"

The next batter, Guy Zinn, also slammed my first pitch to him, right at Swacina. And the big guy let it go right through him for an error that allowed Simmons to score the tying run from second. So I hollered as loud as I could:

"That's the way to play first base, old boy!"

Swacina was spitting and swearing at me, when I noticed an umpire had called time. Our center fielder, Hy Myers, also a big man, came running in to the pitcher's mound.

"Schacht," Hy growled, "if you don't take a punch at Swacina after the game, *I'll* sock *you!*" And he meant it.

This was just dandy—Swacina weighed about 210 and I was all of 135 pounds. But I had little choice between Myers and Swacina: both of them likely could bounce me like a rubber ball. We lost the game, which made me sore, and when we got to the clubhouse later I was in such a mood that I didn't give a damn.

Swacina was over by his locker, starting to undress, and I stood in the center of the room and said:

"You lousy bum, Swacina, I think you let that ball go through your legs on purpose."

"What did you say?" he snapped.

"You heard me—you're a louse. And as big as you are, I think I can take you." And I started toward him.

Swacina turned to Harry Smith and said: "Harry, if you don't keep this Jew punk quiet, I'll throw him right out the window."

I snorted, "Why you phony, you're afraid to fight."

Swacina just stood there taking it, with the sweat standing out on his forehead. Then Harry Smith stepped between us and sent me back to my locker across the room. The next thing I knew, the player whose locker was next to Swacina's had the big guy in a headlock and was wrestling him to the floor. Hy Myers rushed over, and he and Smith untangled the two. When the ruckus was over, I glanced at Myers, and he winked at me.

I'd learned that my fighter, Joe White, had been matched with the great Mike Gibbons at Boston early in the summer. Finding that the Newark club would be playing in Providence about that time, I arranged to take Harry Smith and a few other players to Boston to watch my "tiger" in action. We hurried there after our first game at Providence.

There, I found out White had been contacted by some of his former shady friends and even was palling around with them again. But I was too excited about the big fight to think twice about it. In the dressing room, Joey was calm and looked in pretty good shape. But I did notice he wasn't particularly overjoyed at seeing me and was kind of quiet when I tried to give him a pep talk.

Finally we got the call we were on. White and I walked out of the dressing room and into the arena, with me behind. I was more nervous than I ever was in a ball game. But as we neared the ring, I suddenly felt something hard shoved into my back, and a tough voice hissed in my ear:

"Take one more step toward that ring, and you're a dead pigeon. You ain't gonna see this fight. In fact, you better leave right now."

I couldn't move. Then he poked me in the back again and I turned and walked back up the aisle, getting only a fast glimpse of a rough-looking mugg with his hands in his pockets. Nobody in the crowd even suspected what had happened.

Shaking from excitement, I waited outside the arena. When it was over, Harry Smith and my teammates came out and said Gibbons had outpointed White, which I didn't need any brains to figure out in advance after what happened to me. They couldn't understand where I'd been during the fight, and when I told them, they all busted up laughing.

I didn't try to see Joe White again. The boxing racket didn't mean so much to me that I should battle mobsters for control of a fighter. So I went back to Providence to rejoin my Newark club and tried to forget all about my career as a fight manager. Anyway I was too busy helping Newark win the pennant.

I wasn't at all happy with the contract the Newark club sent me to sign late that winter. They offered me exactly what I'd gotten in 1913, only $175 a month. Feeling I'd won several important games, including a couple of big ones from Rochester, I decided to hold out for $250 a month. So I sent owner George Solomon a note saying I would not sign the contract and that he should try again.

It was nearly time for the club to head south and still Solomon and I had not come to terms, so Harry Smith persuaded me to visit Solomon at his Newark office to see if we couldn't settle it. We kicked it around for about an hour, and finally Solomon talked me into signing a contract calling for $200 a month. After the formalities were over, he and Smith excused themselves and went into an adjoining room to discuss, they said, other business. Strolling around the office, looking at paintings on the walls, I happened to glance at Solomon's desk and saw a sheet of paper with all the Newark players' names on it, with their intended salaries marked alongside.

Next to my name was—$250.

Let me tell you I burned. Snatching the $200 contract which I'd just signed off the desk, I ripped off the bottom of the page containing my signature, and threw the rest of the contract into the wastebasket.

A few minutes later, Solomon and Smith returned. The owner offered me a cigar, saying with a smile: "Well, Al, here's hoping you have a good season."

"Mr. Solomon," I said, "I signed a contract a little while ago, but it's no good anymore. Because it's in the wastebasket."

"I don't understand," he said.

I just leaned over the desk and pointed at the "$250" next to my name on the roster.

Then he understood, and cried: "I can have you thrown out of baseball!"

I said, "Go ahead," and walked out the door.

So I went home and started worrying. If my bluff flopped, I might be washed right out of baseball. But two days before the club was to leave for spring training, Solomon called me to his office. Saying Harry Smith had talked him into it, he gave me a $250 contract to sign. I left there whistling merrily, not just because I'd gotten what I wanted, but because I now realized I must be highly regarded for the club owner to meet *my* terms.

I was really hot that 1914 season. Pitching regularly, I won fifteen games, a very good record both for Schacht and the International League, which at that time boasted such future big league pitchers as Herb Pennock, Babe Ruth, Carl Mays, Ernie Shore, Joe Oechinger, and Leon Cadore. Despite my 135 pounds, I even took to pitching doubleheaders.

Smith, though a good manager, never stopped his practical jokes. And nobody escaped. During one series in Toronto, many of the players bought duty-free jewelry for their wives or girl friends at the Ontario Jewelry Company. Myself, I'd bought my sister Esther a small diamond ring for a hundred dollars which must have been worth a lot more. Next, we moved to Montreal, and before the first game there, everybody locked his valuables in a large trunk in the dressing room, as was the custom.

When we came into the clubhouse after the game, the trunk had been broken open and was empty, and one of the windows was smashed. The players went wild, running around in all directions, until someone thought to call the police. The cops arrived and started a big investigation, but they couldn't come up with one clue.

When the cops had gone, and everybody was sitting with heads in hands, moaning and swearing, good old Harry Smith started laughing. We all looked up and right away we knew we'd been sucked in again. Sure enough, he had all our stuff. He was so pleased with the success of his gag, he even paid for the broken window in the clubhouse, which he'd done himself, of course.

Right then I made up my mind to give him some of his own medicine. Our next series was in Buffalo, and as I was approaching the ball park the second day there, due to pitch that game, I noticed a horse-and-vegetable wagon parked outside the players' entrance. Immediately I knew this was what I'd been waiting for. I walked over to the Italian vegetable man, who was eating his lunch and feeding the horse, and said:

"Hello, there! How would you like to see the ball game today?" When he looked at me suspiciously, I added, "I'm one of the players."

"I no see game," he shrugged, nodding toward his wagon full of vegetables.

"You will," I said, "if I can borrow your horse. . . . How much do you make a day selling vegetables?"

"Mmmm . . . 'bout t'ree dollas," he said.

"You can knock off the rest of the day. Here's three dollars," I said, nonchalantly peeling three singles from the roll of five bucks I had in my pocket. "You let me use the horse for a few minutes, and I'll take you into the park."

We unhitched the nag, which was skinny, sway-backed, flea-bitten and droopy-eyed, and led her through the delivery gate and under the left field bleacher. Then I got hold of a small Negro boy sitting in the bleachers and gave him one of my last two dollars to carry out instructions I whispered to him. This prank might break me, but if it played right it would be worth it. In the dressing room, I sent our clubhouse boy on a final errand.

I warmed up before the game as usual, then ducked back into the clubhouse. As visitors, Newark batted first, and when the side was out, our team took the field and waited for me to come out to pitch.

In a moment, the whole ball park was roaring. For there came Schacht from under the left-field bleachers, wearing a lady's print dress with a bright red ribbon around my head, aboard a broken-down horse, led by a colored boy. My caravan made its way slowly to the pitcher's mound, where I gracefully slid off the horse, removed my kingly robes and discharged my "lackey." Then I turned to Smith, who was catching that day, and, bowing, said:

"This is for your benefit, my dear sir."

Harry was laughing so hard he could hardly stand up. After a few minutes, when the horse was off the field, I settled down to pitch. I got shelled out in the second inning—and Smith was still laughing.

The next morning in the Buffalo *Courier*, Jack Yellen, then a sports writer and now a top song writer, wrote:

". . . Al Schacht was aided and abetted in getting to the pitcher's box by a horse. But when knocked out in the second inning, he had to leave under his own steam . . ."

That incident should have given me a tipoff that it would be lots easier for me to make the fans laugh in baseball than get the batters out.

It also prompted Harry Smith to really go to work on me. The next time I pitched, a very hot day, about the second inning I began to notice a terrible odor around the pitcher's box. I knew I was perspiring, but I didn't think I stank that bad. Even in the dugout, one player sniffed, wrinkled his nose, and said: "Geez, somebody's arm must be dead."

I was a dope not to catch on. Harry had slipped limburger cheese inside the sweatband of my cap.

One thing struck me before long, however, and that was although I was pitching pretty good, big league scouts might get to think of me more as a screwball than a promising pitcher. Also, in those days, two or three losses in a row, and you were in danger of being canned. Ballplayers came and went all the time, and ball clubs didn't bother carrying losing pitchers for very long. So I got to a point where losing a game would sober me up quite a bit.

I never could win at Montreal, for some reason always losing tough, close games in that ball park. One afternoon there, I had them beat, 3–2, with two out in the ninth inning, when Dan Howley, the Montreal manager, got up off his bench and shouted to me:

"We'll still get you, Schacht. You know you can't win here."

I just chuckled, because this time I was sure I had it won. A pinch hitter, McGraynor, came up and singled. And then Tom Madden belted a ball far over the left field fence, and Montreal had won again, 4–3.

Stunned, I stood motionless on the mound as all the players disappeared into the clubhouse. Finally, after about five minutes I entered our dressing room. The first thing I heard was Dan Howley hollering from next door:

"I told you we'd get you, Schacht, I told you we'd get you!"

In a sudden fury, I grabbed a wooden camp chair and smashed it against a steel locker. Howley only laughed louder.

"Go ahead, break another one!" he bellowed.

I did. I broke six chairs before some of the players, who sympathized with me, calmed me down. But that wasn't the end of it—next day, the owner of the Montreal club, Sol Lichtenheim, handed Newark's traveling secretary a bill for eighteen dollars for the chairs. And I had to pay it.

It's funny, but it probably always will be true in baseball that some pitchers will beat certain opposing clubs and never beat others. It must be in the mind. For example, while I never could win at Montreal, it was just the opposite against Baltimore, which consistently had the strongest team in the league then. Baltimore manager Jack Dunn, who in my opinion was one of the best judges of young ballplayers I ever met, developed such great athletes as Babe Ruth, Ernie Shore, Joe Boley, George Earnshaw, Tommy Thomas, Fritz Maisel, Merv Jacobson, Jack Bentley, Max Bishop, Bob Shawkey, Alan Russell, Jim McAvoy, Mose Grove, and many others. And yet, I almost always stopped Baltimore cold.

It would drive Dunn out of his head to think that a fresh, skinny punk like me could have such a hex on his great team, and he always acted like he'd enjoy cutting my throat.

Baltimore was the last minor league stop before stardom in the majors for a big, spindly-legged fellow named George Ruth. He'd come along as a pitcher—and moved up to the big leagues as pitcher—but it was in Baltimore that Jack Dunn first tried doubling Ruth as an outfielder because of his great hitting power. I happened to be pitching the first game Ruth started in left field. He hit a line drive off me that hit the right field fence so hard it bounced all the way back to our second baseman.

Ruth, who was called George then—I think it wasn't until he got to the majors that they started calling him the Babe—already was proving he was a playboy and quite a character.

Actually, I can thank Babe Ruth, indirectly, for learning something that surely extended my pitching career even farther than it might have gone. I was so impressed by his tremendous shot off me the first time I faced him, which he'd hit off a curve ball, I asked one of Newark's veteran pitchers, George Bell, to show me how to throw a "fadeaway." This was the unusual pitch Christy Mathewson had demonstrated to me years before when I was a kid working out with the Giants mornings. The fadeaway, now called a screwball, as I said before, breaks the opposite way of a curve—that is, when a right-handed pitcher throws it to a left-handed batter, instead of curving *in* to the hitter, it snaps away, as a left-handed pitcher's ordinary curve would.

Bell made me work on that pitch until I could fire it through the eye of a needle. And from then on, I had little trouble with most lefty batters, including Babe Ruth. I never really pitched very often against the Babe, maybe about twenty times altogether, but he never got more than four or five hits off me. And no homers.

Years after the Babe retired, we discussed things that had happened to us in baseball, and he said:

"You're lucky you weren't in the majors long enough to pitch to me."

"You big bum," I said, "I pitched to you all right, in the majors and minors, and maybe I wasn't a great pitcher, but you never hit a home run off me."

To me, the Babe was a great man, and I intend to say more about him later.

When the 1914 season was over, a friend of mine named Sammy Smith who was a former ballplayer and pretty good singer, suggested that the two of us could make some money in theaters in Newark.

I liked the idea right away, because I'd had a yen for the stage ever since I'd seen the great minstrel man Eddie Leonard, in vaudeville. Leonard was considered one of the greatest of all "mammy" singers, and his best number was a song called "Rolly Bolly Eyes," which was a hit with vaudeville fans all over the country. Whenever he appeared in the Bronx, I used to sit through two or three performances, and I told myself that if I ever got on the stage the first thing I'd do would be impersonate Eddie Leonard singing "Rolly Bolly Eyes."

So, when Sammy Smith approached me to team with him, at least one number was in the act immediately. We decided that Sammy would sing a song straight, then I'd come on with "Rolly Bolly Eyes," and we'd wind up with a comic dialogue featuring baseball gags. After a few rehearsals, we booked ourselves at a burlesque house in Newark, in the olio (between acts) of the show.

We were lousy. At least I was. But the show must have been lousy too, for it closed our third day there.

We received sixty dollars—but almost didn't get it. The manager of the theater shoveled all the receipts into a bag on closing night and tried to beat it. But I caught him and demanded Sammy's and my money. Later, the two of us walked over to Kelly's boardinghouse, where most of the girls in the show were staying, to find out what they planned to do next. While Sammy waited outside, I walked into the parlor to find old Mrs. Kelly demanding her rent money, and all the girls fluttering around nervously. Several of them asked me if I could help them get to New York where they could scrounge something to eat.

Feeling sorry for their predicament, I passed out most of our sixty dollars and left. When Sammy and I got to the Hudson Tubes for the ride to New York, he said:

"Where's my thirty bucks?"

Sheepishly, I said: "The girls were in a jam and had to get to New York to eat, and . . ."

"And?" he said, lifting one eyebrow.

". . . and we've got six bucks left. You can have three."

Sammy just shook his head sadly. He wasn't angry or anything—but that was the end of my vaudeville that year. I went back to Levy & Company for the rest of the winter.

During the 1914 season, a new "outlaw," the Federal League, which was backed by a few millionaires and had ambitions to become a third major league, had begun making "raids" on the majors and high minor leagues. They offered much higher salaries than most ballplayers were then getting, and players were jumping their contracts left and right to get in on this gold rush.

The Feds set up a team in Newark and in '15 it got so strong, and was murdering our attendance so badly, that we were directed by Ed Barrow, then president of the International League, to move our whole franchise to Harrisburg, Pennsylvania.

After our first game at Harrisburg I got a telegram from Jack O'Connor, my former manager, who was now managing the St. Louis Federals.

It read: AUTHORIZED OFFER YOU THREE THOUSAND DOLLARS BONUS AND FIVE HUNDRED A MONTH YOU JOIN OUR CLUB. COME RIGHT AWAY.

I'd never seen five hundred dollars a month, as this was twice as much as I was getting. And I certainly had never seen three thousand dollars. I sat in the hotel lobby from 5 to 11 P.M. wondering what to do. That money sure was a temptation, but I didn't want to ruin my career by jumping. The big question in baseball then was whether the Federal League would hold up, and if not, whether jumpers would be allowed to return to their former clubs. Finally I decided to make the break. Going up to my room to pack, I ran into umpire Red Rority and told him what I planned.

Early the next morning I received another wire, this one from Ed Barrow: DO NOT JUMP. SPECIAL DELIVERY LETTER FOLLOWS.

That afternoon, which was an off-day for our club, the letter arrived. In it, Barrow advised me to reconsider jumping because, he said, "all those who have done so will never be able to return to organized baseball."

He concluded: "I will personally see to it that you are sold to the big leagues if you do not jump now."

So I unpacked. I bore down harder than ever the rest of the season, to prove to Barrow that I really was ready for the majors.

During a series in Toronto that season, the club secretary came to me and said:

"A fellow named Jim Thorpe is joining us from the Giants, an outfielder. Can he room with you?"

I was very happy to say yes, because I knew Jim Thorpe was considered the greatest athlete of all time, having played football at Carlisle and just recently winning everything in sight at the Olympic games. I figured he'd be more than okay as a roommate, and also as a bodyguard.

Learning Jim had left the Giants in embarrassing circumstances —manager John McGraw had lost patience one day and called him "a dumb Indian," and Jim had blown up and threatened to throw little McGraw out a window—I tried to put him at ease when we were introduced by saying:

"I hear you run pretty fast. Well, if you want track practice, you'll get it when I pitch, because you'll be chasing plenty of line drives in that outfield."

But he just grinned shyly and didn't say anything. Jim was the biggest man I'd ever seen, especially next to me, standing six-foot-two and weighing 210 pounds of solid muscle. In about a week, when we'd gotten acquainted, I started calling him "Big Injun" and he called me "Li'l Injun"; he said with my nose I looked like a Jewish Indian.

Jim's biggest fault, I found out, was that he didn't know how to drink. He'd go out on the town, get a few shots of firewater under his belt, and barge into our room about 1 A.M. talking like the real Indian he was. And then he'd get playful, and rough.

One night he barreled in about one, flipped on the lights, shook me awake and, with his wide grin, boomed:

"Big Injun say Li'l Injun go out with Big Injun"—pointing to the door.

A little annoyed, I said: "Big Injun better come to wigwam. Li'l Injun pitch tomorrow, Big Injun must chase baseballs. Come, get rest."

He ripped my covers off me, grabbed me by the pajama shirt and dragged me out of bed, and, with one huge paw, shoved my fanny out the window.

"Which way Li'l Injun want to go out—this way, or that way?" he said, nodding toward the door again.

I quickly said, "That way." I got dressed and we went downstairs. But when we got out in the street, Jim said, in perfect English:

"Okay, now you can go back to bed. I just wanted to show you who's boss of that room." And he grinned like a big kid.

As a ballplayer, Jim could run, throw and judge a fly ball as well as anyone, I thought. But he'd had little pro experience before joining the Giants after his great Olympic victories. McGraw had signed him mainly as a gate attraction and Thorpe had never learned to hit the curve ball.

He was a big, good-natured giant, not too quick-witted, who wouldn't hurt a fly. He always let his friends kid him, just taking everything with his toothy smile. I often wondered just how much he could take, and when I found out it scared me.

I was pitching one day at Jersey City, and, because Jim misjudged a line drive, we lost. He had leaped at the last moment, and the ball smashed him in the mouth, which required several stitches afterwards. Heading back to Newark, Jim, two other players and I had a twenty-five-minute wait at the West End station of the Jersey Central, so we stopped into a nearby saloon for a couple of beers, taking a table in a back room. Three tough-looking guys had another table. We recognized them as bleacher regulars, and they also recognized us and started ribbing Jim mercilessly.

Jim felt bad enough as it was, having lost the game and with his lip hurting, and finally he muttered: "Those guys talk too much."

Realizing Jim was getting mad, I called to the other table: "You fellas better lay off."

Just then, one of their bunch returned from the bar with some beers, turned toward Jim and said loudly: "Maybe I should give one to the big Indian. He needs it."

I could see that Jim was about to boil over. I dashed out front and yelled at the bartender: "There's some guys back there looking for trouble. You better get them out before they get murdered . . . !"

As I'm speaking, I hear a crash. Racing back inside, I see two of the wise guys stretched out on the floor, cold as a mackerel. And Jim has the third nailed to the wall with one hand about to split his head open with a chair. The rest of us grab him and pull the chair away from him. But he still hauls off and belts the punk, who drops in a heap.

Then Jim says, "Let's go," and walks out.

My old friend Joe Judge, whose teams I'd played for on New York's sandlots, had gotten to the big leagues, but was sent down to Buffalo of the International League by the Boston Red Sox because he wasn't hitting. Joe was a great fielding first baseman, but even after he joined Buffalo he was still in a batting slump.

We got together for a bull session before a Harrisburg-Buffalo game, talking about old times, and I noticed Joe looked worried.

"Al," he said, "I'm thinking seriously of quitting baseball."

"Are you nuts?" I said. "You're one of the best first basemen around."

"I'm not hitting worth a damn," he moaned. "I couldn't stick with the Sox, and here I'm only batting .200 and not even playing regular. I got a beautiful gal I want to marry in Portland, Maine, and a good job waiting for me there if I want it. If I thought Donovan" (Patsy Donovan, Buffalo manager) "was planning to let me go, I'd quit right now."

I thought for a minute, then said: "Joe, if you knew for sure Donovan wants to keep you on the club, would you give it another try?" He said yes, but he could never ask Donovan himself. So I said: "I got an idea how to find out what Patsy's got in mind. I'll let you know tomorrow." And I hurried away before Joe could protest.

That evening I buttonholed Donovan in our hotel. "Patsy, Joe Judge, who is a good friend of mine, has been offered a good job in Portland, Maine, and they're holding it open for him. But he doesn't know what to do because he doesn't know where he stands with you. I'm not telling you how to run your club, but if you plan to let Joe go he'll quit baseball, and I wish you'd tell him right away or else he might lose out on this job.

"Personally," I said, "I think Joe Judge is going to be a great ballplayer, and you'd be foolish to let him go."

Donovan looked surprised. "Why, I have no idea of getting rid of him," he said. "He hasn't been hitting, but he's a hell of a first baseman. And one of these days, he'll break out of that slump. No, sir, he stays with my club."

When I told Joe the good news the next morning, he seemed encouraged. That afternoon we were scheduled to play Buffalo a doubleheader and I got permission to pitch both games.

Joe Judge, the weak hitter—that ungrateful bum—belted me for three hits in the first game to beat me singlehanded 1–0, and three more in the second to beat me again, 2–1. The rest of that season he burned up the league with his bat and was soon brought back to the majors by the Washington Senators. Good Samaritan Schacht stayed in the International League.

The 1915 season closed for me on a comical note. In a game against Buffalo, I somehow reached first base—how, I can't imagine. Taking a short lead off the bag, I heard a colored fellow in the bleacher behind me holler:

"Mistuh Al, don't you wonder off theah too far. Tha's virgin territory for you."

Everybody laughed, including myself, and I turned to make some reply, when the Buffalo pitcher, Bader, snapped a throw to first, trying to catch me napping. Instead of sliding, I sort of fell across the bag—and the ball hit me in the hip.

The first baseman, Jackson, thinking the ball had sailed past us, started peering wildly toward the stands. And the witty colored fellow encouraged him, calling, "There it goes, Mistuh Jackson," pointing far down to the bullpen.

In the confusion, I sneaked the ball, which had been lying under me, into my hip pocket and lit out for second. Joe McCarthy, later the great Yankee manager, was second baseman on that club, and he cried: "Where the hell is the ball?"

Carlson, the third baseman, also was shouting for the ball. Rounding third, I was tiring, because it was the first time I'd ever had a chance to run all the bases. I made a big slide into home plate, and as I did the ball bounced out of my pocket.

"You're out!" hollered the ump.

"Whattyou mean?" I protested. "The catcher dropped the ball!"

"I saw it drop out of your pocket, you bum," he said. "You're out for interference."

The next day, I got a wire from league president Ed Barrow fining me fifty dollars for my little joke.

Before long, I was battling Barrow yet again. Because that fall the Federal League disbanded, the big league moguls having bought them out. And wouldn't you know it?—all the ballplayers who'd jumped organized ball for the Feds returned scot free to their former clubs, with no penalties. Furthermore, I was asked to take a cut in my new contract.

I went straight to Barrow, angrily demanding:

"Is this the great deal I was supposed to get? By not jumping, not only am I out $3,000 and $250 a month extra, but I'm not sold to the majors as you promised. I'm even losing money."

Barrow said the situation had gotten out of his hands. I stayed sore, and he got tough. I probably was lucky to finally get out of his office without a punch in the nose.

I worked at odd jobs that winter, and realized once and for all that there was no kind of work I cared for as much as baseball. So, still aiming to make the majors, I signed up again with Newark which was back in New Jersey again under new ownership, and immediately developed my first sore arm.

The season opened and two weeks went by, and I still hadn't thrown a ball. Meanwhile, the team was playing bad baseball, the weather was cold, and the fans were staying away in mobs.

The new owners called me into their office one day and said:

"We're sorry about your arm, Al. But if you can't pitch, we don't think we should carry you any longer. We'll have to suspend you, without pay."

"But my arm will come around," I said desperately.

"Of course, of course. And when it does, you come back and show us."

Just like that.

chapter 9

Instead of settling for any old job, I spent all spring and early summer exercising, working out, trying to get the mysterious kink out of my arm. Mom, who by now sympathized with me and my baseball, was very understanding and never pressed me to go to work. To help contribute something, I borrowed money from Billy Gibson, lightweight champ Benny Leonard's manager. But my brother Lou was carrying practically the whole burden.

Then, about July, in desperation I made an important move: I went to see John McGraw, manager of the Giants, at his little office in the Polo Grounds. McGraw didn't remember me as the scorecard boy who used to hang around the Polo Grounds every day eight years before, but he knew about me as a pitcher, having expressed interest in buying me in 1914 when I was with Newark. Sitting there opposite the stocky little guy who was considered the toughest and best manager in baseball, I laid my cards right on the table.

"Mr. McGraw," I said, "I know you were interested in me a couple of years ago. I think if given the opportunity I can prove to you now that I can help the Giants, providing my arm comes around."

"What's the matter with your arm, Al?" he said.

"I'll be damned if I know, but it's bad—I couldn't throw a ball across this room right now. The new owners at Newark are losing plenty of dough, and since I wasn't helping the club, they suspended me.

"Here's my idea," I continued. "I believe with the way things are at Newark I can get my unconditional release for a song. If I get my release, you can sign me, and if I don't make good by next year, you can ship me back to the minors if you want. If my arm comes around you've got yourself a pretty good pitcher—dirt cheap."

McGraw toyed with a pencil for a few seconds. Then he said:

"Go find out what they want for your release, Al."

When I went to see the Newark owners, they said they'd give me my release for nothing! I reported back to McGraw. He signed me. I knew the main reason why he did—McGraw always was searching for a Jewish ballplayer to draw more Jewish fans—but I didn't care, I was with the Giants.

McGraw was great to me. He signed me for three hundred dollars a month, and, knowing I hadn't been paid for three months, gave me a five-hundred-dollar bonus out of his own pocket. Not only that, when the deal was completed, he told me:

"I don't expect much from you for the rest of this season. You just work out the way you think best for that arm. You won't even have to pitch batting practice if your arm can't take it. The only thing I ask is that you report for all games like everybody else on the club."

Shortly after I joined the Giants, they went off on their famous twenty-six-game winning streak. The boys weren't tense or jittery as the string got longer and longer, but when they finally did lose it was because of bad, sloppy baseball. I'll never forget the scene in the clubhouse after that game.

McGraw stormed in quivering with rage. "You," he rasped, sweeping the room with his hand, "are nothing but a pack of goddam, lousy boneheaded bums. Not once did you hustle today. Errors I don't mind; they're in the game. But when you miss signs, and run the bases like drunks, and throw the ball all over the goddam place, you all ought to be shot. Big-league ballplayers—ha!" He spit on the floor, then turned and went into his private office, slamming the door.

The dressing room was as still as a tomb for several minutes. Then we heard it through his office door—the toughest man in baseball was weeping like a baby.

Following the season, McGraw sent me to an osteopath for my sore arm. Twice a week I visited the osteopath for heat treatments and massages, with the ball club paying the expense.

What with these treatments, and not having gone near a baseball all winter, when spring training time rolled around my arm felt okay. The team left by train for Marlin Springs, Texas, on Washington's Birthday, 1917. The first night on the train, the boys got up a crap game in the washroom, using tiny dice someone borrowed from a kid. If McGraw had found us, we all would have been docked our pay, because he hated gambling. After playing half the night, when I woke up the next morning I couldn't raise my arm to comb my hair! You can imagine what went through my head the rest of the trip: if this is what happens from just shooting crap, what will happen when I throw a baseball? I brooded for the rest of that long trip, feeling I was coming to the end of my career.

McGraw held a meeting in the Arlington Hotel in Marlin Springs before our first workout, laying down his training rules, which weren't easy. He told us we'd get up each day at 8 A.M. and go right to the ball park after breakfast. We'd dress in a bathhouse next door to the hotel, and there'd be no cabs, trolleys or buses to the field. Following the afternoon workout we'd all *run* back to the bathhouse.

Picture me, all of 132 pounds, running two miles to the ball park, pushing a baseball all day with my sore arm, and running back two miles. That was all right, I told myself, for big guys like Jim Thorpe, who had rejoined the Giants, and others who needed to lose poundage, but not for little Al. So one afternoon, as we left the field, I lagged behind the rest and hitched a ride on the back of a passing hay wagon, relaxing and congratulating myself for being so clever.

But damned if the wagon doesn't clip-clop right past the Giants puffing along the road, McGraw with them, as he always was. McGraw glanced up and saw me sitting in the hay, but he didn't say a word—until the next morning. Then, at the regular team meeting, he said: "When I make a rule, I expect everybody to follow it. My rules are not made to be broken. And when a busher breaks 'em, that's even worse." Staring straight at me, he snapped: "Schacht, if I catch you—or anybody—hitchhiking again around here, I'll send you back home faster than you can say, 'Thanks for the ride.'"

When the meeting broke up and the players were filing toward the bathhouse to change, I went to McGraw and said, "I didn't hitch that ride to be a wise guy. But Mr. McGraw, with my 132 pounds, if I have to keep running like this every day, in another month you won't be able to see me. I'll just disappear."

He laughed, saying, "That may be, but the rules apply to everybody."

Then he looked serious and asked: "How does your arm feel?"

I had to tell him the truth. "It's about the same as when I first came to you—lousy," I said, shaking my head sadly.

"Well," he said, "if you still don't feel like pitching batting practice, just let me know when I can call on you. I don't want you to pitch until you think your arm can stand it."

Here's a guy who hires me knowing I have a dead arm, sends me to a doctor all winter, and then, after bawling hell out of me for taking advantage of him, all but nurses me himself and even begs me not to work unless I want to. And his reputation was that he was tough to live with both on and off the playing field!

After we broke camp at Marlin Springs, we began an exhibition tour with the Detroit Tigers, playing them in various towns in Texas. The Tigers had the great Ty Cobb, who was the most fiery, aggressive player who ever lived, bar none.

As the tour wore on, everybody could see the feud starting to boil between Cobb and the whole Giant team. When Cobb ran the bases, it was every man for himself. The Giants rode him viciously, especially Buck Herzog, the second baseman, who wasn't exactly a sissy himself.

It was during a game either in Dallas or Waco, Texas, I don't remember which, that Cobb slid into second base and Herzog massaged him between the eyes with a ball and, for good measure, our shortstop, Art Fletcher, fell heavily on top of him. Ty didn't say anything then. But the next time up he singled again, and this time when he stole second he slid in with his spikes flying, cutting Herzog.

The pot boiled over. Herzog, though he was shorter than Cobb, furiously challenged Ty to a fight after the game in Buck's hotel room. Cobb was pleased to accept the invitation. He brought along the Detroit catcher, Oscar Stanage, as his second, and Herzog had

Heinie Zimmerman, our third baseman. They stripped to the waist and went at it, and Cobb mauled him something awful. When the "seconds" stopped it, Herzog had taken a bad beating and might have been ruined for good if the fight had continued much longer.

Cobb's manager, Hughie Jennings, finally had to send Cobb to Cincinnati to work out alone instead of finishing the tour with the Tigers. It was a smart move, because I'm convinced that otherwise something serious might have happened.

McGraw stuck with me until May of that year, still hoping my arm would come around. But it didn't.

He called me to his Polo Grounds office one morning.

"Al, I have to cut down the roster to get under the player limit," he began, and I knew this was the hook. I'd been with him for almost a year but might as well have not been, for all the work I was doing. "If you think you'd like to try to work the trouble out of your arm at Rochester, I'll send you there at the same salary. Mickey Doolan, the manager up there, knows about your arm. I've told him all about it. He'll help any way he can."

With no other alternative, I agreed to go back to the International League at Rochester. It was either that or quit baseball altogether, because no one else was going to give me a chance or be as patient with me as McGraw had been.

I'd always been an overhand pitcher. But unable to throw overhand without my arm feeling like it would come off, I tried to teach myself to pitch underhand at Rochester. There have been only a few successful underhand pitchers in baseball, but I wasn't one of them. But while it was a rough season for me, at least I was pitching again.

Probably my blackest day with the Rochester club was in a doubleheader we played at Richmond. I was sent in to relieve in the sixth inning of the first game, and in the ninth, with the score tied, 2–2, and two out, a guy named Reynolds, Richmond's catcher, whacked a home run over the left field wall, and they won, 3–2.

I was naturally in no mood to talk to anybody. As I passed the grandstand on the way to the clubhouse, muttering to myself, some loudmouth yelled from the second row:

"Why don't you hang it up, Schacht! You're through!"

Without thinking, I said a few things which I couldn't possibly repeat here. About five minutes later, we're all moping around the clubhouse, when the door busts open and a big guy in street clothes marches in.

"What the hell are you doing in here?" barks Mickey Doolan, who felt pretty angry himself.

"I'm the sheriff," the big guy drawls, showing his badge. "I have to lock up your pitcher, Schacht."

"Lock him up? For what?" Doolan cries.

"The mayor's wife is sitting in the stands, and she says she heard Schacht just now use foul language on a spectator, and she swore out a warrant for his arrest."

Doolan shoots me a dirty look, then snaps to the sheriff: "Okay, okay. But wait till after the second game, willya? We might need him to pitch."

The sheriff thinks this over. "Well, all right . . ."

"Okay, now blow," Doolan says.

The score was tied again in the second game when Doolan called me in to relieve in the seventh inning. Who's the first batter I have to face but the same Reynolds. You guessed it—bango! over the left field fence again, and they're ahead. I'm kicking the dirt on the mound, Reynolds is trotting around the bases and the Richmond fans are going wild. When the noise dies down a bit, Doolan stomps halfway in from shortstop, and bellows toward the grandstand:

"Where's that sheriff? . . . You can have him now!"

The sheriff actually came out on the field to get me. But the mayor's wife must have felt sorry for me, because she withdrew the charge on the spot.

I was somewhat encouraged by my experience at Rochester the last half of the '17 season. Not being able to throw the ball hard any more, I'd learned to be cute. And I knew of many pitchers who seemed finished because of arm trouble but had come back by "pitching with their heads."

The United States was in the Great War, and many players already were getting ready to leave for service. I knew I would be called any time, but was sure I couldn't possibly pass the physical, because by now I'd lost almost 50 per cent of my hearing. Between the draft and my uncertain baseball status, I had no idea what was in store for me in the next year.

One day I received a telegram from a Tom Keady, who said he was baseball and football coach of Lehigh University and also manager of the Bethlehem Steel Company baseball team at Bethlehem, Pennsylvania. He wanted me to play ball for Bethlehem and offered me five hundred dollars a month, which was actually two hundred dollars more a month than I'd ever been paid as a professional. It seems the steel company heads thought that a baseball team would be a good morale booster for the defense employees, so they formed a "steel league" made up of various branches of Bethlehem Steel—such as Wilmington, Delaware, Fall River, Massachusetts, Steelton, Pennsylvania, and another outside of Baltimore. Most of the players in the league were recruited from professional minor league clubs, guys who were turned down for military service or were waiting to be called.

I'd told Keady I'd be glad to play for them if they'd also give a place on the team to my old pal, Dolly Stark, who'd become a pretty fair ballplayer. Dolly got a utility infielder's job, and he and I moved to Bethlehem, Pennsylvania.

In order for me to "earn" as much as five hundred dollars a month, the company felt it should give me an official title as a sort of cover-up, so they made me a "consulting engineer." And the first day I reported, I was introduced to all the legit engineers as the new consulting engineer. None of the other employees knew who I was or why I was really there, yet.

After several days of nosing around, one afternoon I happened to stroll through Shop No. Two, where huge cannons were being assembled. A group of workers were setting up a big crane, which they called the "million-dollar crane," and I stopped to watch the operation, which seemed pretty important, although I had no idea what the hell was going on.

They were trying to get the crane balanced in a certain spot high above the floor, and were concentrating on a thick steel cable and electric pulley on the right side of the crane, which was supposed to level it off in just the right spot but wasn't quite making it. One of the engineers in on the problem spotted me watching and came over to me and said:

"Mr. Schacht, we're having a hell of a time with the right wing of this crane. We've been working on the damn thing for two hours now, but it won't seem to level off where we want it. Have you got any suggestions?"

I glanced at him quickly to see if he was pulling my leg. But he looked serious; he really thought I was a consulting engineer. So, clasping my hands behind me and frowning thoughtfully, I said:

"Why don't you try the cable and pulley on the left-hand side? That might do it."

"Say, that might be an idea at that," he smiled, all excited.

That really surprised me, because I was only spoofing. But in ten minutes they'd hooked the crane up as I'd suggested, and I was dying to see how it would work. After fifteen minutes of jockeying, they went up and measured the crane's line-up again, and now it balanced perfectly.

The engineer called. "Thanks a million, Mr. Schacht!" and I walked modestly away, figuring that I better get out of there while I was still ahead.

The following Saturday, I was slated to pitch against the Steelton team, and this same engineer was at the game, sitting with Dave Petty, a big shot in the company who'd given me my title, Consulting Engineer. When the engineer heard my name announced as pitcher and saw me warming up, he stood up, his eyes bulging, and cried to Petty, "Why that goddam consulting engineer is only a ballplayer!" They got to kid him unmercifully at Bethlehem Steel for a long time after the story came out. Whenever he ran into a problem everybody said to him, "Go see Schacht, he'll take care of you."

I'd pitched only a few games, without my arm hurting as much as it had, when I got my draft notice. As I say, I was sure I'd be rejected for my hearing; but if by chance I wasn't, the Schacht family would really be in a mess, because Lou also expected to be called.

Dave Petty asked me how my family would make out if I was drafted and I confessed that was the one thing I worried about. I could hardly believe my ears when Petty suggested he could rent a house at Bethlehem for my mom and the kids and send a company truck to New York for the furniture, and would even give my brothers jobs at the plant if they wanted.

When I got back to New York the next day, I excitedly told Mom about Petty's idea and she seemed pleased by it. Then I told her about my draft notice, but so she wouldn't worry I said if I did go in the Army it would just be to play baseball. We started getting everything together to move her and the kids to Bethlehem.

I went to the draft board for my physical, and when the doctor who was chairman of the board was making out a form on me he asked if I had any physical defects.

"I'm hard of hearing," I said.

His eyes narrowed as he looked up at me. "You hear me now, don't you?" he said.

"Sure I do," I replied. "I said I'm hard of hearing, not deaf."

"Frankly," he said, "I think you are stalling."

"If you weren't a quack doctor," I steamed, "you'd check my ears to find out whether I'm lying or not."

He glared at me for a moment, then wrote on the form that I was okay for induction.

I reported for assignment June 1, 1918, at Fort Slocum, which is on an island just a few miles off New Rochelle. I discovered just before I got there that my orders called for "examination only."

It was exactly 12 noon when I stepped off the ferry at Fort Slocum. I was walking up the path from the dock when a soldier stopped me.

"By God!" he cried, "Al Schacht! Are you coming in the Army?"

I didn't know him, so I figured he'd seen me pitch. Sure enough, he said excitedly:

"Our company has a championship ball game this afternoon. How about pitching for us?"

"I'm sorry," I said, "but I'm just here for a physical, and if I pass I think I'm headed for Georgia."

But he insisted on bringing me to meet his company commander, a Captain Davenport, right away. When the captain heard the soldier's idea, he called in a sergeant.

"Take *Mr.* Schacht over to the dispensary, sergeant," he ordered. "He has to be examined immediately."

A little bewildered, I followed the sergeant to the hospital. There, a doctor, a major, worked me over from head to foot. When he'd finished, he turned to the sergeant and said, "I'll have to reject this man. His hearing is too bad. You'd better tell Captain Davenport."

So the sergeant called the captain on the telephone, and in a few minutes a *master* sergeant came busting in and went straight to whisper in the major's ear.

The major looked at me and said, "Schacht, step down to the other end of the room, will you."

Then he hollered at the top of his voice, "Sixty-seven!"

I could have heard that if I was in Asia. I said, "Sixty-seven."

"You pass," he said.

Maybe I should have answered, "Seventy-two," or "Twenty-nine," or something else. Because now they had me. The war was getting serious.

By twelve-thirty I was Private Alexander Schacht. At one-thirty I was wearing a uniform—a 2d Company baseball uniform, pitching against former New York Yankee hurler Ray Fisher and his 6th Company team.

If I'd lost that first game, they'd have found my ears bad again and canned me back to civilian life. Unfortunately, I won, mainly because for the first time in two years I'd been able to pitch normally with hardly any pain. It was a hell of a time for my arm to come back to life, just as the Army had grabbed me.

They fixed it so I would be made permanent party man at Fort Slocum, not subject to overseas duty. I was lucky, because three fourths of the personnel at Slocum were Regular Army men, and it was rare for a recruit to be assigned as permanent party. I was given two jobs on the base: one was checking in draftees from the New England states; the other was kitchen police.

I mentioned to Captain Davenport one day, "If I have to keep peeling potatoes, I don't see how I'll be able to pitch for this man's army," because by then I was playing not only for the 2d Company team but the post team. He laughed and said, "The only way you can keep out of the kitchen is to become a non-com." I said, "I'm not even a Pfc. yet." But before long, the papers returned from Washington officially okaying me as permanent party at Slocum, and I was made a Private First Class. Later still I made corporal and even got to eat at the officers' mess by posing as a football player.

I've always maintained it was I who won World War I for our side, because when I went in the Army we were losing, and when I got out we had won. Not only that, but the Armistice was signed on my birthday, November 11, 1918. Everybody at Slocum got a pass that day, and we all went to New York. Broadway was a madhouse—there was a big parade, and thousands of people milled around, laughing, shouting, blowing horns. Everything went, including kissing strange girls and hugging other men's wives. It was the wildest and happiest celebration I'd ever seen.

I made up my mind to try to get out of the Army as fast as possible, to get back to baseball the following spring. I was eager as a kid again, my arm was not hurting at all any more. What's more, Mom moved the family back to New York from Bethlehem, getting an apartment on Wheeler Avenue in the East Bronx, and I wanted to spend a little time with them before going away again.

By February 1919, I was still stationed at Fort Slocum. Only a skeleton crew was left there now—it looked like everybody was discharged but me. Getting more anxious every day, as baseball season drew nearer, I went to Captain Davenport and said:

"What in hell's holding me up? Do they expect another war and want to save themselves the trouble of drafting me all over again?"

"I'll give it to you straight, Al," he said. "According to what I've learned about your last physical, they found your hearing is now only 60 per cent of normal. But when you entered the Army your hearing was . . . ahem . . . *listed* as normal. So now your case apparently is making the rounds of the Surgeon General's office in Washington. I'm sorry—but you get the picture."

I got it all right. Evidently the Army was afraid I might sue the government for the loss of my hearing, which, as far as official records showed, I'd suffered while in service.

About the middle of March the situation hadn't changed. I was on pass in New York, and ran into a Mr. Brown, who I knew as ward captain of my congressional district. He laughed and said:

"Well, you must really like the Army to stay in."
"Like it? I can't get out!"
"What do you mean?" he said surprised.
"Oh, something to do with my hearing," I said.
"You really want out?"
"Damn right," I swore. "I want to play ball again."

That was all we said about it, and I forgot the conversation. But less than a week later a communication was delivered from the Army's Governors Island headquarters to Fort Slocum that I was going to be discharged at last. My memory is a little hazy on this point, but I seem to recall signing a paper waiving any disability claim against the Government. April 1, 1919, I said good-by to Fort Slocum, and the Army.

I had no time now to visit at home. The day after my release, I went straight to Newark to see if my old club would take me back. But Newark had long since written off Schacht as a sore arm pitcher, so I signed with their hated rivals, Jersey City. It wasn't easy because no one was convinced that my arm had come back.

My first start was against Newark, of all teams, and I whipped them. I beat them three straight games that season without a loss, bearing down harder against that club than any other. My arm felt great, and that season, with a last-place ball team, I won nineteen games and lost sixteen.

About midseason, I began to get ideas about more money. Not only was I the club's best pitcher, but they were depending on me to bring in fans too. No matter what day of the week I'd already pitched, when we were in Jersey City on Sunday, I pitched again. One Sunday, I tackled Bill Donovan, our manager, at his boardinghouse.

"Bill, I'm doing all the pitching on this club, right?" He agreed. "I think I've proved there's a good chance of me being sold to the big leagues, right?" Yes. "So I think I ought to get more money than two hundred dollars, as that isn't enough for me to get by on."

He said, "That's not up to me, Al. But I'll arrange a meeting for you with Mr. Moran at his office in New York."

A few days later I had the appointment. Frank Moran's office was in the Vanderbilt Theatre building. Besides being a very wealthy coal and lumber tycoon, he also owned several theaters and spent a lot of his time around them. I remember then at the Vanderbilt Theatre a hit show was playing, *Sally, Irene and Mary*. When I walked into his office over the theater, two show girls were there. Moran asked me to sit, then proceeded to babble theater talk with these flashy dolls for a full hour while I waited.

Finally they left, and Moran started right out talking about baseball and telling me how much money he was losing on our ball club. I could see he knew damn well why I was there and was trying to con me before I could even open my mouth. Then Bill Donovan opened the door and came in, smiling, "Did you fellas get together yet?"

With that, Moran said, "Well, what's on your mind, Al?" After an hour of making me listen to theater talk and another half hour crying on my shoulder, he finally asks what's on my mind. So I gave him a piece of it, just like I'd told Donovan.

"How much do you want?" Moran said.

"I should get at least a hundred dollars a month more."

Turning to Donovan, Moran said: "Do you think he's worth it?"

"I think he certainly is," Bill replied.

"All right, Al," Moran said, "at the end of the season I'll give you a lump sum equal to a hundred extra a month from now until the end of the season."

I didn't want to come right out and insult the man. So instead of telling him to put it in writing, which would look like I didn't trust him—between you and me, I *didn't* trust him—I said:

"No, no. I want it from the *start* of the season, and I need it *now*. That's why I'm asking now. By the end of the season, a rich uncle might die and leave me a fortune, and I won't need extra money. No, sir, what you give me later is not helping me now."

He stared at me, his eyes wide. Then he relaxed and smiled: "You win."

He not only paid me a hundred dollars for each previous month, but gave me the extra money for the remaining months in advance.

After all that, you'll never guess what happened the very next game I pitched—I got pounded, 18–1. So help me. Here's the story. . . .

We had moved up to Buffalo for a series the day after my great business transaction. Our first day there was an off-day, so Ben Egan, my catcher, invited me to his farm at Sherrill, New York. We were not only late getting back to Buffalo but we stopped for a beer at one of the local taverns.

The next afternoon at the ball park, Donovan cornered me in the dugout and said:

"Don't think I didn't see you and Egan sneaking out of that saloon at one-fifteen this morning."

I tried to tell him exactly what had happened, but he wouldn't listen.

"All I know is," he said, "I saw you coming out of that saloon at one-fifteen. So—you are pitching today, mister."

"I only pitched two days ago . . ."

"You are pitching today."

It was either because of lack of sleep or just rotten pitching, but I got some going-over. By the fifth inning, the score is 11–1, Buffalo, and I'm still in there. The crowd is heckling me and hollering, "Take him out! Take him out!"

Before going out to pitch the sixth, I pleaded with Donovan: "If you wanted me to learn a lesson by getting a beating, you've got your wish. But why do I have to keep taking it now?"

Bill just said, "You'll keep pitching if they score a million runs."

I blew my stack and yelled, "I hope they do, damn you!"

"That'll cost you twenty-five bucks," he said.

I was so mad I cracked back: "Why don't you make it a hundred?"

"I just did."

Now I'm wondering if he's trying to get Moran's dough back for him. I stormed out to the mound seeing red. Disgusted, I accidentally hit the first batter in the back with my first pitch. The crowd kept hooting, "Take him out!" When I walked the next two batters to fill the bases with none out, I realized I was losing complete control of myself. Then all of a sudden I found myself chuckling.

Calling time, I walked slowly up to home plate, and made a speech to the grandstands.

"Ladies and gentlemen, all during this game you've hollered, 'Take him out! Take him out!' I just got through talking with my manager, and I want him to take some blame. He won't take me out. Now you'll notice there are three men on base. I will show you how to get out of this hole. I thank you."

Striding back to the pitcher's box, I wound up and threw one pitch to the next hitter. He slammed it far over the left field wall for a grand slam home run, all the other runners trotting home ahead of him. Then I walked halfway to the plate again and said to the stands:

"Folks, I always keep my word. The bases are now empty. I am out of that hole." And I bowed low. They gave me a big ovation.

Over in the dugout, Donovan was doubled over, laughing. Later, he removed the hundred-dollar fine—but I had to finish the game.

It was now mid-August, and I couldn't understand why no big league scouts seemed much interested in my fine comeback. I wondered if it was because I was still so skinny and light, or maybe because I was clowning on the field more than ever and they were leery of taking a comic seriously. Anyway, I decided to take things into my own hands, because I knew, if no one else did, that I was ready for the majors.

I picked up a copy of *The Sporting News*, the weekly newspaper known as the "baseball bible," and read where Clark Griffith, manager and vice president of the Washington Senators, was in bad need of pitchers. The club was doomed to the second division, and Griffith wanted to start rebuilding, the story said.

I got an idea. I cut out a clipping from the Jersey City newspaper telling of another victory for me and sent it to Griffith with a short note. I did this every time I won during the next couple of weeks, sending him five clippings and letters in all. The messages read something like this:

Dear Mr. Griffith,

Inclosed please find a newspaper clipping telling of the fine work of a pitcher named Al Schacht of the Jersey City ball club in the International League. He's without a doubt the best pitcher in the league. I've been watching baseball for a good many years, and I think I know a pitcher when I see one. Please smarten up and look this fellow over. He will do your club a lot of good.

Just a Fan

The pressure was too much for Griff. He scouted me himself. I didn't know it, but he was watching the day I blanked Binghamton, 2–0, for my tenth shutout.

A few days later I received a telegram:

YOU ARE NOW PROPERTY WASHINGTON BASEBALL CLUB. YOU'LL REPORT HERE IMMEDIATELY FOLLOWING INTERNATIONAL LEAGUE SEASON. BE READY TO PITCH AGAINST DETROIT.

CLARK GRIFFITH

I jumped for joy. I was a big leaguer at last!—something I'd been waiting for since 1908 when I first sold pop and peanuts at the Polo Grounds.

I've often said that Griffith bought me for $18 down and $9.00 when I made good. Actually, it's true that in those days players were purchased on a sort of lay-away plan—Griff bought me for $2,500, paying Jersey City $1,000 outright, with the balance due if I still was with the Washington club by the following June 1. And there was plenty of doubt about any young pitcher sticking with a major league club that long. They didn't fool around with you in those days. If you reported from the minors at 2 P.M., started your first game at 3, and got knocked out at 3:15, you might be on your way back to the minors by 3:30.

I arrived in Washington—September 20, 1919. The Washington *Star* had a story about me which amused me. I was only going on twenty-six, but I'd been pitching so long apparently everybody thought I walked with a cane. For the *Star* article's headline read:

AL "RIP VAN WINKLE" SCHACHT
JOINS WASHINGTON CLUB

If *they* thought it had taken me a long time to reach the big leagues, imagine how long it had seemed to *me*.

chapter **10**

When I reported to Mr. Griffith I was grinning because I figured he'd remember me from when I'd come up to his Cincinnati club from Walton long ago. But in nine years he must have seen a lot of rookies coming and going, and he didn't seem to know me.

"Oh, yes . . . Schacht," he said. "Well, son, you work out a little today, but don't tire yourself. I may need you."

We were playing the Detroit Tigers, and what a bunch of bombers they were!

There was Bobby Veach in left, hitting .360; Ty Cobb in center, hitting a mere .400; and Harry Heilmann, first base, at .325. About the only guy any way connected with that club not hitting over .300 was the assistant groundskeeper. And to think I might make my big league debut against this club!

Griff had a habit of never letting his pitchers know until just before game time who was going to pitch any given day. This day, three of us were allowed to take batting practice with the regulars, which meant any one of us would be the pitcher against the powerful Tigers. After hitting a few, I went to the dugout and asked George McBride, our shortstop and team captain:

"How does a guy know when he pitches on this club?"

McBride said, "About twenty minutes before the game, Griff will reach in the ball bag for a new ball. He'll call out a pitcher's name and toss the ball to him."

I watched the manager. In about five minutes, he dug down into the ball bag, then straightened and looked toward the bench. I stiffened. But he called, "Courtney!" and tossed the ball right past my nose (which is one hell of a toss).

Courtney pitched a great game—for eight innings, holding the

Detroit sluggers to just one run, and we lead, 2–1, as the Tigers bat in the top of the ninth. Then the leadoff hitter socks a three-base hit, and a moment later Cobb singles and the tying run is across. A base on balls; and another, and now they got three on base and still none out.

Griff looks up and down our bench and says, "Where is that young fellow who just joined us today?"

"Here I am," I answer in a small voice.

"Run down to the bullpen and warm up," he says, "I may need you quick."

By the time I get to the bullpen and toss about three pitches, Courtney has three balls and one strike on the next batter, Harry Heilmann. Griff calls time and waves for me.

With the score tied, nobody out and the bases loaded, I'm to make my debut!

When I reach the mound, McBride comes in from shortstop and says, "Kid, just get the ball over." I reply, "Don't worry, I'll get it over."

My catcher, Charity, trots out to say: "What do you wanna throw, a curve ball or fast ball?"

"What the hell's the difference?"

He goes back behind the plate, and for the first time I see Harry Heilmann standing there with that big bat, and he's got an expression on his face like, Sonny, you sure look cute.

I glance around the infield, and it looks like there's more people on base than there are in the grandstands. I stand there, deliberating, taking all the time I can—hell, I want to stay in the big leagues as long as possible. While I'm deliberating, Cobb, the runner at third and fastest man in the league, is prancing up and down the base line, trying to make me nervous. He isn't helping me any, I'll tell you that.

Finally I go into my windup and put everything I have on a curve ball. I got it over all right but it never reached the catcher. Heilmann hit a wicked shot off my third baseman's ankle, almost crippling the poor guy, scoring what proved to be the winning run.

The very next day we played the St. Louis Browns, and Griff let me pitch. We beat them, 4–3. The Browns weren't a bad club in those days, for they had George Sisler, who I think probably was the best first baseman ever. He usually batted about .400, but he didn't get a hit off me that day.

I was walking on air after winning my first start in the American League.

Four days later, on the last day of the 1919 season, I started again, and whipped the Boston Red Sox, 6–2. The Washington club wound up in seventh place, but I had a nice 2–0 record.

When I returned home after the season, I was the toast of the East Bronx. Mom and the kids treated me like a king, including Lou, who was married and had his own home now.

The guys in the neighborhood welcomed me with open arms too, but they seemed different. We were all older, of course; but the guys who were still single were much wilder than we had been in our younger days. They wanted me to join them right away on their all-night parties.

But my hopes were too bright for the next baseball season. I was flying high, and felt I couldn't afford to louse myself up by breaking training. Instead, I packed up and went upstate to Walton, New York, to visit Fay Darling again.

Fay was several years older than me. He owned a hardware store. I stayed with him from about mid-November through January of 1920. I'd saved some money to live on, so all I did was take long walks and go fishing. I ate three solid meals a day and got plenty of rest—it was the first time since God knows when that I had an opportunity just to do absolutely nothing.

The main reason I kept going back to Walton to visit was sentiment: I'd started in organized baseball there, for four dollars a week and board, and as I'd moved up in baseball and now that I was a big leaguer at last, the townspeople, who'd always treated me swell, were real proud of me and practically took me in as their own.

I got taken in another way too. In January, I received a contract from the Washington club, which Mom had forwarded from home, offering me I think $275 a month, which was only $75 more than they'd given me breaking in the previous fall. But I thought I deserved at least $350 a month. So now, after only two winning games as a big leaguer, I become a holdout. I guess I took the cake for gall, writing back to Mr. Griffith that his contract was not satisfactory to me.

I received no answer by the end of the month, so, with my money running low, I decided to head back to New York. The night before I was to leave, I made the rounds in Walton saying good-by, and when I stopped into the local pool parlor, a couple of the guys said:

"How about one last game of pill pool, Al?"

That's when I got took. I lost my last twenty-one dollars. The next day I wired Griffith: SEND ME FIFTY DOLLARS ADVANCE MONEY AND I'LL SIGN FOR TWO SEVENTY-FIVE.

I didn't know it then, but the way things were with Griff, he might easily have wired back, YOU SEND THE FIFTY DOLLARS AND I'LL JOIN YOU. He actually didn't have fifty bucks to send me. The Washington club, which wasn't doing very well either on the ball field or in the pocketbook, was in the middle of a big changeover. Griffith, who was vice president, business manager, and a minor stockholder in addition to field manager, was dissatisfied with the way the officers were running the franchise, and he made up his mind to gain controlling interest and remake the club. He'd just got through hocking his insurance and selling his ranch trying to raise the necessary cash, when who wires for fifty smackers but Schacht.

I didn't hear from Griff, so I borrowed money to get home to the Bronx. Finally I settled with him on the contract, after considerable haggling, and he signed me at $325 a month, my highest salary to date.

In February, joining some other players in Washington, we took a train to the club's Tampa, Florida, training base. I felt in great shape, but after all my healthy living during the winter, I'd gained exactly two pounds—for me this was nearing the heavyweight division, about 138.

It was in Tampa that spring that I first got to know Nick Altrock. It was the beginning of a clowning partnership that would become famous both in baseball and vaudeville, and would lead to my own individual success as baseball's "Clown Prince" and as a restaurateur. Many people who watched Altrock and me and, I hope, laughed at our antics, might be interested to know that almost from the beginning we never liked each other—and in the later years of our partnership, *we never spoke.*

Until I joined Washington, Altrock was the recognized clown of the American League. He was the first base coach, and the fans used to love the way he'd clown at first base during infield practice, juggle baseballs and mimic umpires during games. When he appeared with his cap sideways on his head and his big plug of tobacco popping his jaw, they loved it. And so did Nick.

He was a former American League pitcher, and a pretty good one. A left-hander, he probably had his best year in 1906 when the Chicago White Sox, who were known as the Hitless Wonders, upset the favored Chicago Cubs in the Series. Nick had such a clever pick-off move to first base, they say he used to purposely allow runners to get on base just so he could pick them off and give the crowds a thrill.

I guess he felt secure as baseball's number one clown until the day I came to Washington. Back in September before I joined the club, my old pal Joe Judge had said to the other players: "Wait'll you see *this* screwball!"

I suppose from that moment on, Nick had had his eye on me. At Tampa, some of the other players got Altrock and me together occasionally to gag for them, but Nick was anything but friendly. This seemed stupid to me because at that time I was planning to stick in the American League as a pitcher, not a clown.

Some organization staged a benefit show in a hotel in Tampa, I forget what for, and they invited Altrock to perform. Then, hearing also that I had a reputation for being funny, they came to me and asked if I'd team up with Nick that night.

I dreamed up a number for us, a singing burlesque of a scene from the *Lucia* Sextet, but I had to talk Nick into doing it. His type of comedy was mostly mugging, while I always leaned toward planned routines, gags. We rehearsed for a few minutes before going on—it was the *only* time in our long partnership that we ever rehearsed a number—and got a pretty good response from the audience. But I saw that our styles didn't blend; nor did I think that we'd ever see eye to eye on comedy or anything else.

I knew for sure Nick and I would never hit it off a few weeks later when I first saw what he was like with too much to drink. He spied me in the hotel and insisted I go out drinking with him. I refused. He shouted I was nothing but a "Jew kike bastard!" I knew he was under the weather, but I didn't like it. I never did.

Breaking camp in Tampa, we had a series of exhibitions with the Cincinnati Reds of the National League on the homeward trip. The Reds were the world's champions, having upset the powerful White Sox in the 1919 Series. The first game with them was in Miami. If I'd had any money and sense just then, I'd be a millionaire today.

A former ballplayer named Doyle approached some of us at our hotel saying he was a real estate man and that he had some lots he'd like to sell us at Miami Beach. About twenty players from the two teams went with him to inspect these lots. There was no beautiful causeway across the bay from the mainland to Miami Beach then, just a bumpy string of rocks that had been leveled off. And Miami Beach was a long stretch of nothing but sand, rocks, weeds and shrubbery. The only civilized thing we saw was Fisher's Pavilion, a rickety building with a small beach for bathers. It was the most barren, desolate spot I'd ever seen.

Doyle announced we could buy lots along the beach for from $150 to $300 a piece, any lot we wanted. Then, to me he added: "I advise you to buy ten or so. This is a potential gold mine."

I laughed, "Who the hell would ever want to live in this goddam place?" And the other players agreed. So we turned around and went back to Miami.

Some of those parcels of land we laughed at are now worth about twenty-five thousand dollars each. If I had bought ten lots when Doyle recommended it, right now I'd probably be rolling in dough and own a beautiful home on the beach.

The funny thing was that when we left Miami by train soon after, we threw the biggest crap game you ever saw in the baggage car. The Cincinnati team was known as the best bunch of crapshooters in baseball, and some of the boys won and lost enough money to buy every lot in Miami Beach.

The tour north was great for me. It was plain Griff planned to use me as one of his regular starters, and I was showing I appreciated his confidence. Pitching three or four innings every few days, as starters do in spring exhibitions, I was headed for a big season.

Opening Day was in Washington. To me, the stadium was like heaven; it was a strange, thrilling new world, with the roar of the thousands of fans, the banners, the bands, marching to the flagpole in center field. Both teams lined up along the first and third base lines while President Woodrow Wilson threw out the first ball. Then the National Anthem; and watching the flags flying on the stadium roof, I was all goose pimples. I said to myself, what I wouldn't give to start this game!

I knew damn well no one but Walter Johnson could pitch for Washington on Opening Day.

Next we moved on to Philadelphia for the Athletics' opener, and this time I got my chance to pitch. Only two of us pitchers took batting practice before the game, and Griff tossed the ball to me. Philadelphia manager Connie Mack didn't have much of a ball club, but I still bore down all the way, and with a little luck beat the A's, 7–0. Now I was really in the big league.

My record was 5-and-1 when I lost my second, in Boston. The day after that defeat, I saw my first no-hitter. Johnson pitched it. While he was in his fourteenth season with Washington, he still was by far the fastest and best pitcher in baseball. I'll never forget the ninth inning of that game: Boston still without a hit, had two out when somebody hit a drive down the first base line that looked like good all the way.

But Joe Judge made one of the greatest fielding plays I ever saw. Literally sliding on his belly, he knocked the ball down, then touched the base with his fingers before the runner got there. Johnson's no-hitter was saved.

In the clubhouse later when we were congratulating Walter, someone cried, "Speech!"

These were his exact words: "Goodness gracious sakes alive, wasn't I lucky!"

That's the strongest language I ever heard Walter Johnson use.

In fact, the Washington club had later on what we playfully called "the cussin' battery": Johnson's worst was "goodness gracious sakes alive!" and catcher Muddy Ruel's, "dog-gum it!"

It's impossible for me to say how awed I was being on the same ball team with Johnson, a guy I'd read so much about and admired from afar for so many years. I resolved to find out just what kind of man he really was.

Johnson originally came from a farm in Kansas, and he later bought himself a farm and was a farmer when he died in 1946. The fact is, the big good-natured guy was a hick all his life, but a wonderful hick.

According to the story, this is how he first came to the majors: Baseball heard about a powerful, rawboned farm boy in Kansas who could fire a ball, and Washington sent a scout to look him over. The scout wired back: "This is the fastest man I've ever seen pitch." So they signed him.

He reported to Washington, all six foot two and 190 pounds of him, in a tweedy suit two sizes too small, wearing a derby hat, also too small, and carrying a paper bag containing only his spiked shoes and a supporter. They sent him in to pitch right away, and he lost 2-1, because he couldn't field a bunted ball and the other team discovered it and drove him crazy with bunts.

It was the custom then for the teams to travel between the hotel and ball park in a "tally-ho," a horsecar. After that game, Johnson, in his confusion, missed the tally-ho and was left alone at the park. So, in his uniform and spikes, he clattered along the streets of the capital looking for the hotel—which was four miles away.

On the way, the big rube got caught up in a noisy parade of colored people, and, too embarrassed to slip away, he marched in the middle of the parade for blocks and blocks, until he finally came within sight of his hotel. By this time he was desperate enough to make a break for it.

Maybe he didn't swear, and he might have been a simple country boy, but could he pitch! He threw sort of sidearm-underhand and had only one kind of pitch, his fast ball. In baseball they say if a pitcher keeps throwing the same ball over and over, sooner or later the hitters will catch on, learn to time it and belt his ears off. You couldn't prove it by Johnson—he didn't mix 'em up, had no curve ball or slow change-up pitch, no trick delivery like a spit ball or shine ball or mud ball, just the fast ball. And with the batters knowing he would throw only the fast ball, he'd still bang it past them time and again.

It's a good thing Walter had fine control. For if he had been scatterarmed, or had been suspected of "dusting off" batters, as many pitchers do, I doubt if anybody would have showed up to hit against him.

On dark, cloudy days, his fast ball was almost invisible, and opposing players wanted no part of Johnson. It was remarkable how many grandmothers died or children got sick on days like that when Walter was due to pitch. I remember one game against Cleveland, it was overcast and drizzly and Johnson was, as they say, firing aspirin tablets. A Cleveland batter named Chapman, who later got killed by a pitched ball, got up, and Walter exploded a strike past him. Then another sizzler for strike two. Chapman shook his head, dropped his bat at the plate and walked back toward his bench.

Billy Evans, the umpire, called, "Come back, Chappy, you got another strike coming."

Chapman said over his shoulder: "You can have it, I don't want it."

He did go back, but when he waved at that third strike he was nowhere near home plate.

But for all his power, Walter sometimes could loaf when pitching. For instance, if he had a club beaten by two or more runs, and a batter facing him happened to be in a slump, I know Johnson would often lay a pitch right down the middle so the guy might connect for a hit. Maybe he'd get himself in a jam that way and have to bear down harder to get out of it. On those occasions the other team always knew Walter was ready to burn them in when he'd bend down and pick up a handful of dirt and let it sift through his fingers.

They called him "Sir Walter" and "The Kansas Cyclone," but my favorite was "The Big Train" because he was so big and threw a fast ball that practically smoked, and could pitch all day without much refueling. Walter never drank or smoked, and his only pick-me-up was an ice cream soda. He was a faithful family man. He was a quiet, retiring type, but if anyone came around with any kind of plea or cause to support, Walter would show what a softie he was and go out of his way to help out, financially or otherwise. He also was stubborn as a mule, for once he made up his mind about something, nobody could change it.

There was the time, and long before I joined the club, when he lost to the Yankees in Washington and all the newspapers came out with stories that as great as Johnson was, he couldn't beat the Yanks. His manager then, Joe Cantillion, told Walter not to think anything of such stories, but the idea bothered him. So the next time Washington went to New York, Johnson asked to open the series. It was on a Friday.

He shut out the Yankees that day. And when the papers still said he'd been lucky, he came back the very next day, Saturday, and shut them out again. To prove once and for all it wasn't luck, he blanked them for the third straight game on Monday, allowing fewer hits than he had on Friday. I guess the only reason he didn't pitch Sunday was because Sunday baseball was prohibited in New York at that time.

After this third shutout, Walter said to Cantillion: "Great Scott alive, I hope they stop saying I'm lucky now."

In 1925, when I was a coach with Washington, we were in our second straight World Series, this time against Pittsburgh, the National League champion. The two teams split the first six games. The day of the deciding game, in Pittsburgh, was chilly and rainy. Johnson, who was nearing the end of his career, was due to pitch but was in bad shape, with charley horses in both legs, which had to be strapped up in elastic bandages. We were hoping the game would be postponed so Johnson could get an extra day of rest.

Looking out at the muddy field, somebody said, "It's too wet out there. There'll be a lot of lousy ball playing today."

Johnson, who was in real pain, said, "Let's play it. It's just as tough for the other guys as it is for us."

We played, and it was pitiful. Picture Johnson, hardly able to move his aching legs, rain drops and perspiration streaming down his face, having to call for sawdust now and then so he could grip the slimy baseball, pitching almost on courage alone, as Pittsburgh rattled line drive base hits off him and our team kept making errors which had him in trouble every inning. But he still made it close, and it was only on a fluke hit that we lost that game and the Series.

Afterwards, reporters flocked into our dressing room to get a statement from the weary Johnson. All he said was: "The best team won."

There was much guessing later about why manager Bucky Harris didn't take Johnson out. Bucky said, "If this club was going down in this Series, I wanted to go down with the greatest pitcher who ever lived."

But, to get back to 1920, Johnson's no-hitter came at the end of June. It was doubly exciting because he was having a comparatively poor season, later suffering with a sore arm. So Griffith, knowing Walter was still the number one drawing card of the Washington club, decided to profit by his great performance in Boston and advertised that he would pitch against the Yankees in the big Fourth of July doubleheader in Washington.

At that time ten thousand people at a Washington ball game was a terrific crowd. On this July Fourth, the doubleheader was split into morning and afternoon games. Johnson was to pitch the second game, and the biggest crowd of the year turned out to see him in action—eighteen thousand people.

But about an hour before game time, Griff called the team in the clubhouse for a meeting, and he looked grim.

"Johnson can't pitch," he said sadly. "Not only is his arm bothering him again, but he strained a muscle in his groin. . . . Five years ago I advertised Johnson would pitch, just like today, and almost the same thing happened. The fans stormed the box office demanding their money back. . . . And we've got a bigger crowd today," he groaned, pacing back and forth.

"Men, I'm in a desperate spot"—he gazed slowly around the room— "And so is the pitcher who has to take Johnson's place. . . . It's between Ericson, Courtney, Shaw and Schacht. . . . Who wants the ball?"

The dressing room was silent for half a minute. Nobody stirred. Just the breathing. Then a voice shattered the stillness:

"I'll pitch it, Griff."

The voice was mine. It startled everybody, including myself. Griff stared at me—he must have been thinking, A rookie like him? —then came over and handed me the ball. Gripping my shoulder, he said:

"If you win this game today, Al, as long as I have anything to say about this ball club you'll have a job with me. I mean it. I don't care if you don't win another game this season—you've got to win this one!"

I walked out the door to the field, kicking myself for my big mouth. Because what Griff didn't say was what would happen if I didn't win.

The Yankees had begun to build their "murderer's row" reputation, with hitters like Babe Ruth, Bob Meusel, Duffy Lewis, Wally Pipp, Ping Bodie. Excitement was running high.

It was twenty minutes until game time when I started unlimbering near home plate. There was no reaction from the crowd at first; but when ten minutes went by and they still didn't see Johnson warming up, an angry murmur started rumbling through the stands.

Then the announcer was at the center of the diamond with his huge megaphone.

"Batteries for today's game!" he shouted. "For New York, Shawkey pitching and Ruel catching . . . For Washington, Schacht pitching and . . ."

He never did get to announce our catcher. As soon as they heard my name, the crowd let loose with a thunderous "B-o-o-oooooo!" Then the pop bottles and seat cushions started flying—*at me*.

It took me only a half second to realize I was a sitting duck standing out there alone, so I raced into the dugout and under the stands to complete my warmup. In a few minutes, after the field had been cleared and the game was ready to get going, I snuck back to the pitcher's box without being skulled. But they continued to jeer and hoot; and I couldn't blame them. They'd turned out, a record crowd, to see the great Johnson pitch, to pay him tribute for his no-hitter, and instead found a busher trying to fill their idol's shoes.

The Yankees' leadoff batter walked on four straight balls.

Now the bottles and cushions really flew. The fans must have been just warming up the first time, because now they were throwing better than I was. It took fifteen minutes to clear the field again.

But the Yanks failed to score that first inning. I held them in the second too, and in the third. Meanwhile our boys pushed across two runs, and in the fourth we led, 2–0. Then the Yankees filled the bases with only one out.

Up stepped Babe Ruth—and I struck him out on three pitches. Next was Duffy Lewis, and I also got him for the third out. As I walked back to the dugout, one lonely fan applauded. It must have been my brother.

By the eighth inning, we were ahead, 4–1. But the Yankees again got three men on bases with one out, and Ruth and Lewis coming up again.

I got them both on pop-ups. Then I staggered through the ninth, and we'd won, 4–1. And now they were standing, cheering me.

The Washington club went wild, carrying me on their shoulders and slapping me black and blue, as though we'd won the World Series. We were whooping it up in the clubhouse when Griffith dashed in. Laughing deliriously, he threw his arms around me and cried:

"Al, you were great, just great. And what I said before still goes—I don't care if you don't win another game the rest of the season!"

And, friends, I got news for you. I *didn't* win another game that season. A few days after my great triumph, I was sent in to relieve in a game against Detroit. I got to first on a base on balls (which was about the only way I could ever get on base). O'Rourke, the next batter, dropped a sacrifice bunt in front of the plate to move me to second. Oscar Stanage, Detroit's catcher, grabbed the ball and fired it to second to head me off. It was a high throw. I slid into the bag head first. Shortstop Donie Bush leaped up to snag the ball and crashed down heavily on me. A grinding pain ripped through my right shoulder, and I rolled over moaning.

Our club trainer ran out to massage my shoulder, and the pain lessened a bit. But when I tried to pitch the next inning, it was just like two bones rubbing together. So I asked Griff to take me out.

I didn't know it right then, but my promising big-league pitching career was just about finished.

chapter 11

The ball club sent me to a couple of doctors in Washington after my accident, but nothing much came of the visits. They told me I'd torn a ligament in my right shoulder and that it didn't look good for me pitching again. Griffith finally sent me and Johnson, who came down with a sore arm right after the no-hitter, to a famous specialist in Rochester, New York, a Dr. Knight. With me it was a case of Griff hating to lose a promising rookie; with Johnson, it was losing the meal ticket.

Walter and I took the train from Washington to Rochester. Walter was dejected, this being his first sore arm in fourteen big-league years and it puzzled him, and he didn't talk much. As for myself, I was getting used to it and I made myself clown around to buck him up. But when we got to Rochester, I became a little nervous myself and Walter snapped out of his own low spirits to encourage me.

But I was afraid I'd reached the last of my nine lives.

Dr. Knight concentrated on massage and heat treatments as he treated us at his home every day. After only three days, Johnson got restless and packed up and went back to Washington. I stayed in Rochester for a week, still going to the doctor every day. But when, at dinner one evening, I found I couldn't even slice a piece of steak without sharp pain, I decided to give it up too. The night before I was to return to the club, I sat in the hotel lobby for hours. *Suppose you can't pitch ever again. What are you going to do?*

What *could* I do? Work a sharpening machine in a razor blade factory? Sort shipments for an exporting house? Run deliveries for a jeweler?

I was not yet twenty-seven. How could a guy be a has-been at twenty-seven?

Griff had promised there'd always be a job for me, I remembered. Maybe I could coach . . . clown . . .

Something stirred in me.

From Washington I went to Youngstown, Ohio, to see what Bonesetter Reese could do for me. Bonesetter Reese was well known in baseball, and all over the world, as a near-miraculous healer of injured bones. He'd originally been a steelworker around Youngstown, but once when a fellow workman broke a leg on the job, Reese set it for him on the spot. It mended perfectly. Some local Youngstown ballplayer heard about it and went to Reese with a bad arm, and Reese cured it. It wasn't long before these stories spread through baseball, and players from everywhere started going to him for treatment. Reese quit the steel mill and became a Bonesetter.

He was an old man about sixty when I met him, and looked to me the image of pictures I'd seen of Mark Twain, the author—long, thick white mustache and white hair.

Reese examined me and said he couldn't help me because I had a torn ligament, which was not his specialty. But he told me that massage would only irritate my shoulder more and recommended that I use heat on the sore area in the hopes the ligament would mend.

I pitched very little the rest of that season, mostly in relief roles, and even then I considered myself lucky to get anybody out. Favoring my aching shoulder, I had to pitch in a herky-jerky sidearm motion instead of my straight overhand style. It felt awkward and I had no rhythm, and my control and "stuff" were off. But I was desperate to stay on as a pitcher, and it was better, I felt, to throw with some pain than not to pitch at all. When you have a sore leg, you can't run but you can hobble; and when you have a sore arm, you can't pitch but you can throw—it's that simple.

A month after my accident, I conned Griff into letting me start against the Chicago White Sox, the 1919 American League champs. I'd just returned from Youngstown, and Griff greeted me with:

"Well . . . ?"

"Feels pretty good," I fibbed. "I think I could start again."

Before the game, Griff held his usual team meeting in the dressing room to go over the weaknesses of the opposing hitters. As far as I could see, this great White Sox club didn't have any weaknesses.

"Let's see," Griffith began, ". . . Weaver, we'll skip him. . . . Risberg, we'll skip him. . . . Collins, let's skip him. . . ." (He's just skipping a bunch of .300 hitters, that's all.)

"Ah," Griff said, ". . . Jackson. He's the fellow I want to talk about, Al. Joe Jackson is the best fast ball hitter in the league. You try to make him hit your screwball. I don't care if he hits it out of the park—but *no fast balls* to Jackson. Got that?" Then he dismissed the meeting without mentioning the rest of the White Sox.

"What's the matter," I kidded George McBride, "ain't those other guys gonna play?" He laughed and said Griff probably would go over them with me in the dugout just before game time.

While I warmed up, Umpire Billy Evans passed on his way to his position at home plate, blowing air into his big rubber chest protector, and asked:

"How's your arm feel now, Al?"

With a straight face I shot back: "You better blow up that chest protector good. I'm gonna gun my fast ball not only past the batters but my catcher too."

I got knocked out in the first inning.

Weaver hit my first pitch for a single. My next pitch, Risberg singles. Collins pops up, also on my first pitch, and I'm beginning to suspect they're gunning for me. One out, up steps Jackson. My catcher flashes me the sign for the fast ball. We plan to kind of crowd Joe with the fast one, setting him up for the screwball. So I throw the fast ball—evidently it didn't crowd him enough, because a second later the ball is bouncing off the right center field wall and Jackson's got a triple and two runs are in. On four pitched balls.

Griffith had me out of there before Jackson slid into third base. Shuffling toward our bench with my head down, I heard Billy Evans call out, "Hey, Al! Look!" He was unscrewing the valve of his chest protector and letting all the air out. "I don't have to worry now," he laughed.

I tried to pass Griff without looking at him, but he grabbed my belt and pulled me around.

"You're not getting away with this so easy," he raved. "I bought you because I thought you were a smart pitcher. . . . In the meeting I told you not to give Jackson a fast ball. And you throw him a fast ball right away! You go to the clubhouse," he glared, "and look in the mirror, and you'll see the dumbest pitcher in the American League."

Was my face red! But I was mad enough to reply:

"Well, Mr. Griffith, there must be a helluva lot of dumb pitchers in this league, because Jackson's only hitting .385!" But I went and looked in the mirror anyway.

During the spring of 1920, there'd been some fantastic rumors floating around the training camps that the White Sox had "dumped" the World Series to the National League champs, Cincinnati!

The rumors said simply—"The Sox threw the Series," that was all. None of the players in the big leagues seemed to believe it. The Sox had a great ball club, one of the greatest ever put together, and it certainly had been an upset when Cincinnati won the Series, five games to three. For my part, I felt if a powerful club like Chicago was to lose on purpose, there had to be more than two or three players involved—and I just couldn't get it through my head that there could be so many dumb guys on one ball club.

During 1920, after our Washington club had received a pasting from the White Sox one day, I rode back to the hotel on a trolley with some of the Sox players mentioned in the rumors—Joe Jackson, Happy Felsch, Eddie Cicotte, and Swede Risberg. They were then battling Cleveland for the American League lead, and, still impressed with the way they'd belted us around that afternoon, I said to Jackson:

"You fellas got nothing to worry about. I don't see how Cleveland can beat a great ball club like you guys have."

"You're right, Al," Joe said, "we oughta win all right."

But they didn't. Cleveland won the pennant, and after the scandal broke in the front pages later, I remembered that conversation and wondered. . . .

No one knew then that after the Series in October 1919, Charles Comiskey, owner of the White Sox, who'd been heavily favored to win, made a statement that certain of his ballplayers would never play for the club again. That's when the gossip first began to get around about a "fix." Comiskey asked for a private investigation to dig up the facts. But Comiskey's old friend Ban Johnson, who had founded the American League and was its president, wanted no investigation.

Johnson figured the less found out about such horrible things, the better. So, with no investigations, the guys Comiskey threatened would never play for him again did play in 1920. But the rumors persisted, until finally some smart sports writer came out with a series of stories about the fix, giving the names not only of the players involved but the fixers. One of the fixers was Arnold Rothstein, who threatened the reporter and told him he'd wind up in an alley if he wrote any more stories.

Comiskey finally started his own investigation, offering ten thousand dollars to anyone who could testify against any of the White Sox players. I believe the first to speak up was Rube Benton, a New York Giants pitcher, who said he'd got a tip before the 1919 Series that he could make a pile of dough betting against Chicago because some of the Sox had been fixed by a Pittsburgh gambling syndicate. He also said the Giants first baseman, Hal Chase, had made about forty thousand dollars betting on the Series.

Then Sox pitcher Ed Cicotte confessed he'd received ten thousand dollars, which he found under his pillow the night before the Series opened. (Cicotte got knocked out of the box in the first game.) Cicotte said Chick Gandil, the first baseman, had cooked up the idea with the gamblers, which didn't surprise many people because he was a hard-boiled guy and kind of a sharpie.

The confession that was the hardest to believe was by "Shoeless"

Joe Jackson. One of the greatest hitters of all time, Jackson apparently had a great series in '19, winding up with a big .375 average for the eight games. But after confessing at first, Jackson later denied his part in the fix—he denied it to his dying day. Another surprise was Buck Weaver, White Sox second baseman and a great competitor and a guy who would rather win than eat. It turned out there were eight in all and all of them were barred from organized ball for life.

To me, the saddest part of all was that the "Black Sox" affair also uncovered a bunch of other incidents, which resulted in more scandal. Baseball was in a bad way.

The sport might never have recovered, in fact, if it hadn't been for two men: Kenesaw Mountain Landis and Babe Ruth. Landis was the federal judge who had once made headlines by slapping a sensational $29,000,000 fine on the Standard Oil Company. The baseball magnates asked him to become the first High Commissioner of the game, and the way he cracked the whip right off the bat helped swing baseball back onto the right path.

In 1920, the Babe hit fifty-four home runs; the next year, fifty-nine. He was something new in baseball, the long-ball slugger. (It is true that the official baseball was hypoed up for distance about this time but no one had ever hit as many as thirty home runs before Ruth came along.) More than anyone else the Babe made the fans forget the Black Sox.

I never told my mother or the rest of the family about my bad arm, or anybody back home. Because I felt if anyone was to worry about it, I wanted to be the only one. Mom was getting too proud of me for me to shock her with this bad news. Besides, I didn't fully believe I was washed up yet. I had the notion that my arm was not dead but just ailing again and that I might get rid of the trouble like I did the last time.

After the season, I spent most of my time visiting osteopaths for more treatments and working out in a gymnasium in the Bronx. I'd test my shoulder by swinging my right arm from different positions, and throw a ball now and then when the arm felt okay. One thing I noticed was that if I threw sidearm, like I had at the end of the 1920 season, there was no pain. The big question was, could I make another comeback with this delivery?

But it wasn't going to be all or nothing for me this time—if I couldn't make it pitching anymore, I would knuckle down to my clowning. That was already in my mind. But because Altrock and I were still teammates, I realized I'd have to work with him for a while whether we got along personally or not.

When I arrived at Tampa for spring training the following February, one of the players shook hands and playfully pulled me toward him. I thought my whole arm would fall off, there was that much pain. But I talked myself into believing I could work the soreness out under Florida's hot sun.

After about two weeks, my unnatural style of delivery was pretty noticeable. George McBride, who'd just been appointed manager while Griffith bought a controlling interest in the club and moved himself upstairs, said to me:

"Your arm must still be sore, Al, the way you're throwing."

"Naw," I shrugged, "I'm just taking it easy on my shoulder during training. Don't want to put too much pressure on it yet. I'll be throwing my old style soon as the season gets under way."

The night before the club was to break camp I had a frightening experience. In bed, I was struck with a terrific stomach attack. I lay awake all night, twisting and doubling up with the intestinal pains. Finally, about daybreak my roommate heard me moaning and got scared and called the club trainer. The trainer took one look at me and ran for a doctor. The doctor examined me briefly and ordered me rushed to Bayside Hospital. About 7 A.M. they carted me out of the hotel on a stretcher to a waiting ambulance. Even that early, Mr. and Mrs. Griffith were in the lobby with a few of the players, and they all stared at me without speaking.

At the hospital, the doctors studied me, but they couldn't seem to discover what had hit me. They put me in a room to be kept under observation.

I'd had these attacks before, though not nearly so severe, so I wasn't surprised when the pain started to subside by early afternoon. By 3 o'clock I was feeling fine again and getting restless. The club was due to head north that evening, and I got to worrying about missing the train.

"Nurse," I called at last.

"Yes?"

"Could you get me the afternoon newspapers, please?"

She said, "Sure," and left the room. I jumped out of bed, pulled my clothes on and went out the window, which was on the second floor overlooking the roof of a porch that ran around the hospital. I crawled across the roof and shinnied down a pole. With only a few cents in my pocket, I took a trolley back into town.

When I strolled into the hotel lobby, Mrs. Griffith was coming out, and I thought she'd fall down when she saw me.

"Al!" she gasped, stepping back. "For a moment I thought I was seeing a ghost. When you were carried out this morning, you looked as white as a sheet."

"Al . . . what in blazes are you doing back here?" said Mr. Griffith, who'd come up.

"I'm okay," I blurted out. "They looked me over and . . . it was just something I ate, I guess."

"Well . . . do you think you can make the trip north with us?" Griff said.

"You bet."

He looked doubtful, but I talked him into believing I was okay and should travel with the team. But he said he wouldn't let me pitch, and ordered McBride not to use me even in exhibition games for a couple of weeks.

On the road back to Washington, since I wasn't allowed to pitch, I was made a temporary coach. And the ham started pouring out of me. It was during that trip, I believe, that I got my real start as a baseball comedian. Altrock and I took to clowning together before the games, with me at third base and him at first.

We also roomed together, on the way north. Not that either of us asked for it; it was just a club policy that coaches room with coaches. But we rarely spoke to each other, unless it was to argue. Nick was surly with me off the field, but even then I realized that there was a chance we might remain together on the Washington club and team up as a comedy act. So I kidded him along.

Whenever our fooling around on the field went over pretty good with the fans I'd tell him, "Nick, you looked great out there today," and he'd grunt and try not to show he was pleased. Sometimes I'd dream up a new idea, but he hated to try anything new.

"Nick, I think I got something good. Listen . . ."

"Aaah, the hell with that stuff," he'd scowl.

So I'd say, "Listen, Nick, you'll look great in this."

And he'd think about it, then say, "Yeah? . . . Well, what is it?"

Considering that Altrock probably hated my guts from the beginning, it's amazing that we were gradually able to develop a pretty good act.

By the close of that training season, I was throwing pretty good, sidearm. But there were times, pitching to different batters in tight spots, I would have given anything to be able to fire a fast ball like I used to.

Just before Opening Day, we were playing the Giants an exhibition at the Polo Grounds in New York, and I went in to relieve in the sixth inning with the score tied. We battled down to the twelfth with the score still tied, and as I walked to the mound for the bottom of the twelfth, Frank Frisch, the old Fordham Flash and the Giants star second baseman, said:

"Al, aren't you gettin' hungry?"

"Sure," I grinned.

"Look," he said, "we both live in the Bronx, and we're close to home from here. I'm gonna send you home for dinner."

I laughed at him. But he was first up for the Giants in the inning, and sure enough, he smacked my first pitch into the right field seats for a home run, and the Giants win.

As he's trotting around the bases, Frisch calls to me, "Well, that's it, Al. Let's go home to dinner."

Exhibition game or not I was sore as hell losing. But when I cooled down it occurred to me maybe, having pitched six scoreless innings against a powerful team like the Giants, I might get by after all with my herky-jerky delivery.

But as the season wore on, it became plain I would never again be a good pitcher. The way I'd taught myself to throw now was just not good enough to fool major league hitters. I was used mostly in relief, and sparingly at that, and in fact, the only thing that kept me in the league at all was my ability to pitch to left-handed batters with my screwball, which was still tricky.

That season, I witnessed a great baseball fight between Ty Cobb and Umpire Billy Evans. Cobb by this time was managing Detroit in addition to still playing the outfield.

In this game, Cobb was on second base when the batter hit a grounder to our shortstop. On the long throw to first, Ty tore around third and headed for home. He made a hard slide, crashing into our catcher, Gharity, and knocking him two feet from the plate. Gharity's mask went one way and his glove the other, but he'd held the throw from first and tagged Cobb. Evans called Cobb out. Ty was sure he was safe and was furious, and he and Evans exchanged harsh words. It was the third out, and when Cobb got to his position in center field he made a gesture at Evans that Billy didn't like.

His next time up, Ty was called out on strikes, and he blew up. He and Evans roared at each other nose to nose. Finally Billy challenged Cobb to meet him in the umpires' dressing room after the game.

All the other players were excited, anxious for the game to be over to see the big fight. Naturally, our club hoped Evans would knock his ears off. After the game, guys from both teams piled under the stands and waited. Evans stood at the head of a short flight of steps leading from the passageway to the dressing rooms. When Cobb came in from the field, he was white with rage.

They started to go into the umps' room, but the "Audience" objected, arguing it was barely big enough in there for the umpires to dress, much less for Evans and Cobb to battle. So, after about five minutes of wrangling, it was decided they'd fight in the areaway outside the dressing rooms.

Evans was everybody's favorite. Not just for sentimental reasons either. He was about six-foot-one and strong, and had a reputation of being somewhat of an authority on boxing and able to handle himself. Cobb was about the same size, but he was no boxer.

"How do you want to fight?" Evans said to Cobb.

"I'm no fighter," Cobb snapped. "You challenged me. Everything goes."

"Okay," said Evans, removing his blue coat.

Billy then took a stance like an old-time boxer, with his left fist stuck straight out. Cobb, his hands at his sides, kind of circled around him. You could tell he was scheming, just like he did on the ball field. He maneuvered Evans so Billy's back was to a steel stanchion. Suddenly Cobb lashed out and socked Evans flush on the jaw, and Billy's head smacked back against the pillar and he slumped to the concrete floor.

Like an animal, Cobb leaped on him and grabbed him by the throat. Growling and cursing, he might have choked Evans to death if Hank O'Day, one of the stadium groundskeepers and a very strong Irishman, hadn't pulled Cobb off. O'Day had to pry Cobb's fingers from Evans' throat. The rest of us couldn't move, we were so stunned.

The next day, before the game, Evans went into the Detroit dressing room and said to Cobb, "You licked me yesterday . . . but it might be different next time," and walked out. They never did bury the hatchet as far as I know.

Since I didn't get to pitch very often and spent most of my time in the bullpen, I appointed myself bodyguard for ex-President Woodrow Wilson. Since leaving the White House, Mr. Wilson, who was always an ardent baseball fan, came to many of our home games. Griffith was happy to give him permission to park his big sedan inside the ball park in the home club's bullpen, which was down the right field line in foul territory, not too far from home plate. A chauffeur drove the car in through the right field gate, and the former President and Mrs. Wilson sat in the back and watched the games.

Any of us players who happened to be in the bullpen would stand on either side of the car, our job being to protect the Wilsons from stray foul balls. It was plain Mr. Wilson's health was failing him fast. I noticed his right arm and hand trembled constantly. And he talked in such a soft, low voice it was often tough for me to answer his questions because I couldn't hear him well.

When he asked one day, "Do you mind if I call you Al?" I took that as a cue to be less formal and started telling him humorous baseball stories, which he seemed to get a kick out of. He usually stayed right to the end of games, and I would say he probably knew his baseball better than the average fan. He seemed most interested about the different types of pitches that pitchers threw.

Once I told him, "Mr. Wilson, if I was pitching you wouldn't have to worry about any foul balls coming this way—when they hit 'em off me, the balls always sail over the fences, in fair territory."

"I'd love to see you pitch some day soon," he said.

"If you really do," I said, "you better be here in the first inning or you might miss me."

Mr. Wilson never did get to see me pitch after all.

As the season continued I worked less and less until it became obvious that Griff and McBride had given up on me. I finished with a 6–6 record and knew I was through as a big league pitcher. In September, Griff sadly told me he'd have to send me back to the minors, to New Orleans of the Southern League. He said he'd tried to get some other big league club to claim me, but because of my sore-arm reputation nobody would. However, Griff reminded me he'd watch out for me, as I knew he would.

About a month before the season's close, I got Griff's permission to organize a post-season barnstorming tour featuring almost our entire Washington team.

We had to get Landis's okay to make this tour because we were to play industrial teams some of whose players had jumped minor-league contracts. The commissioner wired me back that if we played against any team which fielded any "ineligible" ballplayers we'd all be subject to a thousand-dollar fine. So, to protect the Washington players, and myself, I wrote letters to the business managers of the clubs I'd booked, quoting Landis's exact words.

We were scheduled to start our barnstorming tour at Chester, Pennsylvania. My star attraction was Walter Johnson. Walter didn't have to come along, because he often got as much as a thousand dollars for pitching post-season exhibitions and he damn well wouldn't get that with us; but he knew his presence might draw more customers and extra money for the other boys, so he was willing to split the loot like the rest of us. We were getting a fifteen-hundred-dollar guarantee, or 60 per cent of the total receipts, whichever was the larger sum.

When we arrived at the field for batting practice, the first thing I did was check the Chester club's batting order. Wouldn't you know it!—they had at least four ineligibles whose names I recognized from the Commissioner's black list. I handed back the line-up without saying anything, yet.

About twenty minutes before game time, I went to the box office and said to their general manager, "I must get our fifteen-hundred-dollar guarantee before the game." When he looked like he might object, I reminded him, "It's in the contract."

Then, with the money, I went back to the field and collared young Willie Carroll, the club's assistant trainer, who was traveling with us. Giving him the fifteen hundred dollars, I said, "Willie, take this and beat it out of here. I'll meet you at the railroad station later. Don't come back here, and don't budge from that station."

The grandstands were jammed just as the game was going to start, most of the fans having come to see the great Johnson, who was going to start for us. When the Chester manager and I brought our respective line-ups up to home plate for the umpires to check, I saw he still was set to play his four ineligibles.

"I'm sorry," I announced, "but we can't play."

"What!" the Chester manager cried, his mouth hanging open. "What do you mean?"

"You know our agreement. Still I see you plan to play four ineligibles."

Getting panicky, he pleaded, "But I got nobody to replace them now. . . . We'd have to give the people their money back."

"Listen," I said, "your general manager and I both have signed contracts which say 'no ineligibles will play' against us. My part of the bargain was that I bring the full Washington team, including Johnson. Well, I got 'em, just like the contract says, and I expect you to go through with your end of the bargain.

"I'm not gonna let any of our players get fined a thousand bucks," I added.

Then he tried to bluff me. "I won't give you your fifteen hundred dollars."

"Oh yeah?" I laughed. "Well, my man is waiting at the railroad station right now with that fifteen hundred dollars. . . . And now I think I'll make a speech to the fans and tell them this whole story."

If I had it figured right, the fans wouldn't stand for ineligibles keeping Johnson from putting on his show. So I made my speech, and I was right. The crowd hooted, "Let's play ball! We want Johnson!" And the Chester manager was on the spot.

Finally he said, "If you don't let these four guys play, I got no catcher." Without hesitation, I loaned him one of our catchers, Val Picinich.

Johnson pitched a great five innings, at the end of which we led, 2–0. Then I came in to finish up; but Chester got two off me, and in the bottom of the ninth it was tied at 2–2. With two out and one man on base for Chester, Val Picinich stepped up and belted a two-base hit, driving home the run that beat us, 3–2. My own catcher.

When we got to the dressing room, Picinich came in and, a little embarrassed, asked, "You gonna dock me for breaking up the game?"

I laughed, "Don't you worry about being docked. But we all better start worrying whether we can find Willie Carroll with that money."

But we arrived at the railroad station to find Willie sitting in a corner of the waiting room with both hands tight in his pockets. He said he hadn't moved an inch for three hours, protecting the fifteen hundred dollars.

We went to Philadelphia to lay over a couple of days before resuming the tour the following week end. But at the Delphia Hotel I received a telegram from a dear friend of mine, George Maines, a former newspaperman who had gone into advertising and promotion and managed various entertainers. He asked if I could go to New York to talk about entertaining with Altrock before every game of the Giants-Yankees World Series.

Excited as a school kid, I rushed to New York, where I met Maines and Altrock. George said he'd approached Jake Ruppert, the Yankee owner, about the idea and that Ruppert had given his okay. The plan was for Altrock and me to do our stuff the mornings of the games to entertain the early bleacher arrivals right up to game time.

Nick and I walked into the Polo Grounds clubhouse about 10 A.M. Opening Day (the whole Series was to be played at the Polo Grounds because Yankee Stadium was not completed yet), but when we started to tell Miller Huggins, the Yankee manager, what we were going to do, he blew his top.

"No sir," he roared, "there'll be no clowning as long as I have anything to say about it." And he stomped off.

We didn't know what to do then. We're hired to entertain, but the Yankees don't want us. Nick and I were standing with Capt. Til Huston, Jake Ruppert's partner, trying to straighten out the mix-up, when Giant manager John McGraw came along. I hadn't seen Mac in a while, and told him what was happening.

"Hell," McGraw said, "if the Yankees won't hire you, consider yourself hired by the Giants."

The Yankee officials came over to discuss this move, and it turned out they'd thought, particularly Huggins, that we intended to clown on the sidelines *during* the games. Learning the true facts, they apologized, and the misunderstanding was cleared up.

So we missed getting out that first morning. The following day, Altrock and I started with exactly three routines—a burlesque prize fight, a pantomime tight wire walk and a "band concert" in which I directed the 71st Regiment band (which still plays at World Series in New York). We had to invent new gags as we went along because many bleacherites arrived as early as 8 A.M., and the players didn't start coming on the field until about noon, so the fans would get a little restless around ten, when we appeared. The most popular thing we did in the mornings, it developed, was a "community sing" in the bleachers, with me leading the band. I wore a battered top hat and tail coat over my baseball uniform. I'd only worn the outfit once before, in 1914. But it was to become my costume from then on.

Before the game, during the second infield practice, Altrock got on first base and I on third, and we played ground balls and pop-ups like a couple of drunken sailors. Next came our feature stunt, a burlesque of Ruth St. Denis's "Death Dance"—she was a popular dancer whose big number was a dramatic dance with a live snake—with me taking the part of Ruth St. Denis and Altrock my slave. Instead of a snake, though, I had a string of frankfurters; and where Ruth St. Denis used to wind up by sticking the snake in her mouth and dying, I took a bite of a frankfurter, barked like a dog and died like a dog.

The next day, we added a couple more routines, for instance the slow motion pitcher (me) and batter (Altrock). It was the first time anything like this had ever been done at a World Series, or in baseball. All the newspapers had glowing reports about how well Altrock and Schacht went over. We each received two thousand dollars, a grand from both clubs.

Life had taken a new turn for me.

chapter 12

With the newspapers around New York giving Altrock and me so much good publicity, the Keith vaudeville booking office decided to latch on to our "hot" act before we cooled off. An agent came around to see us and asked if we'd like to play a few houses in New York and in the area. I had to finish my barnstorming baseball tour first, and did, rejoining the Washington players for three more games. This was without Walter Johnson, who, during the layoff, packed up and went fishing and hunting for the winter. When I got back to New York, Altrock and I went to the Keith office in the Palace Theatre building on Broadway and signed contracts.

We were scheduled to appear at five theaters—the Fifth Avenue, in downtown New York; the 125th Street Theatre uptown; and in houses in Yonkers, Mount Vernon and Jersey City, all Keith theaters. We were signed for what they called a split week, three days at a theater, and we were to get eight hundred dollars per.

Keith's assigned a fellow named Tommy Gray to write an act for us. And what did he come up with but a sketch in which Altrock and I were supposed to just stand and trade jokes back and forth and sing a few songs! I objected right away. We weren't that kind of a comedy act; we should be doing pantomime like on the ball field. That's how we'd got a name, not by telling jokes. But the office insisted, and finally I gave in, having gotten little support from Altrock, who was hypnotized by the money. And I couldn't blame him, because it certainly was too good to resist.

This Gray had never seen us perform in baseball, I soon found out, and here he was writing an act for us. The way he had it, and Keith's went for it, was for us to wear our baseball uniforms on stage. During our two-day rehearsal, I fought with them again over this, saying:

"Dammit, it's silly for us to wear baseball uniforms doing this kind of act. If you're gonna make us wear our uniforms, you oughta let us do our baseball act, pantomime."

But we lost out on this beef too, and opened at the Fifth Avenue Theatre, headlining the show along with another comic, Johnny Dooley. As I feared, we had a lousy act—although I must say the Fifth Avenue drew a real tough audience. The theater was in the middle of the dress manufacturing district (known as the "garment center" in New York), and it seemed when business was slack the salesmen would sneak in to watch the show for a couple of hours, with their bundles and sample cases. One matinee, Johnny Dooley had me in stitches by stopping his act and remarking to the audience:

"I wish you salesmen would come in without your samples under your arms. Maybe then you'd be able to applaud."

After that, we played the 125th Street, Yonkers and Mount Vernon houses. After our first performance at Mount Vernon, a Keith's agent came backstage and informed Altrock and me our engagement in Jersey City was canceled. I wasn't surprised. Though I suppose if we hadn't been making so much money they might have kept us on. Anyway we were finished in vaudeville for a while.

In fact, it took us a long time to live down that experiment and get back into show business, because we were then marked down as a bad act, as most ballplayers were who tried to make a fast buck on the stage. The difference was, I *knew* we had something, even for vaudeville; and we proved it years later.

During the winter, I'd let Clark Griffith know I didn't intend to report to New Orleans, where he'd said he wanted to ship me. I figured in the condition I was in, the heat down there wouldn't be so good.

Of course, my brothers, who knew something about baseball, suspected I was through as a big league pitcher. But the way the money was rolling in for me—and would continue to—they must have thought I was still on my way up instead of down.

Towards the end of that winter I had my appendix out in an emergency operation. After I got out of the hospital, I got restless and made up my mind to go to Washington to see Griff, hoping he might be able to make a deal for me to get back in the International League. I was sitting with him in his office, shooting the breeze, when the telephone rang. It was somebody from the Reading, Pennsylvania, club of the International League, asking if Griff had any pitcher he'd care to sell to them.

Griff paused, then, eying me, said, "How about Al Schacht?"

They must have been interested, because after a short discussion, Griff was all set to wrap up the deal. But he told the party to hold it for a second, and said to me, "Fix your own terms with them, Al."

I was flabbergasted. First, while I'm sitting right in the office, I hear myself all but sold to a high-class club; and to top that, Griff is letting me make my own salary terms. I assure you, this was an unusual thing for a club owner to do and a mighty nice gesture by him.

But my mind quickly got back on the beam and I grabbed the phone. The man from Reading said they'd pay me $450 a month. I said $500. So, before I'm even sold to their club, I'm a holdout.

Glancing at Griff, I added into the phone, "If you won't pay me $500 a month, the deal is off." Now I'm even taking the deal away from Griff, and his eyebrows are shooting up a notch at a time.

When I got through talking, I was promised $500 a month. Believe it or not, this was more money than Griff had ever paid me for pitching with his major-league club! When I put down the telephone and described the deal to him, he just shook his head in wonderment.

"See, Griff," I said with a grin, "you been holding me back from making real dough."

I reported to Reading immediately, to manager Chief Bender, the former great big-league pitcher, and within a couple of days he named me to pitch at Jersey City. Remember, this was only about three weeks after my appendicitis operation.

For the first six innings, I was great, allowing only one hit. But by the seventh my strength was gone, and Jersey City bashed me all over the lot and Bender had to take me out. After the game, Bender and I were leaving together, and The Chief said:

"You know, I never seen a pitcher go to pieces so quick after pitching so great for six innings."

Without thinking, I blurted out, "What the hell, I just got out of a hospital."

"What!" he said, disbelief all over his face.

"Sure, I got operated on for appendicitis three weeks ago."

He just stared at me without speaking. Then I realized what a damn fool I was to tell him that, because maybe he'd hop on Griff for pulling a shady deal, selling Reading a piece of broken merchandise.

But Bender didn't do anything about it—not until a few days later, when I made my second start. A batter hit a line drive back at my right knee, and instinctively I threw my bare pitching hand down to deflect the ball. It smashed my open palm against the knee. The ball dropped a few feet away, but I couldn't even untangle my fingers to pick it up. The hand was broken.

The club trainer sent me to a doctor who set the bones, stitched up the wound and dressed it, saying to lay off any exercise with the hand for a couple of weeks at least. When the club heard about me being on the shelf for a couple of weeks, the camel's back broke. They made a federal case out of me.

Going to Judge Landis, the Commissioner of Baseball, they protested that Griff had sold me to Reading when I was in no condition to play, naming my recent operation as one thing and now my broken hand as another. Landis wrote me a letter, asking for my side of the story, and I answered right back that Griff had had no idea I wasn't in shape; all he knew was I wanted to work, and he sold me strictly on the basis of what I'd told him, which did not include mention of my operation. As for the broken hand, I added, what the hell did that have to do with Griff anyway?

Landis ruled in favor of Griffith and me, and my sale to Reading stood.

One day, after about a week of inactivity, I noticed a swelling in my right armpit, and my whole arm was starting to ache and throb. I moseyed into the Reading clubhouse looking for one of the players who'd used to study medicine. When I described the condition, he said:

"Boy, you better go see the doctor right away. You probably got an infection."

I went to the doctor who'd treated me, but after listening to me and looking at my hand, all he said was, "Well, suppose you come back tomorrow and we'll see how it is."

My arm hurting worse every minute, and puffing up badly, I said to myself as I left his office, This guy might be a quack. I better try another doctor just to be sure.

Finding another doctor's shingle in the neighborhood, I went in and told him my troubles. He warned if I did have an infection, he'd probably have to scrape the bones. I told him to look at it. When he removed the dressing, he whistled.

"If you'd waited until tomorrow," he said, "the poison in this hand might have raced through your whole system. Why, we might have had to take your whole arm off!"

I nearly fainted at that. He went right to work; giving me an anesthetic, he reopened the wound where my hand had been split open, carefully scraped and dug out all the pus and infection, and redressed it. In a few days the swelling and ache was all gone. But even after the injury was completely healed, the rest of that season the middle finger of my right hand stayed numb. Now, along with everything else, I was Three-finger Schacht on the pitching mound.

Shortly after this mishap, I ran into Bugs Baer, the famous humorist, and he proceeded to write a column in the New York *Journal* about all my injuries in baseball and my illnesses. The title of it, as I recall, was something like "Talk About Your Hard Times In Arkansas! . . ." He couldn't have known, naturally, that a couple of beauts were yet to come.

After about three weeks, I returned to the club and resumed my pitching turn, wearing tape across the inside of my fingers and palm.

We had a first baseman on that Reading club named Sam Post, a tall, skinny guy who was unusual because it seemed he could hit well only in the early innings of games. Well, about the fifth inning of a game with Rochester I was touched for a single by the first man up. As I was getting ready to pitch to the next batter I whirled and gunned a quick throw to first, trying to catch the runner napping. But Sam Post must have been napping instead, because my throw hit him square in the chest.

A moment later, I whipped another throw over to first again. And again the ball hit Post in the chest. I said to myself, I can't be that quick. There's something screwy here.

After the inning, on the bench, I sat next to Post and said, "Sam, maybe we ought to change the rules and put the batters at first base. Seems like I got more stuff throwing over there than pitching to home plate—you can't even hold my throws."

When Sam looked at me, I saw his eyes were sort of glazed. Then he laughed his head off at my remark, and I smelled a rat. I smelled more than a rat. A fast investigation turned up this story: Sam had a habit of strolling behind the grandstand for a smoke between innings. There was a big brewery right behind the ball park, and Sam had made arrangements to have someone sneak him a scuttle of beer between every inning. By the fifth inning, he'd be cockeyed. That's why he got so lousy late in the games.

Towards the end of that season, I was pretty well disgusted. I was in miserable shape and not getting any younger, and I just couldn't seem to pitch good any more. My record for Reading was worse than so-so, and my future in baseball appeared very dark. My only hope now was to somehow stay in baseball until I got a chance to put my long-range clowning idea to work. The truth is, I was doing more clowning on the field that season than ever before.

For example one day between the games of a doubleheader in Baltimore—my old nemesis, Jack Dunn, was still manager there—I put on a burlesque golf exhibition. Instead of a golf ball, I used a ten-cent "Rocket," which looks like a real baseball and is regulation size but is only stuffed with sawdust. After the act, I shoved the Rocket into my hip pocket and forgot about it.

In the fifth inning of the second game, our starting pitcher, Gordonier, was getting his lumps, and Chief Bender told me to run down to the bullpen to warm up and be ready to finish the game. Finally, when Baltimore got three men on base, with none out, I was waved in. (Somehow I was always pitching with three men on base, whether they got there off me or some other pitcher.)

In those days, you could still use tobacco or licorice juice to discolor the ball when pitching, making it tougher to hit of course. So as I reached in my back pocket for my licorice, my hand felt the ten-cent Rocket I'd put there. I smiled to myself, This is it.

When I got to the pitcher's box, I had the Rocket in my glove, and picking up the real ball left on the mound by Gordonier, turned my back to the grandstand and sneaked the good ball inside my shirt. Then I motioned to Nig Clark, my catcher, with the excuse to go over our signals. When he came out, I said in a low voice:

"Don't laugh, Nig, but I got a ten-cent Rocket in my hand." A big grin spread over his face. "Don't ask for any fancy pitches," I said. "I don't want this ball fouled out of the ball park."

The first batter to face me is Joe Boley, Baltimore's shortstop, who later played great ball for the Philadelphia Athletics. He swings with all his might, and the ball goes *pffft*—a little pop fly to the second baseman. One out. Next is Lena Styles, their catcher. He hits the first pitch with all his might too, and it goes *pffft*—a little pop-up to the shortstop. Two out.

When I got the ball back this time it's a bit lopsided, and I have to mold it back to shape with my hands. Up comes Baltimore's pitcher, Rube Parnham. We used to ride each other, so I swagger up to him and say:

"What're you doing with that bat on your shoulder? It's not gonna do you any good."

"You just throw the ball up here," he sneers, "and I'll knock it down your throat."

I laugh, "You won't even hit it out of the infield." He don't know I got a ten-cent Rocket.

I pitch the ball, and he hits it with all his might, and it goes straight up above me, wobbling in the air like an egg. I wave my infielders away and make the catch myself for three out.

But Parnham, having heard the dull thud as he hit the ball, and seeing it wobbling in the air, goes running back to the plate umpire, Bill McGowan (now in the American League), screaming to see the ball I'd thrown. Meanwhile, after catching the pop fly, I go into my shirt for the good ball, knowing I have to leave a ball in the pitcher's box after retiring the side, and I sure can't leave the phony. But the good ball has worked around to the back of my shirt and I can't reach it without unbuttoning my uniform. So I walk toward the bench, figuring I'll get another good ball there and throw it out to the mound.

By now, the other guys who've hit the Rocket, and Jack Dunn, are also charging Ump McGowan. He hollers over to me, "Lemme see that ball!" But I can't find a good ball around the dugout and all I have is the lopsided Rocket, so I roll it to him. It bounces up like a football, this way and that way, and as McGowan reaches for it, it flops off to one side.

"Come up here!" he roars to me.

I walk up, saying, "What seems to be the difficulty here?"

Right away Parnham and I get in a terrific argument, and he wants to punch me in the nose. Finally:

"I'll confess. I pitched a good ball to Boley and Styles," I lie, "but I tricked Parnham. There's only one ruling you can make, Bill. I made an illegal pitch. Which means I gotta pitch over to Parnham . . . and I can pitch to this guy all day long. He couldn't hit the side of a barn."

"That settles it," McGowan says. "Bring your team back on the field."

Everybody goes back to their positions. The bases are still loaded, two out. Soon as I get to the box, I reach into my shirt. The crowd is suspicious of me, chanting, "Watch him! Watch him!" Parnham calls, "Just a minute. I want to see the ball again." But this time it's the real ball.

I get two strikes on Parnham, and I feel if I could strike him out I'd give a million dollars. And I do strike him out. So he's the third out again, and now I got a record: four putouts to retire the side. As I pass Parnham on my way to the bench, I gloat:

"Here, you big rube, look at the ball."

He looks, and seeing it's the McCoy, he gets so mad he fires it all the way over the grandstand.

And McGowan fined *him* twenty-five dollars.

Nick Altrock and I worked the 1922 World Series, again between the Giants and Yankees. And that Series, I got one of my best—and queerest—breaks in my comedy career.

The night before the opening game, Buck O'Neill, a sports writer, and I went to see a popular movie called *Blood and Sand*, starring Rudolph Valentino, who, I don't have to explain, was then the great lover of the screen. There was a scene where Valentino, playing a bullfighter, was out to kill this bull to win the love of a señorita sitting in a box seat. The scene made quite an impression on me and gave me an idea.

Leaving the theater, I said to O'Neill, "I'd like to reproduce that bullfight scene as our feature stunt tomorrow."

"What'll you use for a bull?" he asked.

"I haven't figured that out yet."

On the way home, I stopped off at a speakeasy near my home for a beer. The bartender, who knew me, asked what gags I planned to use at the Series, and I told him about the bullfight and that I needed to come up with something that looked and acted like a bull, but not a real bull.

"There's a fella named O'Hara," the bartender said, "who's the watchman at the lumberyard near here, where the old Bronx Oval used to be. He has a pet goat roaming around there. What about that?"

This sounded like it could be it, so early the next morning I went to the lumberyard. Finding the gates locked, I looked around for O'Hara, but he was nowhere to be seen. So I climbed over the fence. There was the goat, sure enough. Thinking it must be tame and friendly, I started toward it; but he ran like hell the other way.

I chased that damn goat all over the lumberyard, and I was huffing. Finally I opened the gates from the inside and went out into the street and rounded up four young kids. Then the five of us cornered the goat, and I grabbed a length of rope and tied it around his neck.

I dragged him along the sidewalk, looking for a taxi. One came along, and I managed to shove the goat inside and slam the door, puffing "Polo Grounds" to the driver. On the way, the goat billied, or bayed, or whatever it is goats do when they wail; he was unhappy as hell, wanting out of that cab. Then the driver said over his shoulder:

"Mister, you wanna know how to keep that goat quiet? . . . Just get some cabbage leaves and feed him an' he'll shut up like a clam."

So we stopped by a vegetable store, where I bought a head of cabbage, and the rest of the trip I kept stuffing cabbage leaves into the goat's mouth. By the time we got to the Polo Grounds, three-quarters of the cabbage was gone. Getting out of the cab, I turned to pull the goat by the rope again, but he fooled me by strolling onto the sidewalk and following me like a devoted puppy. When I realized I had the rest of the cabbage in my hand, and he was trailing the cabbage, not me, the light dawned—I had the answer.

It was about a quarter to ten, and some of the Giant players were already sitting in the clubhouse playing cards. I asked George Kelly, the first baseman, and outfielder Ross Youngs if they'd take a few minutes to come out under the bleachers and help me in an experiment.

They held the goat, while I, stuffing the cabbage leaves in my hip pocket, leaving some hanging out, stood about twenty feet away with my back to them.

"Let him go," I hollered, snapping my fingers. The goat charged toward me, and I whirled around and threw several little sticks of wood at him, just like a bullfighter throws swords at the bull. The goat screeched to a halt. We repeated this a few times, and the same thing happened each time: he'd head for the cabbage leaves in my pocket and pull up when I tossed the sticks at him. That settled my problem about getting the goat to charge me like a bull. I tied him to a girder under the stands and went to meet Altrock.

Nick and I performed our usual stunts for the bleacherites the rest of the morning, and clowned in infield practice after noon. Then shortly before the first game of the Series was to start, we presented our feature number. With the peak of my cap turned up and a red bandanna tied around my head, I strode out to the center of the diamond, standing motionless alone on the wide, empty field. Altrock went to a field box and sat down demurely. He was my lover, and to prove it he had a rose in his teeth, just like in *Blood and Sand*. If I could kill the "bull," I'd win his love. At that point, however, I was more concerned about whether my bull would go along with the act.

The public address announcer recited our scene to the big crowd. I bowed deep. In one back pocket I had the cabbage leaves, and in the other a bottle of ketchup. The players on the Giant bench had the goat, and he was giving them a rough time, busting to dash out on the field. Then, at my signal, they let him loose.

Good old goat, he charged out at me just like a rampaging bull. When he got near, I swiveled sideways like a toreador and tossed my "swords," the little wooden sticks, and at the same time sprayed ketchup at him, which was supposed to be blood. He circled around me and charged again, and I "stabbed" him again. After a couple more passes, I let him come up close to me and start nibbling at the cabbage leaves in my hip pocket. As he took a bite, I darted around, grabbed him by the neck and wrestled him to the ground. After a tremendous struggle, and with great courage, I subdued the savage monster and staggered to my feet, exhausted. Nick, my lover, tripped out to me and planted a big smooch on my forehead and coyly handed me the rose. Everyone in the stadium was applauding, and we bowed gravely.

Suddenly there was another burst of laughter from the crowd, and glancing out the corner of my eye I saw the goat to my right, bowing with us. In wrestling with him, I must have wrung his neck and he was trying to loosen it, the crowd thinking he was bowing too.

Our act over, Altrock and I walked across center field to the clubhouse, and the goat trotted along behind all the way. In fact, we had a hell of a time getting rid of him, which we had to do because that gag couldn't have been repeated in a thousand years. Even today, people who witnessed the stunt still ask me if that was a trained goat, especially because of the way he followed me to the clubhouse.

But he was just after the last of that cabbage.

After the Series, somebody from a professional basketball team in Buffalo, New York, inquired if Altrock and I would perform between halves of a game there, for money naturally. And this inspired me again. A barnstorming basketball team made up of well-known baseball players! Basketball was becoming popular in this country by leaps and rebounds, and I was convinced immediately this could turn into an off-season bonanza for baseball players who could handle a basketball. It surely had never been done before, and we could probably book games all over the country, starting, say, in December. But we were leery about billing any such outfit as Schacht & Altrock, so I got together with Eddie Holley, a friend of mine who was a former ballplayer and then a baseball scout, who could handle bookings and financial arrangements. And, rounding up some ballplayers, we named ourselves the Holley Majors. We'd play anybody, anywhere, with the added attraction of me and Altrock putting on a show between halves of every game.

On the team were Dolly Stark; Snooks Dowd, who'd been with Detroit and Philadelphia; Val Picinich, the Washington catcher; Alex Ferguson, who pitched with the Red Sox; myself and a few others I can't recall now. We weren't very bad, but we weren't too good as a basketball team, either. Holley booked games all through New England, a different town just about every day, and we each averaged about a hundred dollars a week plus expenses. Because some of the players were big leaguers, and Altrock and I entertained at intermissions, we drew pretty good crowds.

It was fun, and I even got by with some clowning during the games. I played at guard. I don't think we had a single game in which there wasn't at least two arguments.

We had a young fellow playing center who was only a busher in baseball but knew his basketball. We called him the Traffic Center, because when he'd get the ball he'd point to where we should go before he'd pass it off; and he held that ball until satisfied we were in the right positions to start working our plays. He didn't realize it, but he was doing the rest of us a good turn, since we were older and not really in good enough shape to be constantly running up and down the court; and him holding the ball, we got a breather.

In late February, we disbanded for the season. I made a mental note that this could be good the following winter too; maybe if we got a better club together.

One thing that had been troubling me all winter was whether or not the Reading ball club would even bother to send me a contract for 1923. It was surely very questionable if I could ever make another big-league comeback; but even after the unfortunate season I'd had with Reading I hoped they might take my injuries into consideration and give me a fair trial this spring, to see what kind of shape I was in before deciding what to do with me.

When I got home to the Bronx from my basketball tour, the Reading contract was waiting. I at least expected a cut in salary, but they were offering me the same money. I was thankful, but I didn't deserve it.

There was also a message from Clark Griffith, inviting me to spend a few weeks working out with the Washington club at Tampa. To this day I still don't know if Griff had any intention of bringing me back to the majors if I was physically able, but you can imagine how fast I hopped a train for Florida.

Griff plainly liked me, and, particularly since the day I'd saved his skin by pinch-pitching for Walter Johnson against the Yankees and winning, he always seemed to be trying to give me a break. But even Griff had a hard time being diplomatic after I'd worked out two weeks with Washington. I still didn't have full control of the middle finger of my pitching hand that had been broken the previous season, and I couldn't throw the ball with any authority. I hadn't told Griff about that injury, but he could tell something was wrong with me again, and when we sat down for a long chat one day I finally told him.

"Al," he said, measuring his words, "maybe you ought to give up pitching. You've had so much tough luck. Have you thought about it at all?"

From things he said, I got the impression he might be considering hiring me as a coach, though he didn't come right out with it. Showman that he was, and is, he probably was thinking Altrock and me as a permanent team might help draw extra customers for the club, which was not doing well. This 1923 season, Griff was trying his third manager since he'd quit the job himself—first there'd been McBride in '21; next season, Clyde Milan; now Donie Bush—he was that hard pressed for improvement. I privately agreed with him about Altrock and me; our comedy was good enough for two World Series and was certainly good enough for the Washington club.

But inside, I battled against really giving up pitching, even though I was so discouraged by all my physical ailments. If ever there was a guy who loved to pitch, who lived, breathed and dreamed it, I was him. I think standing out there alone on the pitcher's mound, trying to outguess and outthink a hitter, is a tremendous thrill. The will to work hard and to win makes pitching a fascinating science, and a satisfying experience. Especially those times when, by your own cleverness and resourcefulness, you work yourself out of tight jams. You feel like you've conquered the world.

So, with a small spark of hope about my pitching still alive, I left Tampa and went north to Henderson, North Carolina, where the Reading club was in training.

The difference in the living accommodations alone was enough to sour me when I arrived: after the beautiful hotel the Washington club stayed in at Tampa, the Reading team's joint looked like a barn. To make it worse, as I was checking in, Frank Gilhooley, one of the players, greeted me with:

"Abbott, the new manager, already is passing remarks about you. He said, 'When this Schacht reports, he'll find out he's not gonna do any clowning on this ball club. If he don't cut it out, I'll send him so far away a post card won't ever reach him.' That's his exact words, Al," Gilhooley grinned.

I'd heard about our new manager. Spencer Abbott was supposed to be an old-school-type manager, a tough bird, who ruled his club with an iron fist. He'd been around, and while never much of a ballplayer himself, he'd had good success managing in the Southern League, although he never seemed to last very long with any one team. From the way Gilhooley spoke, I could tell he and maybe some of the other players didn't think too highly of Abbott already.

The next morning, I decided the first thing I'd do was try to find out just what was behind the unfriendly attitude Abbott apparently had toward me. I had a suspicion he was putting on a big show for the other players to establish his authority right off the bat, using me as his stooge. Even before I'd met him.

Meeting him in the lobby of the hotel, I introduced myself as friendly as I could.

Right off he snarled at me: "If you try any clowning here, you won't stay long with this club. I'm not managing any clowns, see?"

"Listen," I snapped back, "you can't stop me from clowning. All you should be interested in is whether I can pitch good enough to stay with this club. If I *can* pitch, clowning or not, you ain't gonna fire me . . . see?"

The fact is, the way he glared at me, I already felt fired. For the first time in my baseball career, I knew what it was like to have my manager against me.

That first morning at the ball field I had a real rhubarb with Abbott. A couple of photographers and a reporter from the local newspaper approached me in the field, looking for pictures and an interview, and Abbott ran over, angrily trying to chase them away.

"Boys," I said loudly, "if you want pictures, go right ahead and take 'em." Turning to the young reporter, I added, "And you and I can go in the clubhouse right now and I'll give you any story you want."

Abbott stared at us, his face red, then stalked off without another word.

During the rest of the training season things were tense between Abbott and me. Finally we broke camp and headed north, opening the season in Reading. I didn't have to be a psychologist to realize I wasn't wanted on that club nohow—but I also knew Abbot didn't dare fire me too fast because it so happened I was very popular with the Reading fans for my clowning. What Abbott was waiting for was for me to get my ears pinned back a few times while pitching, which would be all the excuse he'd need to lower the boom. And this was very likely to happen, because I was getting close to where I was lucky to finish a game much less win one.

When the team made a bad play in a tight spot, or an umpire would call a close play against us, Abbott would get so excited, he'd grab the water bucket and heave it way out on the field. This led to the chance Abbott was waiting for to bounce me. It was a day only a couple of weeks after the season had begun when I got knocked out of the box. I could see the vicious pleasure Abbott took in yanking me out of the game. Then came a crucial play, for me. On a hit to the outfield, with an opposing base runner steaming around third, our catcher let the ball go through him; to top it off, he lost it in the dust and couldn't find it. So the runner scored and the man who'd hit the ball swiped an extra base.

Abbott was beside himself. Sparks flew out of his ears. Then he stormed about the dugout, wild-eyed, looking for the water bucket.

"It's here," I called from the end of the bench. Jumping up, I picked up the bucket by the handle and said, "I'll throw it out for you."

And I did . . . all the way to the third-base line.

"Get off the bench!" Abbott roared. "Go in the clubhouse. I'm gonna see you're released this time, mister."

Smiling happily, I nonchalantly walked to the dressing room. The tension was over.

Right after that, the club went on a road trip, and I was left behind, although I hadn't been released yet. I was just hanging around for a few days when a man named Bill Fischer came looking for me at the hotel. Fischer was general manager of the Binghamton club of the New York-Pennsylvania League, a Class B league.

"I hear you are going to be released?" he said.

I said yes.

"What do you plan to do?"

"Well, I don't know," I said. "I haven't been released *yet*."

"Well," he said, "I'm here to make you an offer to join our club. . . . George F. Johnson of the Endicott-Johnson Shoe Company sent me down here specifically to get you."

"To tell you the truth," I said, "I've been thinking of giving up pitching." I dreaded the idea of sinking to a lower class league and finding I'm not able to pitch even there.

"Mr. Johnson wants you more for your clowning than your pitching. Most of the fans in Binghamton work at the shoe factory, and Mr. Johnson thinks you could do a good job entertaining them. . . . Oh, you'll pitch some, but mostly you'll coach at third base and put on shows before the games."

I was wavering. When he offered me a fifteen-hundred-dollar bonus and the same salary I got at Reading, I couldn't resist. So Fischer made arrangements to buy my contract from Reading that very day, and that night the two of us left for Binghamton, New York. I always felt whatever he paid Reading for me was too much. Spencer Abbott probably thought so too.

I should have brought a picnic basket to Binghamton, I had that good a time that season. I wouldn't say I had a great record pitching, only pitching about once a week, but the weather was cool and pleasant in upstate New York and the fans and the club were swell to me. I clowned every day, and every so often went to the shoe factory to entertain the employees. Once when I won an important ball game, Mr. Johnson, who was quite a fan himself, sent me a check for two hundred dollars to buy myself a new summer outfit.

Right after the season, Altrock and I clowned at the World Series again, which was the third meeting between the Yanks and Giants, the Yanks winning this time for their first Series victory. They've hardly stopped since. That year, by the way, was when Yankee Stadium was first opened. It was my third straight Series clowning, and I'd like to add that I've worked every one since 1921, first with Altrock and then alone, right up through 1952, except for the World War II years when I went overseas to entertain the troops.

During the winter, I reorganized our basketball team, the Holley Majors. This time we were a much better club, and we started drawing bigger guarantees in the towns we were booked in. We also did not confine ourselves to New England any more, branching out into the Midwest. Snooks Dowd still played, Dolly Stark and me; but we added Al Kellett, a Philadelphia Athletics baseball player; Ray Keating, who used to pitch for the Yankees and Boston Braves; a fellow named Nat Hickey; two brothers from Philadelphia whose names I can't recall, and the guy who really made the club that year, Stanley (Bucky) Harris.

Bucky was a fiery, hard-driving athlete. In 1918, he'd come up to the Washington Senators from Buffalo of the International League, a second baseman, about the same time I arrived from Jersey City. He'd reported with a broken finger, but never told Griffith. I'd always admired his aggressiveness on the baseball field, though we had clashed in the International League. I was pitching against Buffalo one day when Bucky lashed a wicked line drive in a tight spot which might have meant the ball game if it had gone for a hit. But it was caught for the third out. Passing me on the way to his position, Bucky snarled at me, "You goddam lucky punk!" Me being practically the father of the International League by that time, and him only a rookie in his first season, I retorted, "Why, you busher . . . you were lucky to even hit that ball . . . I'm on you the rest of this season." So we became enemies. But when we both were called up to Washington, we shook hands and a close friendship sprung up between us, which has held to this day.

Bucky had become Washington's regular second baseman, and this winter he joined the Holley Majors. He was a former professional basketball player, and a tough one. I'll never forget a game we played at Pittston, Pennsylvania, which was Bucky's home town. After Altrock and I put on our act between halves, we went back to the dressing room, and Bucky said to me, "I'm not playing guard this half, I'm playing center." I had a good idea why he wanted to switch.

Pittston's center was a guy named Kane, about six-foot-two and a solid 190 pounds, who'd been roughing up our boys all during the first half. Bucky, not a big fellow, was burning, and I knew he'd decided to take care of Kane, and I sure didn't want to miss it, knowing how hard he could play at times.

The referee tossed up the ball to start the second half, Harris opposite Kane, but instead of Bucky making the usual pass at the ball, he closed his fist and belted Kane square in the mouth, knocking him colder than a mackerel. The ref immediately chased Bucky from the game.

It was the practice then in many places to have a cord cage strung up all around the basketball court, I guess to protect the players from the fans and vice versa. When the ref cried "Out!" to Harris, Bucky kicked the ball high in the air, and it soared right through the netting and knocked out the lights. The place was in darkness, and no one saw Bucky leave.

It was the next day that Bucky received a wire from Clark Griffith asking him to report to the club offices at Washington at once. When Bucky got there, Griff informed him he was the next manager of the Senators. The newspapers called him the Boy Wonder, for he was only twenty-seven. But he went on to become one of the great managers of all time in my book.

When Bucky wrote the Holley Majors to explain what had happened to him, he added this sentence, addressed to me: "If you ever decide to give up pitching, I'd like to have you as my coach." I thought then that this might lead to the turning point I'd been hoping for.

That winter while I was home for a week, I received a message there from George Weiss, the present fine general manager of the New York Yankees, who was then owner of the New Haven, Connecticut, club of the Eastern League. He'd bought me from Binghamton, offering me even more money than I'd gotten at Binghamton. I had to laugh, because though I was washed up, but good, as a pitcher, and kept sinking deeper into the minor leagues, it seemed the lower I went in organized baseball the more money I was making. They just wouldn't let me quit pitching. Clark Griffith again invited me to work out for a few weeks with the Washington club at Tampa. I had a thousand dollars in my pocket, a new job, and the birds were singing.

chapter 13

My arm felt great. I couldn't believe it; I was pitching like my old self. The Washington club's pitchers had reported to Tampa a week or so earlier than the rest of the team. Bucky Harris, the new manager, hadn't arrived yet, for he was working out with some of the veteran players at Hot Springs, Arkansas. But Griff himself was at Tampa, and he noticed how free and easy I was throwing again. Bucky and the others all arrived by March 1, and training began in earnest.

When Bucky saw how good I looked on the mound, he got me working with Washington's regular chuckers. My fast ball was good and the screwball and curves were okay. Griff and Bucky both watched me closely. One morning, Griff stood behind the batting cage while I was pitching batting practice, and when I'd finished, he walked up and said:

"Al, your arm looks as strong as when you first joined us. . . . Keep up the good work. I'll be watching you. . . ."

To me this meant if I continued my good showing he might bring me back to the American League as a pitcher.

"By the way," said Griff, interrupting my daydream, "don't forget our luncheon appointment at the Kiwanis Club."

"Okay," I said, "but first I want to hit against Johnson."

"I'll meet you at the hotel after practice," Griff said, walking away.

Walter Johnson had taken my place pitching batting practice. With a big grin I grabbed a bat and shouted toward the mound, "Big Train, I can hit you!" and stepped up to the plate to take a few swings.

Johnson, also smiling, wound up and cut one down the middle. To my shock, I lined the ball into right field. I jumped in triumph and crashed to the ground as my right knee buckled. A terrific pain ripped at the knee as I writhed on top of home plate. Johnson came running in, and players gathered around. The trainer hurried out, felt around the knee as I winced, and declared it looked to him like I might have torn a cartilage. They helped me off the field.

By the time I'd sat around, then dressed, my knee was as round as a grapefruit and I could barely walk on it. Knowing I was expected to speak to the Kiwanis Club and had to meet Griff at the hotel, I stopped a Western Union messenger boy and borrowed his bike. Pedaling with my left foot, I inched toward the hotel. Griff was waiting for me on the front porch, and when he saw me weaving along on this bike, he smiled and shook his head, thinking I was clowning again. But when I dropped the bicycle and limped heavily toward him, Griff's expression changed.

"What happened to you?" he cried.

I told him. He studied my face, then walked a few feet away, his hands behind him, eyes on the floor. He came back and said quietly, "Why don't you make up your mind to quit pitching? . . . You just have too much hard luck, Al."

I nodded slowly. "I think you may be right. If this knee doesn't come around, I might be looking for a coaching job. . . ."

A week later, I joined the New Haven club which was training at home. When I dragged my pore ol' broken body up to George Weiss, he took one look at me and nearly had a fit. I was in no condition to be walking around, much less pitching for New Haven. The knee actually was so bad, the torn cartilage would seem to pop out of place if I just sat down too quickly. I kept having it treated with heat, but this only kept the swelling down. Water had developed on the knee.

It got little chance to improve, either. In that Eastern League, we were always on the move, always hurrying somewhere.

One day in a game at Hartford, I was called on to relieve, practically walking in on one leg. The first Hartford batter to face me was a thick-chested, muscly fellow named Lou Gehrig. I'd first heard about Gehrig a few years before when he and my brother Larry had played ball together at the High School of Commerce in New York.

"How do you pitch this big guy?" I asked my catcher, Wilson.

"Throw him close and high," Wilson said. "Try to crowd him."

I pitched "close and high" and Gehrig hit the ball *far* and high outside the ball park for a three-run homer that won the game for Hartford.

The next day, back at New Haven, Weiss called me to his office in the Taft Hotel. "Al, I'm sorry, but I have to suspend you. The club is losing money, and I simply can't afford to carry you like this, in the shape you're in. . . . Of course, when your knee comes around, I'll lift the suspension."

"I don't blame you for suspending me," I said. "I'm ready to give up pitching anyway. But if I could get my unconditional release from you, I think I got a chance to latch onto a good coaching job."

"Well, I don't know," he said. "I paid fifteen hundred for you. If I wait until your knee gets better at least, I might be able to get my money back selling you to some other club."

"Mr. Weiss, you couldn't get ten cents for me as a pitcher now," I smiled. "I'm through. But I do want to stay in baseball. Now, how much would you want for my release?"

"One thousand dollars," he said.

"I'll give you five hundred."

He paused, then said, "All right, five hundred. I don't want to stand in your way. If the club was doing better financially, I'd give you your release for nothing."

I had only two hundred dollars with me—which was all I had, period. So I called Clark Griffith long distance, collect. "Griff," I began, "wire me three hundred bucks quick," telling him the background.

"Keep trying," Griff said. "Try to get Weiss down to three hundred."

"My God!!" I yelled into the phone, "I already weaseled him down from a thousand to five hundred. I got two fish myself. Send me the other three hundred, will you?"

There was a short silence at the other end. Then Griffith asked, "What do you plan to do when you get your release?"

"Join you as a coach," I said.

"I don't know, Al. I've got four coaches now, and the club is in seventh place. We're not making any money down here . . ."

"Look," I said, "let me come down to see you and talk about it, okay?"

"All right," he said.

"Send me the three hundred dollars?" I said.

"Yes. . . . How's your knee?"

"Well, it's not a helluva lot better. I think I'll go visit Bonesetter Reese again before I see you."

When I got Griff's three hundred dollars, I bought my release from Weiss and started out for Youngstown, Ohio. The old Bonesetter heard my story; he asked me to stand up. He pinched a nerve or muscle in my right hip, and my knee, which I'd been unable to straighten since the injury, snapped straight, just like that. He told me to walk around the block a few times, which I did, without limping and without any pain either. The Bonesetter told me to keep up heat treatments. And all he charged me was ten dollars, because I said I wasn't working steady. That's the way he was—if you told him you had no money, he wouldn't charge much; but if he knew a ball club was paying the bills, he charged more, depending on how much dough the club had.

The day I got to Washington and went looking for Griffith was the first Sunday in June and it was raining. It had rained so hard in the morning the scheduled game already had been called off, which made it a bad day to try to see Griff. If there was one thing that drove him buggy, it was a Sunday postponement, because Sunday has always been the best attendance day. But I went to Griff's office and found him, and started right in with my sales pitch as to why I'd be a valuable addition to his coaching staff.

But he hardly let me get more than a thousand words in edgewise. "Al, I'd *like* to make you my third-base coach," he interrupted. He was giving up without a fight.

"It's a very important job," Griff went on. "You'll have to handle signals and exercise sharp judgment directing base runners. I honestly think you'd be a good man for the position. Bucky wants you too. So, if you really think you can handle it, you've got the job."

"Boy, that's swell, Griff," I began. "Now about——"

"I can't pay you much," he said quickly. "We're in seventh place, we're not pulling customers, and if we don't improve pretty soon the sheriff probably will be gunning for me."

I got up. "Griff, it's still raining outside, the game's been canceled, and I know this ain't your day. Suppose I come around tomorrow and we'll talk money, when the sun is shining."

"The club goes to Philadelphia tomorrow morning," Griff protested. "If you're to go with us as a member of this club, you'll have to sign a contract before we leave."

Of course, I'd already decided to settle for almost anything. All I wanted was this opportunity to get back to the big leagues. There was no doubt in my mind anymore about the direction in which I was heading. From now on I was clowning for pay. If I could make good as Griff's third-base coach, I not only was sure to get a better contract from him the next season, but I'd have my foot solidly in the door—for keeps this time.

So I signed his contract right away, for twenty-five hundred a year. After, I said, "Griff, about that three hundred dollars I owe you—don't expect me to give any of it back on pay day, because I haven't gotten any pay in over three weeks now."

"Okay," he said, eying me. "But you're not by any chance going to try to talk me out of that three hundred, are you?"

I laughed, "I'd like to meet the guy who could ever talk you out of three hundred bucks."

But he was wise to me.

The club went to Philadelphia and swept the series there. Then we moved west and blazed through Detroit, Cleveland, St. Louis and Chicago in a great road trip. Before you knew it, in a little over two weeks' time we were sniffing at first place, and the fans in Washington were going wild. When we returned for a home stand, crowds began flocking to our ball park. For the first time in Griffith's long reign, Washington had a pennant contender. And Griff, momentarily at least, forgot about the three hundred dollars I owed him.

In July, we went up to New York to play the Yankees, which was the team we were battling for the lead. The Yanks had won the AL pennant three straight years, and in 1923 had become World Champions for the first time, at last whipping the NL champion Giants.

There is a scuttlebutt around the dugouts in baseball about the tricks of every other club in the league. One of the things we knew about the Yankees was that none of their pitchers would hesitate to throw at you if you crowded home plate too close. As a result the first game of that series at Yankee Stadium became the turning point of the 1924 pennant race.

The visiting team had to pass through the Yankee dugout on their way from the dressing room to the field. As we filed out just before the game was to start, one of the Yankee pitchers yelled, "You guys better stay loose up at bat. Every one of you is goin' down today!"

He wasn't kidding. When our leadoff batter, Joe Judge, stepped up, Yankee pitcher Bob Shawkey fired the ball straight at Joe's head, and Joe hit the dirt just in time to avoid being skulled. Then he grounded out. Sam Rice was next, and down he went as Shawkey dusted him off too. With two out, our manager-second baseman Bucky Harris went to bat with his eyes blazing. On the first pitch, Bucky reached out and just pushed the ball toward first base. He knew first baseman Wally Pipp would have to field the ball and toss it to Shawkey, who was supposed to race over from the mound to cover first. That's one of baseball's oldest plays. But Shawkey didn't cover the bag, for he also knew another of baseball's oldest plays was for an angry runner to tap such a ball on purpose, just to be able to come in contact with the pitcher. Shawkey knew Harris —Bucky would have creamed him.

So Bucky got a free trip to first.

On the next pitch, Harris lit out for second. The Yanks shortstop took the throw from the catcher, and he had the ball in plenty of time to tag Harris out. But Bucky, instead of sliding into the bag, threw himself at Scott, both spiked feet aimed at the shortstop's chest. Scott jumped back in self protection, and Harris was safe.

"What are you tryin' to do, ruin me?" Scott cried.

"You guys wanna play dirty," Bucky snarled, "we can play the same way."

A moment later, Harris scored the first run when somebody got a base hit. Actually, Bucky should have made the third out in that inning. When our side was finally retired, Bucky ran to his position at second base, and Babe Ruth, who was playing right field for the Yanks, paused on his way to the dugout and hissed at Bucky:

"Wait'll I get on base. I'm coming down to second, and I'll *cut your legs off!*"

"Don't worry," Harris snapped back. "I'll *see* that you get on base . . . and I'll be waiting for you."

The first two Yankee batters were outs, and Ruth was third up. Harris took a few steps in from his position and shouted to our pitcher, Tom Zachary:

"Put the monkey on!"

So Zachary intentionally gave Ruth a base on balls.

On the very next pitch, the Babe starts down towards second like a runaway freight train. Harris races over to take the catcher's throw. Ruth hurtles through the air to give Bucky the business, but Bucky gives him the old basketball hip in midair, and damned if the next thing you know Ruth isn't rolling toward center field.

The Babe picks himself up, shaking with rage, and everybody's holding their breath wondering if he'll go after Harris. Bucky's standing by second base with the baseball tight in his fist, and he's watching the Babe to see what his next move will be. Ruth hesitates, then, kind of smiling a little, turns and walks to his position in right field.

We won the game. And I've always felt Bucky Harris's guts and aggressiveness that day led to us taking the pennant that season.

Right after that game, my old neighborhood pal, Harry Ruby, who'd become quite a songwriter ("Three Little Words," etc.) met me, and we went home to the Schacht house for dinner. Harry is a terrific baseball bug, and with me on the Washington club fighting for the pennant, he was very thrilled about our big win that day. All the way home he jabbered excitedly, replaying every important play of the game.

It was tough to cool him off, but I had to tell him. "Harry," I finally interrupted, "I want you to do me a favor. . . . I know how crazy you are about baseball, especially right this minute, but when we get home please don't say a word about today's game."

"Don't say a word?" he cried.

"Yeah, in fact don't even mention baseball at all. . . . You see, my mother never liked baseball, and while she's used to me being in it now, she still don't know a thing about it. My sister don't know anything about the game either, and my brothers Mike and Larry won't talk about it at home—we have a standing rule, nobody talks baseball in that house unless I start it, and I don't like to because, well, in some ways it's a touchy subject. . . ."

Harry stared at me like I had an extra nose in the middle of my forehead. "You mean to tell me," he said, "that when you get home nobody will ask you if your ball club won or lost today . . . in the middle of this hot pennant race?"

"That's right."

"Why, I can't believe that," he spluttered. "I think that's crazy."

"You'll see," I said. "Just don't break the rule."

We get home, and the family is there, ready for dinner, and no questions. All through dinner we chat about this and that, and still nobody asks me what happened at Yankee Stadium that afternoon. I sneak a look at Ruby every now and then, and I can see he's coming to a boil; he thinks the family is nuts. We're there about two hours, Harry barely having eaten a thing, because he's bursting to talk about that big ball game. Finally he stands up and announces it's getting late and he better start downtown.

"Okay, Harry," I speak up quickly, "I'll drive you downtown." I figure I better help him get out fast before he blows his lid.

We climb into my convertible outside, with Harry still shaking his head in bewilderment, and I'm about to drive away, when the window of our apartment slides open and my mother calls, "Al!"

"Yeah, Ma?"

"So who vun today?"

Harry almost blew his lid all right—laughing.

When the team got back to Washington, we were in first place, and there must have been thousands of fans waiting to greet us at the railroad station. Baseball fever was at its peak in the Capital.

Fans were coming all the way from Virginia and North Carolina, as well as Maryland. The ball park was packed on Sundays, and even weekday attendance averaged about triple what it used to be. It sure looked like Griffith would finally get out of hock.

We were in one of the greatest pennant fights the American League had ever had. There was hardly more than two games between the Yankees and us any time as the season rolled into August. Then the Yanks came to town for an important series. They were hot, particularly Babe Ruth, who was blasting home runs in every park. So Bucky Harris got a brainstorm how we might stop the Babe, or at least slow him down.

The Secretary of the Polish Legation in Washington happened to be a fanatical baseball follower, and he idolized certain ballplayers. Every so often, he'd throw a dinner party at his legation, inviting mostly ballplayers. On the Yankees, the Secretary's favorites were Herb Pennock, Waite Hoyt, Joe Dugan, and the Babe; on our club, outfielder Goose Goslin and myself usually took advantage of such invitations, because "refreshments" were served, despite prohibition.

The Polish Secretary decided to have another party the night before we were to play the Yankees a doubleheader, and Goslin and I were invited, and also the Babe. Bucky Harris, learning about this, took me aside that afternoon and said:

"I want you and Goose to be sure to attend this party tonight. I understand Ruth will be there. You guys stick with him."

"And . . . ?"

"You fellas do your damnedest to keep him out late, all night if you can. Maybe even try to get him potted. If he's got a hangover tomorrow, we got the games half won."

I thought it was a great idea, and so did Goslin, but both of us had our doubts about whether we could really outlast the Babe, who had a solid reputation—and he'd earned it—of being a night owl and playboy supreme.

The party was swell. I drank beer, but kept plying Ruth with champagne, which was no struggle at all, as he swizzled it down like soda pop. At midnight, the other Yankee players at the party left to get back to their hotel before the team curfew; but the Babe, the star of the team, apparently had his manager, Miller Huggins, over a barrel, for he ignored curfews.

Came 3 A.M., and Goslin and I were pooped, although neither of us had let ourselves tie a load on for fear of letting Ruth slip off the hook. The Babe, however, still was having a grand time. He looked like he'd just got his second wind and might carry on for days.

"Al," Goslin moaned, "I'm dead. I gotta get some sleep. We done our job. Whadya say we blow?"

"Yeah, that big guy is just getting warmed up. He'll never be able to play tomorrow."

Before leaving, I reminded Ruth he and I had an appointment early that morning to visit war veterans at the Walter Reed Hospital, and he agreed to meet me in the lobby of the Wardman Park Hotel at 8 A.M. sharp. I figured we had him in the bag; it didn't matter much if a coach like myself didn't get any sleep, but with the Babe staggering around in the outfield and at the plate, the Washington club would be sitting pretty.

About eight o'clock that morning I walked down to the hotel lobby, but Ruth wasn't there yet. In fifteen minutes, a cab pulled up outside and the Babe strolled in. His eyes appeared a little baggy, but otherwise he seemed steady enough.

"Where the hell are you coming from?" I said puzzled.

"I just left the legation," he smiled. "C'mon, let's go over to Walter Reed and get this over with."

We talked with the veterans there until eleven-thirty or so, then we taxied to the ball park. As he went inside the visitors' room I heard him tell the attendant to get him three franks and a coke. He still hadn't slept a wink. When I gave Bucky my report, he grinned slyly.

The Babe only slammed two home runs and a single in the first game of the doubleheader, and another homer and a pair of doubles in the second, to personally pin our ears back in both games. Meanwhile, I was dead on my feet coaching at third base, and Goose Goslin batted eight times without a hit. And we were going to outsmart the Babe.

That was one of the few times Bucky Harris's strategy flopped that season, for on our last swing through the western half of the league in September, we were still in first place. One morning in St. Louis, just before going out to the ball park, Walter Johnson and I were sitting in front of the Kingsway Hotel when Clark Griffith came toward us.

I whispered to Johnson, "Watch this financial talk I'm gonna have with Griff." Then I called cheerily, "Griff, will you sit down a minute? I got something very interesting I want to talk to you about." I knew he was in a good mood as we'd won the day before.

"Griff," I said, "if we win this pennant, and we both know we will, you should be ashamed to take that three hundred bucks from me."

"I knew you'd try to talk me out of that money from the moment you joined the club," he said.

"All I know is," I said, "you were in seventh place when I joined you, and afraid the sheriff would run you in, and now you're in first place. I don't say I personally put the club in first place, but my finger's in the pie somewhere."

"Griff," Johnson laughed, "I'll bet he talks you out of the three hundred."

"Well," Griff said, "let's see how we make out with the pennant."

We were playing in Boston the last week end of the season, with the Yanks playing Philadelphia, and us still just a game or so ahead. The Boston fans were rooting as hard for us to win as our own fans in Washington; in fact, the whole country seemed to be pulling for Washington to clinch its first pennant. The main reason, I think, was that Walter Johnson was such a sentimental favorite with everybody. He'd been a tremendous pitcher for eighteen seasons without ever getting into a World Series. Even in 1924, almost at the end of his career, he'd won twenty-three games for us and lost only seven.

The day we did clinch it, all of us were as tight as bow strings. To make it more nerve-racking, our pitcher got in a real jam during Boston's at-bat in the sixth. The guys on our bench were fidgeting nervously. Especially Altrock. With one man on base, and our pitcher apparently straining to control his stuff, Altrock buried his face in his arms, saying he was afraid to watch. A moment later, after a roar from the crowd, without looking up, he said to me, "How many on base now?"

"Two," I muttered.

A few minutes later the crowd roared again, and Nick asked, "How many on base now?"

"Three," I said.

Then, another roar—we'd got out of the inning without Boston scoring—and Altrock moaned, "How many now?"

"Four," I snapped. It took a moment for that one to sink in, then he jumped up. "Four?" he cried. And the whole team started laughing, breaking the awful tension.

We won that game, and we were American League champions. Our dressing room was a madhouse. Everybody was laughing and shouting and slapping each other on the back. We were probably more excited than any team which won a pennant, because you must remember it had long been said that Washington was "First in war, first in peace, and last in the American League." Griff came in last, grinning from ear to ear and congratulating each player. When he came by my locker, I collared him and said:

"Well, Griff, there it is, we won. How about that three hundred dollars?"

He only laughed again and mussed my hair saying, "Let's see how we do in the Series."

Griff made a short talk thanking everybody on the club for the great job completed, adding: "Tonight, boys, you're on your own. There'll be champagne at the hotel, and we'll have a big party. . . ." Then he turned serious and said, "But *only* tonight. Let's not forget we've got a big series coming up against the Giants."

That 1924 World Series was the most exciting Series I've ever seen, and I've watched about thirty-seven of them. The two clubs had, I think, the best infield combinations of any two teams ever to play in the Series. We had Judge at first base; Harris at second; Roger Peckinpaugh, shortstop; and Ossie Bluege, third base. The Giants had Long George Kelly and Bill Terry alternating at first; Frisch, second; Travis Jackson, shortstop; and Freddie Lindstrom at third base. The Series went the full seven games, and I'd say except for one game, the fourth, which we won, 7-4, each game rode on every pitched ball.

Our ace, Johnson, who won the American League's Most Valuable Player Award, lost twice, but the Series was three and three as we battled down to the final game at Washington. Behind, 3-1, we rallied for two runs in the bottom of the eighth to tie it, and then Harris brought Johnson in to relieve in the ninth. And what a job of clutch pitching old Walter did.

In the Giants' ninth, they had the potential winning run on third base with only one out, but Johnson struck out Kelly and got the next hitter easily. The game struggled along into the twelfth inning, and the same situation arose, and Johnson pitched out of it again.

Then in our half of the twelfth, with two out we got Muddy Ruel to second base. I, coaching at third, worried about whether or not to send Ruel for home in case of a sharp base hit, as Muddy wasn't too fast a runner. I decided to send him all the way if he had any chance to score at all.

Earl McNeely hit a bouncer toward third base. It looked like a routine grounder that would mean the third out—but the ball suddenly took a crazy hop over Lindstrom's head just as he was set to grab it, and it rolled into left field. Ruel came chugging around third, with me waving my arms like a runaway windmill, and scored the winning run. We were the world's champions.

The grandstands exploded. The huge crowd really rocked, everybody hugging and kissing and screaming for joy. Our clubhouse was bedlam, with all the guys pounding one another and lifting Johnson on their shoulders. Anybody who says professional ballplayers don't love to win, like college kids, doesn't know what he's talking about.

When Griffith burst in, tears of happiness were streaming down his cheeks. He dashed about, slapping everybody on the back. But when he approached me, I grinned, "Just a minute, Griff. I can't eat a pat on the back. How about the three hundred dollars?"

"Good God!" he cried, "you can have it!"

Damon Runyon, the great writer, who covered the Series, wrote that he was in Paris when the Armistice was declared in 1918, but that the wild celebration there was nothing compared to Washington after we won the Series in '24. The whole city was in an uproar. It was like the Mardi Gras—dancing in the streets, singing, shouting, bands playing. But while I was as happy as anyone, the celebration presented a problem.

A month before the season ended, I'd promised some people in Rochester, New York, that Walter Johnson and I would go up there and play in a benefit ball game which was to be held for an ailing police captain. It turned out that this game was scheduled for the day after our Series victory, and I had to try to get Johnson and myself aboard a train for Rochester only a few hours after we'd won.

Seeing the mob waiting outside the ball park for their hero, I sneaked Johnson out by way of the center field exit gate. Then we made a run for our hotel, hiding out there until about seven. But apparently the rumor got around that we were headed for the railroad station, for there was a crowd of three thousand waiting for us there. So we ducked around the side and through the station master's office and got on the train without Johnson being mobbed.

The train stopped four or five times along the way during the night and each time crowds were lined up on the platforms to greet the Big Train. At Utica, New York, several hundred people stormed the train and filed through our car to get Johnson's autograph. The poor guy was dead tired, but he sat up half the trip in his pajamas accepting congratulations and signing autographs. And neither of us was getting paid for our appearance in Rochester, either.

The Rochester Ball Park was packed, and I suppose we helped clean up for this sick police captain. Walter was really dragging his fanny when we headed back to Washington. I sort of apologized for having talked him into making the trip after such an exhausting Series, but he just smiled wearily and said, "Al, I wouldn't have missed this for the world."

A short while after the Series, I received a letter asking if I'd speak at a dinner for a fee. I'd done some such jobs for the ball club before, but now it struck me this might be worth getting into in the off-seasons. I always loved to stand up and pop off to an audience and had developed a pretty fair routine, including both serious and humorous baseball stories. Becoming my own booking agent, I began speaking at various functions, getting two to three hundred dollars an engagement.

At a father-and-son sports dinner at Hartford, Connecticut, one night, I had a strange experience. Knowing I had to catch the last train back to New York about 10 P.M., in order to make another train for Chicago, where I was slated to speak at a hardware convention, I asked the toastmaster, Bill Miller, how long he wanted me to speak. He said, "About twenty minutes," and I said, "Be sure you call on me no later than nine-thirty, because I have to catch that last train."

At nine-thirty, Bill started introducing me. He and I had attended high school together, and he knew quite a bit of my background. So he rambled on about me, beginning almost from the day I was born. I was getting fidgety and kept glancing at my watch but nothing could stop Miller.

At long last, Bill finished my life story, at ten to ten, and turning toward me, said, ". . . And now I give you Al Schacht, the Clown Prince of Baseball!"

I got up, cleared my throat, and said: "In conclusion, gentlemen, I want to thank you very much . . ." and ran like hell out of the room for the railroad station.

Which reminds me of another time, many years later, when Jack Dempsey and I went to Syracuse, New York, for a sports dinner. On the way there in the train, Jack, who is a wonderful, wonderful guy but who enjoys pulling practical jokes, repeatedly tried to give me a "hot foot" as we sat in the club car with Joe Williams, the Scripps-Howard sports writer. But I always caught him in time.

At the banquet, on my feet giving my spiel, I didn't notice Dempsey had left his seat. In the middle of a story, I suddenly howled, "Yeow!" leaped a foot in the air, stumbled backward over my own chair and crashed down on the floor of the dais. That bum Dempsey had crawled under the head table, stuck a match in the sole of my shoe and lit it while I was talking. I have to admit it got a bigger laugh than any of the gags I told.

In the summer of 1925, romance popped into my life again, and about time. I'd been dating now and then, with no real interest in any one girl, but now that I was fairly well settled as a Washington coach and clown, and seeing as I was going on thirty-two, I wondered if I'd ever meet the right girl.

About 2 A.M. one hot morning in Washington, I was sitting on the little balcony of my apartment in the Arlington Hotel, trying to cool off, when I noticed smoke seeping out the window of a two-family house across K Street. The lights were out in the house, and not seeing anyone stirring, I figured the occupants must be asleep. Dashing inside my apartment, I put in a call for the fire department, then raced downstairs and across the street to the house.

The front door was locked, so I kicked it in and yelled, "Fire!" In a few minutes, a distinguished-looking gentleman and a girl came running out. Soon the fire engines arrived, and the fire was extinguished quickly with not too much damage. The man and the girl were very grateful.

Her name was Ethel, and she was a knockout, a redhead about twenty years old. And I always had a weakness for redheads. Her father was a congressman—at least I thought he was; it wasn't until some time later I learned he'd *used* to be in Congress but was then practicing law. They were pretty well off, in high society. We got to talking, and I made a date with Ethel when her father left us alone for a minute.

We saw each other several times a week after that. We'd go dancing at the Powhatan Roof Garden, where we'd look out over Washington and talk, she drinking Coke and me near-beer. She was a great baseball enthusiast, and I'd get her and her friends tickets to Washington ball games. We seemed to be getting along pretty good and I thought I was falling in love with her.

But I couldn't be sure. There were doubts nagging me. For she insisted more and more on me escorting her to society functions in the Capital, to dinner dances, parties and such, all at homes of very rich people, her class of people. They always begged me to entertain for them at these affairs, and while they enjoyed my clowning and stories, I began to get the suspicion that they looked down on me a little, that maybe I wasn't really acceptable. I had the vague feeling sometimes that Ethel thought of me as a novelty, a curiosity for her wealthy friends to get a bang out of. And it dawned on me that I didn't think her father knew Ethel and I were dating.

The blowoff came the night we went to a Naval party at Bethesda, Maryland. For the second time in my life, I drank champagne, and too much of it.

When we got to Ethel's house, we stood on the front stoop for a few minutes. Then the door was thrown open, and her father was standing there. He was angry; and when I mumbled something like "Mornin', Congreshman," he got angrier.

"Ethel," he snapped, "do you know what time it is?" And turning to me, he said, "What do you mean bringing my daughter home at this hour? And look at the condition you're in . . ." I wasn't too drunk to see right then he was glaring at me like I was a disease.

"I think it would be better," he said, "if you do not call on my daughter again." Just like that.

I looked at Ethel, but her face was blank. She moved inside the house without a word. The old man stood there, waiting for me to leave, and I finally stumbled down the steps and over to my hotel. I tried to call her a couple of times after that, but she was always tied up, she said.

I stuck to my baseball the rest of that summer, working harder than ever with Altrock to polish our routines. Meanwhile, our club romped home to our second straight pennant, beating the second-place Philadelphia Athletics by eight and one half games. The Yankees, with whom we'd battled so long and hard the year before, sank to seventh place.

I described before what happened to us in the last game of the Series against Pittsburgh, that rainy, muddy day. We'd had them down, three games to one, but the Pirates won the next two. The last day, in Pittsburgh, Walter Johnson pitched for us. The Big Train, in his nineteenth American League season, almost thirty-eight years old, had won twenty and lost only seven during the season, and won two straight starts in this Series, 4–1 and 4–0. But this last game, although our club got him seven runs, the Pirates battered him. In the bottom of the eighth, with us leading 7–6,

Pittsburgh's Kiki Cuyler doubled with the bases loaded to drive in the tying and winning runs.

But, as usual, I managed to squeeze some good fortune out of the setback. That last game of the Series had been held up at the start by the rain, and with the big crowd and both teams just sitting twiddling our thumbs, Altrock and I got an idea for what I think is one of the best gags we ever pulled on a ball field.

The infield had been covered with the usual canvas tarpaulin, and I noticed a pool of water forming around the pitcher's mound, which is higher than the rest of the infield. I got hold of a broom from the clubhouse and broke off the sweeping part, leaving the long stick. Then, taking two bats and a bottle filled with water, Altrock and I removed our shoes and socks and ran out into the downpour to the mound. There we sat down, facing each other, me "rowing" with the bats and Altrock "fishing" with the broomstick. The crowd roared.

Suddenly Altrock got up, as though he'd hooked a big one, lost his balance and started rocking the boat, with me yelling to sit down. He fell overboard, right into the small lake surrounding the mound. Having sneaked a mouthful of water from the bottle, I dove in to save him. Then, grabbing Nick around the neck like a lifeguard, I "swam" for shore (toward the third base line), spouting water out of my mouth.

Next, we got a wooden board and put on an exhibition of high diving off the mound. The crowd loved it. Of course, we never thought the game would be played. But Judge Landis figuring it might rain for days in Pittsburgh, ordered it to go on. So Altrock and I had to hurry into the dressing room to change our uniforms, which were wringing wet. We both grabbed the first uniforms in sight, and they were yards too big (I'd put on one of Johnson's). During the game we looked like a pair of ragamuffins on the coaching lines. But the way it rained all that day, the uniforms practically shrank down to our size. Anyhow, later on we incorporated that rowing and swimming routine into our act.

chapter 14

Nineteen twenty-six was a disappointing season for our Washington club, after two pennant-winning years. We finished fourth, eight games behind the winning Yankees. It was the more disappointing because Griffith had given Bucky Harris a bright new three-year contract calling for $100,000 after we'd won the two straight pennants. One reason we slipped, I'm sure, is that our ace, Johnson, going on thirty-nine years of age, slid to a sour 15-16 record. It was clear Walter was almost through as a winning pitcher. As it turned out, the Big Train had only one more season in him, and not much of a one at that—in '27, he won only five games while losing six.

One event stands out in my mind about 1926, and it had nothing to do with Washington or the AL pennant race. I was hired to entertain at an experimental *night game* in Salem, Massachusetts. I'm not certain now if this was the first night game ever played, but it must have been one of the first. The lights were not the high-powered arcs arranged in banks like today, but simply rows of individual spotlights. The field was not particularly well lit, although I must say I've performed in some minor league parks in recent years where the lights were not much better than they were that night in Salem.

Anyhow, I entertained before the game and then hung around, curious to see how baseball looked at night. A large turnout in the stands showed the fans also were interested. In the ninth inning, with the score 1–1, the home team got a runner at second base with two out, and I went to their manager Tom DeNoville and said, "How about letting me go up as a pinch hitter?" and he said okay.

The man with the megaphone announced me, and I advanced to home plate carrying a lantern. Setting the lantern down on the plate, I turned to the grandstands and made a speech:

"Ladies and gentlemen, I am going to hit for Hoffman. Not that he's a poor hitter, but I happen to be a better one." . . . (If they only knew!) . . . "I don't want to take advantage of this poor pitcher, so I plan to take two strikes and then single cleanly to right field and score the man from second with the winning run, and we'll all go home happy. I thank you."

The pitcher cut a strike across the middle of the plate. I turned to the crowd and hollered, "There's one!" He fired another strike, and I called out again, "There's two! . . . Now ladies and gentlemen, pick up your seat cushions and get ready to go home. I'm gonna break up this game right now!"

The next pitch was a fast ball high and outside, and I stuck out my bat and slapped it sharply to right field. The runner wheeled around from second and scored the game-ending run. I ran back to home plate from first base, grabbed the lantern and blew out the flame. I'll be damned if all the flood lights didn't go off at the same moment, leaving the entire field in darkness. There'd been some sort of power failure. If we rehearsed it for a year, it couldn't have gone off so perfectly.

Which reminds me of another night game when I was coaching with the Boston Red Sox some years later. It was an exhibition in Wilkes-Barre, Pennsylvania. I came to bat as a gag, and just as the pitcher was winding up to throw to me, somebody turned off all the lights. But I fooled them. When the lights came on, there I was sliding into third base.

Altrock and I of course clowned again during the '26 Series between the Yanks and the St. Louis Cardinals. That was the Series that the great St. Louis pitcher, Grover (Pete) Alexander, came out of the bullpen in the seventh inning of the final game and struck out Tony Lazzeri with the bases loaded. The legend has been that Pete was drunk at the time. I've never been quite sure about that although if anybody had the inside dope, I did.

Pete, who was about thirty-nine then, was always a drinking man. He'd won the second game of the Series, 6–2, and the sixth, 10–2, which tied it all up at three games apiece. So, after that sixth game, St. Louis manager Rogers Hornsby told Alexander to go out and relax and have some fun (which Pete was going to do anyway), as he wouldn't be needed any more in the Series, the next day being the last game. This was in New York.

The night before the final game, I'd entertained at a charity bazaar at Roslyn, Long Island, along with some Broadway actors. On the way back, our auto broke down, and it was 3:30 A.M. before I reached the Alamac Hotel, where I stayed during the Series. The Cardinals also were stopping there. When I walked into the lobby, a couple of bellboys were fussing with a guy stretched out on a couch. It was Alexander, and he was stiff. He'd been out celebrating his victory, and now the bellhops were trying to hustle him up to his room but he wouldn't budge.

I knew Pete pretty well, so I shooed the bellhops away and talked him into letting me take him upstairs. He was really pie-eyed, and kept begging me to go out with him for some more fun. I tried to talk baseball to him to keep his mind occupied. Going up in the elevator, Pete repeated over and over, "Al, old boy, always keep that curve ball low on the outside and you'll never have any trouble . . ." I said, "What if you don't have a curve ball?" But he ignored me and mumbled on. At last I got him to his room and flopped him on the bed, out.

The next day, after entertaining the bleacherites all morning, I was resting on the Cardinal bench when old Pete came out of the clubhouse and slumped on the bench near the water cooler. His cap was perched wearily on the side of his head, his eyes were half closed and bloodshot; and he looked like death warmed over.

Jess Haines started pitching for the Cards, and they led 3–2, going into the seventh. Then the Yanks filled the bases with two out, and their hard hitting rookie, Lazzeri, due up. But Haines had developed a blister on one of his pitching fingers, and Hornsby signaled to the bullpen. I could have dropped dead when I saw old Pete Alexander coming in to pitch. He shuffled in slowly, his cap still tilted on the side of his head. I watched him closely to see if he would stagger a little, but he seemed steady. After a few easy warmup pitches, he said okay, and Lazzeri stepped in to hit.

Alex threw a ball, then a strike. Tony slammed the next pitch a mile up into the left field stands, foul by only a few feet. The big crowd was still humming about that when Alex slipped Lazzeri a beautiful low-breaking curve ball on the outside corner of the plate for strike three. The Cards had got out of the inning. Alexander finished the game, pitching two more hitless innings, and the Cardinals won the game and the Series.

Later, in the excited St. Louis dressing room, I congratulated Pete. He still looked drunk.

"Like I told you, Al," he said, "always keep that curve ball low and outside . . ."

I'm still not sure if he was really sober pitching that crucial ball game.

It was before that game that I was approached in the clubhouse by Cash & Carry Pyle, a big time promoter, who offered me and Altrock a proposition. I knew of Pyle as the promoter who'd persuaded the great football star, Red Grange, to turn pro after Red's sensational years at the University of Illinois, and he'd helped Grange make a bundle of money. Pyle said he had a tennis show booked in Madison Square Garden that night featuring Mlle. Suzanne Lenglen. He claimed she was the greatest female tennis player who ever lived. He wanted Altrock and me to join the tour and put on a burlesque tennis act between the singles and doubles matches. He offered us five hundred dollars a week apiece and expenses.

While I'd clowned at tennis on a ball field several years before, I didn't know enough about the game to be able to gag it up, and I asked Pyle for a photo of Mlle. Lenglen, thinking I would concentrate on impersonating her. Pyle had said she was the colorful, temperamental type. He had a publicity picture of her right with him, and I saw she wore a long white dress and a red ribbon around her hair. So after that final game of the Series, I went downtown and found a shop on Sixth Avenue where I bought a white dress and red ribbon.

Mlle. Lenglen's principal opponent was to be an American star, Mary K. Browne. One of the male members of the troupe was Vinnie Richards, a great amateur who had just turned pro. That evening I stood on the balcony of the Garden, outside the dressing rooms, and watched Mlle. Lenglen in her first singles set with Mary Browne. Her mannerisms were very showy, and she did everything with an impatient flourish. She seemed on edge, having lost her temper a bit when the Garden crew was slow preparing the court before the set. She looked like a good subject for my mimicking. The only thing that bothered me was whether the audience would accept me and Altrock. A record tennis crowd had turned out for Mlle. Lenglen's first appearance in America, and most of the box seats were occupied by society people, who might not appreciate our performance, as nobody had ever dared do anything like this before.

When our turn came, Altrock came out dressed in ordinary men's tennis togs, and I pranced out in the white dress and red ribbon around my head. The public address system announced we would show how tennis should really be played. The crowd was silent.

Altrock and I put on an exhibition of the greatest shots ever made in tennis—without a ball and using rackets without strings. I flew around like Mlle. Lenglen, and Altrock flailed all over the place. Then we wound up with a set in slow motion. By the time we were through, I must say the audience was enthusiastic. So was Cash & Carry Pyle and we were in.

The tour was some deal. Nick and I only had to work about four to eight minutes a week, and we were getting five hundred dollars apiece. You couldn't beat that. And everything went lovely for about a month. Until one night in Minneapolis, when bad feeling suddenly sprang up between Mlle. Lenglen and us. This particular night, Mlle. Lenglen, who had been beating Mary Browne regularly all through the tour, was finally getting licked and the crowd was booing her. She got madder and madder, and when she'd lost, stalked off the court to her dressing room under the temporary bleachers. Altrock and I went on next.

Mlle. Lenglen had actually never seen us work, as she always rested between her singles and doubles matches. So, this night, when she heard the crowd laughing and cheering our antics, she snapped to her trainer (he told us later):

"Ze American public, zey are very funnee. Zey do not appreciate ze art of tennis, only ze clowns of tennis."

So that was the start of the trouble. The camel's back got broken only a few days later in Chicago, when we played the Chicago Stadium.

I had entered the stadium shortly before the first set between Mlle. Lenglen and Mary K. Browne and stood watching while three photographers on the arena floor badgered Lenglen for pictures, as she practiced her volleying. Having studied her so often, I could tell she was beginning to boil at these photographers. Finally, in a burst of temper, she blew up and demanded they leave the court. Two of them reluctantly moved off, but one, from the Chicago *American* I believe, persisted in following her around the court pleading for just one more picture.

Mlle. Lenglen stamped about, waving her arms and crying, "No more! No more!" But he wouldn't give up. The crowd was starting to rumble too, half of them calling, "Let him have a picture!" and the other half hollering, "Get him off the court!" It looked like a riot might start. Suddenly, a man wearing a raccoon coat dove out of the crowd onto the court, screaming curses in French, and tried to drag the photographer off the floor. The photographer dropped his camera, and a fight started. The whole auditorium was on its feet, roaring. Then the superintendent of the stadium raced out and pulled both men off the court.

I dashed downstairs, got a cigar box and buttonholed the superintendent and asked him to paint the box black for me, like a camera. When Altrock arrived a few minutes later, I outlined what had happened and what we were going to do—he would be the wild Frenchman. We couldn't find anybody else in a raccoon coat, so Nick used his own overcoat. Then I gave a spectator a few bucks to hold the "camera" and come running out as the photographer.

When Lenglen and Browne had finished their game, I pranced out in my dress and ribbon and began practicing alone in pantomime as Mlle. Lenglen. The "photographer" trailed me around the court, begging for pictures, and I got temperamental, stamping my feet and throwing my arms up in exasperation, shouting, "No more! No more!" Next, Altrock charged out of the stands and tussled with the photographer, and they both got so excited they almost really came to blows. We all got dragged off.

The next day, Altrock and Schacht were on their way back to New York. For Mlle. Lenglen was so furious at our burlesque of her, she threatened Pyle, "Eizer you keep me or you keep ze clowns. You cannot have boz of us." And since she was Pyle's main meal ticket, Nick and I were the ones to go. I guess that time we were a little too funny.

I went back home and spent the rest of the winter making after-dinner speaking engagements.

When I arrived at Tampa, Florida, for 1927 spring training, there were still signs of destruction of the big hurricane they'd suffered there before we ballplayers arrived. The chamber of commerce was planning a benefit show for the storm victims at the Tampa Bay Casino, featuring the great violinist Mischa Elman and the Russian composer, Sergei Rachmaninoff.

There were about eighteen hundred people jamming the Casino, at twenty dollars a head, to hear these great artists. But just before the curtain, Harry Bailey, who was managing the show, got a wire from Rachmaninoff saying he'd missed train connections and wouldn't be able to make it to Tampa in time. Bailey was frantic.

"Don't worry," I said. "You go out and read the telegram, then tell 'em you're very fortunate to have the services of that great French pianist, *Professor Chinini*. That's me."

After Mischa Elman played *Humoresque* on his violin, Professor Chinini was introduced. I'd painted on a little black mustache and a goatee, and as Mr. Elman came off I borrowed his frock coat. Then I went out on the stage and walked solemnly to the piano amid thunderous applause.

"Ladeez and gentlemens," I began, very serious, "I will play for you my favorite composition, *Sunatotra*, which is ze *Hungarian Rhapsody*, ze *Lucia* Sextet and ze *Madame Butterfly* all at once." They applauded like mad.

I sat at the piano delicately, tickling the keys and listening to the tone of each. I whipped out my handkerchief and dabbed my brow, then wiped off the piano. Still nobody snickered or anything.

I hit the first octave of the *Hungarian Rhapsody*, ran my stubby fingers along the keyboard as fast as I could, stopped cold and played with two notes—"ding, ding . . . ding, ding . . . ding, ding

". . . ding, ding . . ." I turned and looked at the audience. To my surprise, they were staring up at me, fascinated. You could hear a pin drop. One old lady had her hand to her ear, trying to make out what I was playing.

So I went through my whole "recital," which consisted of the above about eight more times, just changing the original octaves or chords and making up my own. It even sounded great to me. At the very end, reaching to the far end of the piano for the last crashing note, I threw myself into the orchestra pit. There was one big "Ooooh!" and they all started laughing.

What I'll never understand is how I could fool nearly two thousand people for six whole minutes. Although, when I got back to the hotel later, Mrs. Clark Griffith said to me, "You didn't fool me, Al. I recognized your walk when you first came out. But while you were playing, a woman on my right leaned over and whispered, 'He may be a great French pianist, but his technique is terrible.'"

The less said about the 1927 pennant race as regards the Washington club—and six other teams, for that matter—the better. It was interesting for a while; we finished in third place, which was one notch higher than the previous year. The catch was, we wound up *twenty-five games* back of the incredible Yankees. In fact, the second-place Athletics finished *nineteen games* behind the Yanks. For Ruth, Gehrig & Co. merely won 110 games, the American League record which stood until 1954. Ruth, of course, hit his sixty home runs that season, which is still the all-time major-league high.

But Altrock and I were getting ready to appear before another World Series crowd. The Jack Dempsey-Gene Tunney rematch and the famous "long count" gave us a golden opportunity to work up a burlesque of that fight to unveil during the Series.

We got a break through George Weiss, who by then had become business manager of the Yankees. He liked our long-count burlesque during the Series, and sent us to a friend of his, a theatrical agent named Marty Forkins, who also handled Bill (Bojangles) Robinson. Forkins, on Weiss's recommendation, made the rounds of booking agents, trying to sell us to vaudeville. I imagine Forkins had a rough time at first, as agents are like elephants, never forgetting bad acts, and we'd had a bad act years before when we first tried vaudeville. I don't know how he did it, but Forkins got us booked for fifteen solid weeks, at fourteen hundred dollars a week. Nick and I made Joe Engle, the baseball scout (now president of the Chattanooga, Tennessee, Lookouts), our personal manager.

Engle also acted as ring announcer and referee in the act. We had a regular prize ring on the stage. Altrock played Tunney and I Dempsey. Nick and I would come out and spar around, and I'd finally nail him on the button and he'd go down, with the referee (Engle) shoving me all over the ring trying to get me to a neutral corner. Then I'd walk over to Altrock and hand him a banana to eat and a newspaper to read as he lay on the floor, while I went to my corner and played cards with my seconds. The referee kibitzed on the card game, finally saying aloud to me, "Why don't you leave the queen?" I'd point to Altrock and say, "How about him?" and Engle would stroll over to "Tunney," count "One!" and return to watch the card game. In a few seconds he'd go back to Altrock and say "Two!" and back to the card game. At *nine*, Altrock would get up, and I'd chase him a few laps full speed around the ring, and we'd be having a foot race as the curtain came down.

As we moved across the country, Engle and I both started having difficulties with Altrock. Nick was doing some drinking, and sometimes he'd show up late for the performance, or fumble around onstage. We were getting afraid maybe the big money was going a little to his head.

Ring Lardner had once written a poem about Nick, about his terrific pitching for the White Sox in 1906. Nick took a lot of pride in this poem, and he got to reciting it each show in front of the curtain after our act. Neither the various theater managers nor Engle and I thought it belonged in the act, but Altrock bitterly insisted on his recitation. You could put the lights out on him, and he'd still give out with the poem.

On the bill with us at the old State Lake Theatre in Chicago was a young crooner named Bing Crosby. He was a good-looking youngster, only about twenty-four, loaded with talent. He was sort of quiet then, not the humorist he is now, but anybody who knew anything about show business could see he had a singing style all his own. He was one of a trio known as the Rhythm Boys, including piano player Harry Barris.

One night, backstage, Bing said to me, "Harry has written a number he thinks is great. Listen tonight and see if you like it." It was "I Surrender Dear," and I thought it was terrific. I always felt that that song made him. A short while after I first met him, I was spending some time in California during the winter, and Bing was singing with Gus Arnheim's orchestra at the Los Angeles Ambassador Hotel, and people were going wild over his theme song, "I Surrender Dear."

As we were about finishing our tour in late February, Marty Forkins got in touch with us, asking if we'd play an extra week at the Keith's theater in Washington. The ball club had already reported to Tampa and Engle felt we should get Griffith's permission to stay away longer. So we had Forkins wire Griff:

REQUEST PERMISSION BOOK ALTROCK AND SCHACHT ONE MORE WEEK HERE. SORRY TO DELAY THEIR REPORTING DATE YOUR BALL CLUB.

Griff's answer was:

YOU CAN DO ME BIG FAVOR BY ENGAGING THOSE TWO MENTAL CASES FOR ENTIRE BASEBALL SEASON. LET VAUDEVILLE MANAGERS WORRY ABOUT THEM FOR CHANGE.

chapter 15

That spring of 1928 I came very close to death.

All during the training season, my stomach had acted up again, the trouble becoming so acute that by April I'd lost about twelve pounds, bringing me down to 126. The sharp pains were striking more often, the dysentery got worse, and I couldn't eat. I went to a few doctors, but none of them seemed able to diagnose what was wrong—especially when I informed them my appendix had been removed several years before to "cure" me. When my stomach wasn't acting up it felt numb, and Griff refused to let me get in uniform as we traveled north toward Washington.

During an exhibition game against the New York Giants at the Polo Grounds just before opening day, Joe Engle and I were sitting in the center field clubhouse watching the game and reminiscing about some of the great players Joe had scouted for our club. Suddenly I was doubled up by an awful pain and a few minutes later I went to the men's room and got really scared when I saw I was discharging blood. Joe made me lie down on the rubbing table and called the club trainer, Mike Martin, who probed my stomach with his fingers. I remember the scared look on Engle's face as he watched anxiously. But, naturally, Martin couldn't make out what had hit me; the sharp pain seemed to dig all through my insides.

"We oughta get you to a hospital," Mike said, nodding toward the telephone. "I'll call an ambulance . . ."

"No," I said. "Wait a minute." All I could think of was the long list of doctors I'd already gone to who had just looked puzzled and sent me away as ignorant of my ailment as I'd been. Only a few days before someone had recommended a Dr. Philip Norman, who was supposed to be a great stomach specialist. Fortunately I had remembered it.

"Dr. Norman," I gasped. "Philip Norman . . ."

"You want him?" Mike Martin asked. "Where?"

"Manhattan . . . look in the phone book. N-o-r-m-a-n."

Martin went to call Dr. Norman, and I could hear "Al Schacht . . . Polo Grounds . . . stomach, bad . . . emergency . . ." Dr. Norman said we could come over right away. Someone went with me in the cab, I forget who now.

Dr. Norman ushered me into a private office, as other patients were in the waiting room. He asked me to relate the entire history of my ailment from the earliest I could remember.

When I finished, Dr. Norman studied me gravely and said, "It sounds to me like you may have an ulcer in your lower intestine. We can make sure without any delay." He led me into another room, had me undress and stretch out on a table, and then inserted a long, thin instrument like a periscope and studied my *insides*. Seems a pretty obvious step to take, doesn't it?

Dr. Norman whistled in amazement. "You have *several* ulcers in there," he said quickly. "They're bleeding. You're about to have an internal hemorrhage. I'll have to irrigate you at once."

He moved rapidly preparing the solutions. I noticed he included argyrol in one. He set up the apparatus and sent the liquids flowing into my intestines. I passed out.

Much later, dressed and lying more comfortably on a couch in Dr. Norman's office, I asked if he could cure me.

"Your lower intestine all but dropped out," he said. "But I think I can help you. You'll simply have to follow my prescribed treatment."

A thought struck me. "Does that mean I'd have to stay here in New York?"

"I'd prefer it," he said.

"That puts me in a sort of a spot. My mother lives here, you know. She is a wonderful woman. She knows there's something wrong with my stomach, but if I stay behind when the ball club starts the season, she will worry like hell."

He waited for me to go on. "Do you suppose I could go to Washington with the team," I said, "and enter a private hospital, if they will treat me according to your prescription?"

"Well, that might be all right," he said. "Do you have such a place in mind?"

"Yes."

"Very well. I'll make the necessary arrangements."

So I went on to Washington, registered at a private sanitarium, and started undergoing treatment planned by Dr. Norman in cooperation with the hospital's authorities.

In less than a month, I was cured forever. For at the end of that time, Dr. Norman examined my intestines again and said, "I've got good news for you. You're clear as a bell.

"If you're smart," he continued, "you'll stay on the same eating plan and you'll never have to worry about ulcers again. Actually, this is not a 'diet' but merely a sensible plan for eating. But don't you go around telling other people how they should eat..."

I don't usually. But for those who may be interested, I was cured not by medicines but by proper food combinations. And I've eaten Dr. Norman's way ever since, which is over twenty-six years as I write this. For the first ten days of his treatment, my three meals a day consisted of big glasses of orange juice and milk. Then, when I was allowed solid foods, for breakfast I'd have raw fruit and milk; for lunch, creamed soup, salad with or without French dressing, and black coffee; dinner, sea food appetizer, soup, any kind of meat broiled, baked or boiled, any vegetable well cooked, fruit and black coffee. I was not permitted any white bread, pastries or other rich desserts, no butter or sugar. Also, no snacks at bedtime, but if I got hungry during the day I could munch on some fruit. On this diet I gained twenty-five pounds in nine months.

The unhealthy feeling between me and Altrock continued that baseball season. At Philadelphia one day, the first of two unfortunate incidents occurred.

We were clowning in infield practice, with me at third base and Nick on first, as usual. One of our gags was for me, after whipping a couple of real baseballs across the diamond to Altrock, to give him a signal and then fire a rubber ball which he'd let hit him right between the eyes. This always brought a yell from the crowd. Altrock must have mistakenly thought I gave him the sign, which was to wipe my hand across my shirt front, because he let a *hard* ball crack him on the forehead. He fell in a heap, out cold, with a huge lump on his noggin. When he came around, he glared at me suspiciously. I don't think I ever did convince him I hadn't tried to trick him.

A few days later, in New York, we were doing our burlesqued prize fight on the center of the diamond, with Nick using a pair of first baseman's mitts and me two infielder's gloves. In one sequence of punches, I weaved when I should have bobbed, and Altrock caught me solidly on the chin with the buckle of one of his gloves, sending me sprawling. It cut my chin. "Now we're even," he growled down at me. But I don't believe he meant to do it.

Toward the end of the 1928 season, it looked like Bucky Harris had worn out his welcome in Washington. Our club was just doing so-so, and the fans were riding Bucky. On top of his having gotten that fat $100,000 three-year contract, which might have been the most ever paid a manager up to that time, Bucky had married into society, and the rumors went around that he was getting too high-hat for his job. Sometimes club owners, as much as they might disagree, have to listen to the fans, who, after all, pay the freight. Griff thought highly of Bucky, but you could see he was bothered by all the talk.

As a matter of fact, Bucky was about through as a second baseman and Griff began to figure out how he could get Buddy Myer back. Griff had bought Myer, a shortstop, from the minors in 1925 for thirty-five thousand dollars, which was quite a sum in those days. Myer reported with a groin injury, and though he had one pretty fair year with us in '26, he never really lived up to our hopes, and was traded to the Boston Red Sox the following year. There, through most of 1927 and '28, he developed into a fine shortstop-third baseman, hitting around .300. Griff knew that Myer could be turned into a topflight second baseman to replace Bucky and be the key man on a rebuilt team.

Bob Quinn, then owner of the Red Sox, was willing to trade Myer—in exchange for six of our players, including a top shortstop. We had a pretty good one, Bobby (Gunner) Reeves, but we didn't want to lose him. So Griff sent out Joe Engle to try to buy a shortstop from some Class AAA league club.

We got a telegram from Engle before long—AM SENDING YOU JOE CRONIN SHORTSTOP KANSAS CITY CLUB. TAKE CARE OF HIM.

Cronin arrived a few days later. He was a big, chisel-chinned Irish kid, all excited, and when he said to me, "Gee, I hope I can make good for this team," I didn't have the heart to tell him we only wanted him to throw into the Red Sox deal. The truth was, Engle had bought him for only seventy-five hundred dollars; he was the only shortstop we could get so late in the season for so little money. I'll bet the Kansas City club thought they'd put something over on us at that, for Cronin had hit a weak .240 and was not even considered an outstanding fielder.

I took Joe to meet Griff, introducing him by saying, "Here's your new shortstop." As was the custom, Griff had Cronin sign his contract immediately. After the kid had left, I said to Griffith, "Maybe you oughtn't to send this boy to Boston. He might make good for you." It was just a hunch; I liked the kid.

"What?" Griff snorted, "a .240 minor league hitter?"

"Listen," I said, "you always used to tell me you could judge a ballplayer by his chin. If he's got a solid jaw, he'll be all right, you said. According to that way of judging, this Cronin ought to be sensational—he's got some chin."

Griff laughed me off. But I'd got my motor going and I decided to let it run a while. "You've had Reeves at short for a few years," I said, "and he's not bad, but he's certainly not been any ball of fire for this club. Why not take a look at Cronin while he's here?"

So Griff let Cronin play a few games. Joe finished the season at shortstop. And Reeves was among the six players we traded to Boston for Buddy Myer. The following season, Cronin became the American League's best shortstop. Three years later Griff named him manager. And three years after that, he sold Joe back to the Red Sox for $250,000 and another player. Do you think Griff owes me some money?

That fall, everybody in baseball was guessing about who would be our next manager, for Griff announced he was releasing Harris. I happened to be one of the few who knew beforehand who the new manager would be. For right after the World Series I visited Griff, and he told me he planned to appoint Walter Johnson to the job. "I feel I owe him this chance after all he did for me as a pitcher," Griff said. Walter had quit playing after 1927, and put in a year as manager of Newark of the International League in '28. "I know he'll be a poor manager to start," Griff said, "because I really don't think he's the type. But I'll give him a three-year contract, and maybe he'll pick up enough experience to make a good leader."

As much as I admired and liked Johnson, I also had my doubts about him as manager. It looked like the old story: you can take the boy out of the country, but you can't always take the country out of the boy. As I said before, Walter never changed; he was always the big, good-natured hick, yet with a streak of stubbornness that could hurt him when he had to direct a bunch of hard-bitten pros. I was afraid the players might take advantage of him.

That's just what happened the following season. But Walter's biggest problem was in mishandling his pitching staff, which can be disastrous because maneuvering pitchers (successfully) is about 80 per cent of a manager's job.

Walter had the notion that every pitcher should do as well as he himself had done, which was impossible to my way of thinking. If a pitcher had a bad game, Walter lost patience with him and didn't regain it for a long time. If a guy got into a jam on the mound, Johnson felt the pitcher should be able to power his way out of the trouble, à la Walter Johnson, and so he made the mistake of leaving tired pitchers in the game too long.

We wound up fifth in '29, the Philadelphia Athletics winning the pennant this time. While we were entertaining at the World Series, Altrock and I were asked to perform at a dinner honoring Charles Lindbergh, the flier. Also on the program were Will Rogers and actor Fred Stone and his family. Altrock and I did our boxing routine, with Rogers acting as referee.

That winter, I went back to my after-dinner speaking. The previous winter Engle, Altrock and I had gone out on the vaudeville circuit again. Our bookings were spotty, and we saw that vaudeville was on its last legs. One day I said to Engle, "When this vaudeville dies for good, we can always claim we killed it."

There still was no real romance in my life. And, to tell the truth, it didn't particularly bother me. I wasn't looking for romance, although I was past thirty-six. For I was by now an incurable rover.

Speaking of romance, I could see one blooming early in 1930— but it wasn't my romance. Griffith's pretty young adopted daughter, Mildred Robertson, who worked as his private secretary, had also been what I called my "social secretary." It seemed that any time there was a big social function in the town, I was being invited to help entertain. There were always men or women calling the ball club requesting I appear somewhere, and because I was around Griff's office so much Mildred took calls for me.

It was Joe Cronin who took my social secretary's mind off her work. I'd find him hanging around Griff's office more than ever, and realized that she liked him too. I did all the aiding and abetting I could—as if they needed any help.

Finally, Cupid Schacht got in a hassle with Cronin. It was shortly before Joe and Mildred were to be married, and the club was training in Biloxi, Mississippi, instead of Tampa. Cronin was manager of the club by this time. Griffith had hired a beat-up Ford for the use of the hired help around the ball club; but since I was dating a girl in Biloxi, and not having my car with me, I'd borrow the Ford every chance I got. So did Joe.

One night I took the car and went on my date, not returning until 1 A.M. When I walked into the hotel, the night clerk called me over and whispered:

"You better stay away from Cronin, he's sore as hell."

"How come?"

"He wanted to take Mildred out," the clerk said, "and when he found out you had the car and you said you'd be back by ten, he waited for you. He quit about midnight. He was steaming. . . ."

Next day, before practice, Cronin held the usual clubhouse meeting, and right away he mentioned he'd waited up for me and some of the other boys until after the twelve o'clock curfew. Then he tore into me, in front of everybody, setting me up as an example. "I'll fine anybody who comes in late from now on," he yelled, "and that goes for coaches too."

Joe and I being fast friends, and I sort of his "protector" ever since he broke in with Washington, he always used to ask me after these clubhouse pep talks how I liked them. After this meeting, I didn't give him a chance to ask, not that he was going to.

"You always ask what kind of speech you made," I snapped at him in his tiny office. "I want to tell you right quick that was the lousiest one you ever made." We stood there, glaring at each other. Then I grinned. What the hell, I knew he was a wonderful guy and was just sore about missing out on the auto ride with Mildred. "This is really love, huh?" I laughed. And a smile cracked his Irish puss and he threw a playful punch at me. And you know, he and Mildred were married right on schedule, Ford or no Ford. They have a fine family today.

my own particular screwball 193

In my years in baseball, I'd met a lot of superstitious guys, for many players are that way. They have little rituals they perform, like always touching first base when coming off the field, or wearing the same undershirt all during a winning streak; or things they won't do, like stepping on a baseline between innings, or using the same bat twice. Silly things like that.

But Alvin (General) Crowder was the most superstitious ballplayer I ever saw.

I won't go into everything he did—that might take a book in itself—but there was one incident I'll never forget. One day, he'd misplaced his glove and borrowed mine to pitch a game, and he won. He found his own glove, but the next time he was to start a game, he asked for mine again. I think he won twelve straight, using my glove. He treated it like it was his son. Then a funny thing happened. In one of those slam-bang games where both sides were using pitcher after pitcher, Crowder, down in the bullpen, was called on to relieve. He walked in, but instead of going direct to the pitcher's mound, he strode to our bench and peered around as though searching for something.

General was a quiet man normally, but when he was pitching you could never get a word out of him at all. Everybody was watching him now and finally I asked, "What're you looking for?" No answer. Johnson, the manager, repeated the question a minute or two later, but still no answer. In about five minutes, the plate umpire bustled over. "What's the delay, here?" he bellowed. Crowder ignored him like he'd never spoken; he just kept walking up and down the dugout, looking under the seat or down at the floor. Finally the ump warned, "You guys better come out of the fog or I'm gonna forfeit this game!"

Then it dawned on me what Crowder was looking for—my glove. So I darted into the clubhouse to look for it myself, because we couldn't afford to lose the game by forfeit. At first I couldn't find it, until I remembered all our trunks were packed, ready to hop that night to our next series in another city. I pulled the glove out of a trunk and rushed back to the field. Crowder was sitting stonily on the bench. He just wouldn't pitch without my glove. All the umpires were ranting and raving now, and so was the opposing manager. They were getting ready to forfeit the game to the other team when I tossed my glove to General. He smiled a little, got up and went to the mound.

He got his ears pinned back. Next inning, he went back to his own glove and never borrowed mine again.

Nineteen thirty was the year the depression was hitting the country pretty hard. My brother Lou, who had built a good ornamental iron fixtures business, was hit hard. It was the first time Lou ever asked me to lend him money. I went to Griffith and asked to borrow five thousand dollars, and he gave it to me without a murmur, telling me I could pay it back any way I felt I could. And I was just about earning five thousand a year myself as a coach.

After the 1930 Series, Earle Mack, son of the Philadelphia A's grand old manager, Connie Mack, got together a team of American League All-Stars and booked a month's barnstorming tour throughout the Midwest and Canada. I was asked to go along as a coach, clown and general joker of all trades. This was the first of many such tours by Earle Mack's AL Stars.

It was during this period that I again seriously thought about clowning as a full-time career. I didn't feel I was getting anywhere as a coach and I had no desire to be a manager. I felt the fans were taking my antics as a matter of course. And I certainly wasn't getting paid extra for it. The only times I did benefit directly from clowning was during World Series and when I went out on my own in the off-seasons. But the way the small-town fans turned out to see the AL Stars, and judging by the reception I enjoyed personally, a picture was taking shape in my mind of how a smart guy might make a hell of a business out of just clowning in minor league ball parks. As the tour progressed, I got hotter on the idea, until finally I had to argue myself out of quitting baseball right then and making a wild stab at a new career the following season.

The tour was great for the players, like a vacation almost, and we were all splitting the take. It was October-November, and the hunting season was on in most places we visited. A lot of the players would go out shooting duck or fishing in the mornings and play ball in the afternoons. One game stands out in my mind, at a town in Canada, Lethbridge, where we played in a wide, open field about a mile outside of town. Flat rocks were used for bases; there were no baselines—let's be honest, it was a big cow pasture. There also was no grandstand. The fans who came, and there were a couple of thousand, drove up in automobiles, parked them all around the field, and watched from inside the cars. This was the first drive-in baseball.

It was the only game I ever saw or participated in where you couldn't hear a sound. It was a snappy fall day, and most of the spectators kept their car windows rolled up. It was a weird feeling, like we were playing a secret game. There was only one person I could see, a youngster about ten who was standing on the bumper of a car right behind me near third base. During infield practice, I pulled my usual shenanigans, turning to the kid to say, "Buddy, this show is strictly for you. I hope you enjoy it." He only stared at me glumly. I knocked myself out to entertain that boy. "Would you care for my autograph?" I kidded finally.

He sneered, "Who are you?"

I could have slapped him right in the kisser.

Our ball club was a third-place finisher in 1931 and again in 1932, and although on paper Johnson hadn't done too badly as manager, people close to baseball felt he hadn't gotten the fullest possible mileage out of the material on hand. The one who really mattered most who was disappointed with Walter was the boss, Griff.

One morning toward the end of the 1932 season, I was in Griff's office shooting the breeze when he turned serious and said, "Al, I'm going to have to do something soon which I'd been hoping to avoid. It will break my heart. . . . I feel I must get rid of Johnson." I wasn't too surprised, so I didn't say anything.

"He was my best pitcher," Griff said, "at times my only pitcher, my bread and butter. . . . We've been together so many years. I have actually idolized the man. But I can't kid myself any longer. I don't think he's proved a good manager. . . . It's time for a change." Griff was apologizing more to himself than to me. "I've got to let go the finest man I was ever connected with in baseball. It's not an easy step to take, Al . . ."

After a few moments I said, "Have you made up your mind who'll replace him?"

"I've heard a lot about Oscar Vitt," he said. Vitt was then managing Oakland of the Pacific Coast League. "But I don't know . . ."

A little later, I left Griff there, gazing thoughtfully out the window, rolling a pencil between his fingers. I'd had a flash of a crazy idea.

That afternoon, Joe Cronin was taking a shower in the clubhouse and I joined him. Out of the blue, very offhandedly, I remarked, "Joe, have you ever thought of managing some day?"

He considered the question and replied, "Yeah, probably I'd like to, after my playing days are over. I'd like to stay in baseball. . . . Why?"

"Just asking." I felt Joe would make a good manager, aggressive, alert and a good leader.

The last couple of weeks of the season, the newspapermen had an inkling Johnson might be on his way out and were playing guessing games in their columns. I hated to have to sit on the bench next to Walter, whom I admired so, being the only one besides Griff who knew definitely the Big Train was through. I finally went to Griff and threw my Sunday punch straight from the shoulder.

"You had success once before with a playing manager, didn't you?"

"Harris?"

"Yes. I think Joe Cronin is the same type," I said.

Griff thought about it. "I'm liable to ruin a great shortstop," he said. "Managerial duties might prove too much for him."

"My eye!" I said. "When you made Harris manager, he became an even greater player. . . . Give it to Cronin, Griff." He said he'd think it over.

The 1932 Series was one I'll never forget. The big moment was when Babe Ruth apparently pointed to the bleachers at Chicago's Wrigley Field and then rode a tremendous home run right out where he'd aimed.

my own particular screwball   197

That fall, I toured with the All Stars once again. The guessing still was hot about who would replace Johnson as Washington manager, and with us on this tour was one guy whom I believe was hoping for the job, my old pal Joe Judge. Joe had been with the club for many years and had played a fine first base. I was in the press box during a game at Winnipeg, Canada, when an Associated Press dispatch came over the Western Union ticker, and I interrupted my nonsensical play-by-play announcing over the loudspeaker to report:

"Let me read an important announcement. Joe Cronin has just been appointed manager of the Washington Senators, succeeding Walter Johnson."

Joe Judge nearly fell over at first base. That dampened my enthusiasm a bit, for I liked Judge a lot. But I knew Cronin would make a swell manager. He proved it the next season by leading us to the pennant.

The spring of 1933, as just about every year since I'd been with the Washington ball club, I held out for more dough. Griff and I always were kidding each other, and we'd hassle good-naturedly and usually come to terms in the end—his terms. This year, though, considering I was getting tired of being in what I felt was a rut in baseball, and also with a green manager coming in who needed more help than ever from his coaches, I figured I really had a case. As usual, around January, Griffith sent me a contract to sign. He enclosed a letter, in which he said, ". . . Since the ball club didn't make any money last year, I'll be unable to raise your salary, as you mentioned last fall."

I was determined this season to convince Griff I was worth more and I wrote him back this way:

Dear Mr. Griffith,

I received your contract and letter, and I may say I could have told you the contents of the letter even before opening the envelope. I want to make an experiment with this contract. I plan to bury it in the rich dirt of a rubber plant we have here at home, sprinkle holy water on it, recite a Jewish prayer over it each morning, and when the blooms are raising in the spring maybe the salary figures on the contract will raise too.

This seems like the only way I'll ever get a raise from you. Seriously, this time I'm really holding out.

Sincerely yours,
Al Schacht

When I joined the club at camp the end of February, I was still a holdout. It was probably the only time in the history of baseball that a coach was a holdout. Toward the end of the training period, Griff came to me one day and said, "You know, you shouldn't have your board paid for here because you're really not a member of the club yet. You haven't signed your contract."

"Don't worry," I said, "you'll see it my way soon. Maybe your conscience will bother you some night and you'll sign me at my terms. If I wasn't here, you might forget all about me."

Opening Day, in Washington, I was on the field in pre-game practice when I was called to Griff's office. William Harridge, the president of the American League was there.

"You know, Albert," Griff began, "the rules of baseball are that no one is permitted in uniform during a championship game unless he's signed a contract. It was all right in spring training, but this is Opening Day, and you haven't signed . . ."

I said, "That's not my fault. It's yours. . . . And by the way, is it so tough to sign me up you have to bring the president of the league around?" Mr. Harridge was getting a kick out of this.

Griff placed a contract form on his desk in front of me and said, "Sign this." I looked it over. My name wasn't on it; and there were no salary figures and no date—it was a blank.

"You mean to tell me," I said, "after holding out for nearly four months I'm supposed to sign a blank contract and put myself at your mercy? Do you want me coaching at third base worrying about what salary I'm gonna get and forget all about the base runners?"

"Sign it," he said, trying to cover a smile.

So I signed it. Then he handed me another form, saying, "Sign this too."

I said, "This one is blank too."

"That's a duplicate for you," he said.

"What good is it? There's nothing on it."

"Just sign it."

Then I said, "You got anything else around here you want me to sign?" Mr. Harridge's face was red from holding back his laughter. As I turned to go, I said to him, "Mr. Harridge, you're a witness to this. If Mr. Griffith don't pay me the salary I ask for, I'm gonna blow up his stadium."

Pay day was two weeks later, and I still didn't know what salary I was to get. According to custom, the club secretary, Ed Eynon, distributed the players' checks in our shoes in the lockers while we were on the field. After I got mine and figured out my salary (you sign a baseball contract *by the year,* say five thousand dollars a year, but your "year" only lasts about six months), multiplying the amount of the check by two to get my monthly earnings and then by six to get my yearly figure. It added up to be just what I'd asked for.

Later, on my way out, I passed Griff's office and waved to him and he beckoned me in. We talked about team matters for a few minutes, then he leaned back in his chair and said, with a big smile, "Incidentally, I guess I fooled you, eh? You didn't think you'd get the money you asked for, did you?"

"You certainly did fool me," I grinned. "I thought you'd give me more than I asked for."

That season I got another thrill I'll never forget. I was delegated by the guys on our club to personally present a baseball autographed by all the players to the President; it happened to be the ball F. D. R. had thrown out on Opening Day. I took the ball to the White House and saw Marvin McIntyre, the President's press secretary. He asked me if I'd like to have lunch with the President some day.

Before I knew it almost, I was invited to meet the President of the United States at the Blue Room of the White House. Me! the grubby little Jewish kid from New York's side streets, whose parents had come over on a cattle boat from Russia, eating with probably the most important man on earth and swapping funny stories! There were two other gentlemen at the luncheon, both aides of the President. Mr. Roosevelt said he'd watched me and Altrock perform before the game Opening Day and had enjoyed the act. F. D. R. could really tell a good story himself. I think we both enjoyed ourselves. By the time I left he was calling me "Al," and he invited me to come back again.

The very next night after this luncheon, Marvin McIntyre and I made a date for dinner at the Occidental Restaurant. As we entered, Mac stopped at a table of men and said to me, "Do you know Jim Farley, the Postmaster General?" A big, husky guy with a round Irish face stood up. He seemed familiar, but I thought maybe it was from his pictures in the papers.

"You should know me," Farley smiled. "You pitched semi-pro ball for me at Haverstraw, New York, in 1910. I was manager and first baseman."

"Oh, yes, now I remember," I said. "And you paid me six dollars for the game in a barn where the team dressed."

The 1933 pennant race turned out to be a two-team fight. Sparked by Joe Cronin, who played 152 games out of 154 and batted .309, while doing a swell job of managing, we outbattled the champion Yankees and won the pennant going away, by seven games. Meanwhile, our ex-manager, Johnson, took over the Cleveland club in midseason from Roger Peckinpaugh and finished fourth.

The Giants won the National League pennant. They also had a playing manager, first baseman Bill Terry, and he too, like Cronin, was in his first full season piloting the club. It was a hard-fought Series, with the last two games going into extra innings and the Giants taking both of them. They won the Series, four games to one. It was a disappointing loss to us, especially to Griff, who'd maneuvered so hard for eight years to bring home another flag.

My old songwriting friend from the Bronx, Harry Ruby, who by then had moved to Hollywood to work in pictures, had written me that some movie people were talking about using me in a baseball picture starring Joe E. Brown, to be called *Fireman, Save My Child*. He suggested I go to the Coast and see what gives. So, following the Series I booked passage on a Grace Line ship, the Santa Paula, which would sail down through the Panama Canal and north to California. I figured that way I could go to Hollywood and get a little rest too.

My second day at sea, I got a cable from Griff, who'd learned I was heading for Hollywood in hopes of getting into pictures. He ribbed me:

IF YOU'D WAVED DAVE HARRIS HOME WE MIGHT HAVE GONE ON TO WIN SERIES AND MAYBE YOU COULD AFFORD BETTER CLASS TRIP. HAVE FUN.

I did have fun but the movie part was only a walk-on and I passed it up and came back for another year in baseball.

chapter 16

Nineteen hundred thirty-four proved to be a big year for me. I entertained at my first All Star Game . . . managed the Washington club for a month . . . and left Washington for good.

Our pennant-winning team fell to pieces, and I mean every which way. Where in '33 every break had gone with us and we couldn't do anything wrong if we tried, this season was just the opposite. Nothing went right. Bad luck stuck to us like flypaper. Worst of all, half our stars got banged up and we had to play subs most of the time. Joe Kuhel broke his leg; Fred Schulte also injured his leg; Buddy Myer got hurt; and to top it off, Cronin fractured his wrist. The team got in a rut and slumped deep into the league's second division.

I believe it was a Sunday in early September that Cronin broke his wrist in a game. The next morning, Griff called me into his office and told me I would be acting manager for the last month of the season. Cronin would not return at all, for Griff gave him the rest of the year off. So Joe and Mildred made ready to get married and go off on their honeymoon.

The first thing I had to do as manager was get Griff to bring in some replacements from the minor leagues, our club being shot full of holes, as I've said. Win or lose, I was to finish the season as manager, and I looked forward to it, thinking I'd get a kick out of it. But I also made up my mind right off that even if the club won every game with me as manager, I'd resign at the end of the season. Because I'd never had ambitions to be a big-league manager, I enjoyed clowning and had plans for myself as a clown, but I knew there was no future in managing.

The day after Griff named me manager, I had my final blowoff with Altrock. Nick and I hadn't really spoken for nearly five years, though we'd been coaches together on the Washington club and had continued to clown together. I think Altrock was not happy about me taking over as manager, even though it was only temporary. Anyway, we had a showdown in the locker room. He told me what he thought of me and I returned the compliment. Neither of us were using Sunday-school language and neither of us were whispering. It was a hell of a good row.

I should have quit managing right after our next series. We won three straight. Next stop was St. Louis, and on the train one of our pitchers, Wally Stewart, sat down next to me and said, "Al, you know in my contract it says if I win twelve games I'll get a twenty-five-hundred-dollar bonus. So, I'd like to pitch as often as possible, if it's okay with you."

"How many wins you got now?"

"Nine," he said.

"Okay, let's see," I said. "I'll start you in St. Louis, Chicago, Cleveland, Philadelphia and Boston . . ."

Stewart was a good pitcher, not too big or fast but a real cutie, something like Eddie Lopat of the Yankees now. But he was strictly a seven-inning pitcher. He'd go great for seven, then you'd have to watch him closely because he might start to fade. I started him our first game in St. Louis, and he was doing fine, leading the Browns, 2–1, after seven.

It was a blistering hot, muggy day—and it gets hot in St. Louis, especially on a ball field. As Stewart walked toward the mound to pitch the home eighth and I was headed for the dugout from my third base coaching box, I asked, "How do you feel, Wally?"

"Fine," he gasped. His eyes were just popping out of his head, that's all.

But he got by that inning somehow, giving up a base on balls and getting the side out on three long line drives to our outfielders. Knowing how much it meant to him to win, I figured maybe he'd be lucky enough to finish the ninth inning.

We didn't score any more in our last turn at bat, and it was still 2–1. As Stewart warmed up for the bottom of the ninth, I motioned to Jack Russell, our best relief pitcher, who'd practically won the pennant for us singlehanded in '33. "You go down to the bullpen and get ready," I said. "If Stewart blows and I gotta make a change this inning, it'll be you." I already had Tommy Thomas, Monty Weaver and Alvin Crowder in the bullpen. Not that I didn't trust Stewart.

Almost before Russell could pick up his glove, the first St. Louis batter, Rollie Hemsley, hit a long home run into the left field bleachers to tie the score. I knew Stewart had had it, but Russell hadn't even reached the bullpen yet; also, the next batter was Slug Burns, a left-handed hitter, and seeing as Stewart was lefty and lefties are supposed to have a tough time hitting lefties, I let Wally stay in. Burns singled hard to right on the first pitch. And Russell hadn't yet thrown a ball in the bullpen.

Then began the greatest bit of managerial maneuvering of my short career. Knowing I had to stall so Russell could get heated up, I called time and walked very slowly from the dugout toward Bill Dineen, the home plate umpire.

"Mr. Dineen," I said, "this is Al Schacht, pinch manager of the Washington club, taking the place of Joe Cronin, who, if you don't know it, had his wrist broken in Washington the other day and got married and is now on his honeymoon with Mildred Robertson Griffith.... Now I have two problems..."

Dineen cut in angrily, "Are you stalling for time? I'm not interested in your problems. Are you gonna make a pitching change?"

"Absolutely," I said, "but please don't rush me. Anyway, whatever change I make, hardly anybody will know it, because there's only about forty-five people in the grandstands."

I rambled on, and Dineen got madder, and all the while Jack

Russell was warming up in the bullpen. Then Rogers Hornsby, the Browns manager, stamped up to us and roared at Dineen, "Are you gonna let him get away with this? He's just stalling to let Russell warm up. Make him get a pitcher in here."

I said to the ump, "Hornsby's got a lot of guts coming up here and telling me what to do. Imagine him, a seventh-place manager, trying to tell a fifth-place manager how to run his ball club." Meanwhile, Russell kept warming up.

Dineen blew his top. "If you don't make your change right now," he yelled, "I'm gonna forfeit the game."

"All right, Bill," I said calmly. "But here's my first problem. They tell me you were quite a pitcher in your day, maybe you can help me. I got four pitchers in the bullpen. Which one would you suggest I bring in?"

Out came Dineen's pocket watch, and he started walking away from me around in a circle, studying the watch, and finally said, "I'll give you one minute."

"Okay, Bill, okay. But my other problem is to try to get Stewart out of the pitcher's box." Wally was the kind of stubborn pitcher who never thought he should be taken out of a game and sometimes it would seem like you had to call the cops to make him leave. And I could see this day he didn't want out.

I walked toward the mound, with Dineen following me. "Tough break," I said to Stewart. "Gimme the ball. We're gonna make a change."

Stewart protested, "I put the winning run on first. If anybody's gonna lose this game, *I'm* gonna lose it."

Turning to Dineen, I said, "See, Bill? Here's my problem. We have to get him out."

Russell's still warming up.

Stewart continued to give me an argument. Seeing Dineen about ready to forfeit the game, I snatched the ball from Stewart's hand and said, "You get out of here and go to the clubhouse. I'll see you after the game, mister."

Dineen said, "Who's your new pitcher?"

I stared at the ground and saw he happened to be standing right on the pitching rubber, so I grinned, "It looks like you're ready. You're my pitcher."

That was just about the last straw for Dineen. But before he could bite my head off I pointed toward the bullpen and said, "Eenie, meenie, miney, mo, Catch a monkey by the toe. If he hollers, let him go. Eenie, meenie, miney, mo—Russell!"

Russell got us out of the inning. What the hell, he'd had a good ten-minute warmup. The game dragged into the fifteenth inning. Then, the Browns got a runner to second with one out, and Hornsby put himself up to pinch hit. Rogers had been one of the greatest hitters in baseball history, having hit .400 or better several seasons, although he was now about through as an active player.

I called time again and walked up to home plate. "Mr. Dineen," I said, "one does not pitch to a .400 hitter in a situation like this, so I will now order my pitcher to put Hornsby on first base for free. If anybody's going to break up this ball game, it'll have to be Strange." Alan Strange, St. Louis' rookie shortstop, was batting about .230.

On the first ball pitched, Strange singled cleanly to right center field and the runner scored from second to break up the game. All my masterminding was for naught.

We won our next two games against St. Louis. Then, in the last game of the series, I had another chance to use some strategy, ordering one batter intentionally walked to get at another weaker hitter. But Hornsby crossed me up by switching to a pinch hitter who promptly delivered a hit that won the game for the Browns.

I had a lot of fun managing that month. Of course, our club wasn't going anywhere. Our injuries so crippled us I had to have a pitcher play the outfield some games, and catcher Luke Sewell also played the outfield and most of the infield positions at one time or another. We finished seventh, even behind Hornsby's Browns, whom I had razzed that time in St. Louis.

So my short managing career came to an end. I had no thoughts about pursuing it any further. There were a lot of other things I wanted to do.

I made my report to Griff just before the World Series. During our discussion, Griff said, "Can you imagine? Eddie Collins (then general manager of the Boston Red Sox) called me and asked if I'd sell them Joe Cronin!"

I thought for a moment, then said, "If you got enough money for him, it might not be a bad idea."

Knowing how close Cronin and I were, Griff was surprised. He got on his high horse and made a speech. "Why I've never sold a ballplayer to another big league club. I've traded players or sold them to the minors, but I've never sold a valuable ballplayer outright to another big league competitor. Even when the sheriff was practically camped on my doorstep years ago, and I could easily have straightened things out by selling one or two of the few stars I had, I never even considered doing it then."

"I know, Griff," I said. "But listen. The wolves are already riding Cronin in Washington after this lousy season. And what with him marrying your adopted daughter . . . If you don't sell him for big money now, there might come a time when you'll have to *release* your own son-in-law." But Griff shook his head persistently. He was determined not to sell Cronin.

For the first time, I entertained at a Series alone. It was between the National League's blazing "Gashouse Gang," the St. Louis Cardinals, and the AL's Detroit Tigers. When the Tigers owner, Frank Navin, approached us about working the Series, I told him, "Altrock and I aren't working together any more. So you can have either one of us—take your pick."

"In that case," Navin said, "do *you* want to work?"

"Sure," I said. So I began my solo career. Altrock? He stayed on as a Washington coach. In fact, now almost eighty, he's still with the ball club.

But to get back to that World Series. When Dizzy Dean was warming up before a game, I sneaked up behind him dressed in a Tiger skin and leaped on him. Not even looking around he shook me off and said, "Stop ticklin' me, Al." A little later, I was leading the band, which was behind home plate, and without my knowing it Diz stopped warming up and got in with the band. I didn't notice him until the sourest tuba I ever heard started blasting my ears. Diz was quite a character. And quite a pitcher. He and his brother each won two games that Series to give the Cards the championship. If Diz hadn't been injured at the height of his career not long after this, he might have gone down as the greatest pitcher of all time.

Right after the Series, a fellow named Dave Itzel signed me for a week's vaudeville date at his Fox Theatre in Detroit, a movie house, starting November 20, as I recall. This gave me plenty of time, about six weeks, to tour again with Earle Mack's AL All-Stars. They were already on the road, and I was to meet them at Nuevo Laredo, Mexico, a town right across the Rio Grande from Laredo, Texas. At Laredo, I picked up a temporary passport; the customs officials emphasized I must get it renewed at Mexico City when we passed through there, or else I couldn't get back into the United States.

Earle Mack met me at the railroad station at Nuevo Laredo, and the first thing he talked about was a player on the Nuevo Laredo team, which the Stars had played the day before and lost. "He's the greatest hitter I ever saw," Earle said. "A big colored Cuban, and he hit .750 during his season here—a hundred and eight games no less. Yesterday, he got five for five off Jack Knott (a St. Louis Browns pitcher)."

That day I watched this big fellow in batting practice slamming line drives all over the field. He got four more hits in four at-bats that game. We left Nuevo Laredo then to tour Mexico, but on our way back we played the same team three more games. The Cuban only made out once in fifteen times up. Some of our guys asked him why he didn't leave Nuevo Laredo and come to the States. He said he had a good job at a gas station, and since colored players didn't get much of a break in the U.S. then, he figured he was better off where he was. It's a shame, because he looked like he might have been a tremendous ballplayer here.

At Mexico City, I went to a night club one evening, and met a great toreador—I can't remember his name, and I'm sure I couldn't pronounce it anyway. Right away I got the idea to stage my own version of a bullfight before our game a few days later. I asked the manager of the arena where the bullfights were held if he could get me a tired cow, as I didn't want to fool around with any real bull. He said he'd bring me a white cow, and I said to make sure he got the beast to the ball park well before game time, which was 3 P.M.

One thing I noticed in Mexico, time doesn't mean a damn to most Mexicans. If you make an appointment, say at seven, and the party doesn't show up until ten, nobody thinks anything about it. That's just the way they seem to be, real easy-going. Well, the local ball club advertised that Al Schacht would put on his own bullfight before the game. I borrowed a toreador's outfit, not forgetting my bottle of ketchup, like I'd used the first time I'd done a takeoff on a bullfight from *Blood and Sand* years before.

At two-thirty I expected my bull, the white cow, to be delivered. Nothing. By three the big crowd was chanting, "Al Schacht . . . bullfight, bullfight!" Still no cow. So I decided to chuck it and go ahead with my regular routines. I was pretty sore.

That evening about seven, having dinner at the fashionable St. Regis Hotel, a bell captain paged me. "Señor, you have the telephone message from the baseball stadium," he said. "There is man with a cow . . ."

It was about this time that I heard Clark Griffith had sold Joe Cronin to the Boston Red Sox for $150,000, plus Lyn Lary, a pretty good shortstop who'd played a number of years with the Yankees and one season with the Sox. When I first heard this, I couldn't believe it—first of all because Griff had seemed so determined *not* to sell Cronin the last time we'd been together; and because, while I considered Joe a great player, I felt $150,000 was some bundle of cash to pay for anybody. Then I read about it in an American newspaper. I made up my mind to see Griff as soon as I got back to Washington.

The last few days of the tour, most of us bought souvenirs to bring home to our families and friends. I myself went overboard for about four hundred dollars' worth of stuff. It wasn't until we were back on the train that I found out you're allowed to take only a hundred dollars' worth of Mexican merchandise out of the country. At the same time, I realized with a jolt that I'd forgotten to renew my passport in Mexico City.

When we reached the border, the train stopped, and a Mexican customs man came through the cards to pick up all temporary passports. By now I really had the jitters. We were sitting in the dining car, but I couldn't eat. When the Mexican official came near my table, I tried to make believe I didn't see him. But he stared at me, finally saying, "I see you in Monterrey. You make fun for me."

I decided to bluff it out. "You come with me for a minute," I said confidentially, "and I'll give you some more laughs." We stepped out into the corridor, and I said, "I got no passport. Not only that, I got about three hundred dollars more merchandise than I'm allowed. . . . Now, does that make you laugh?"

He looked at me for a moment, then broke into a wide smile. "I know you no come to Mexico for monkey business," he said, "so I let you go through, don' worry." And he did. When we reached Laredo, Texas, I got off the train and knelt down and kissed the ground.

At that I just about made Detroit in time for my first show. Dave Itzel said, "I've had you advertised for two weeks, and I've been thinking you weren't going to show up. What kind of act you gonna do?"

I'd had no rehearsals or anything, so I said, "I'll build it as I go along."

"Well, do me a favor," he said. "There's an act called Lottie Mayer's Diving Beauties following you on the bill. I want you to take a dive off their high board at the finish of their act, wearing your top hat and tux over bathing trunks."

"I never dove into water in my life," I protested, "and I can't even swim. I'll be damned if I'm gonna learn now. Why, if this nose of mine got full of water, I might never come up. . . . Do I *have* to do it?"

"I'm paying you nine hundred and fifty clams a week. If your act is lousy, yes, you'll have to do it."

I did my first show, consisting of a monologue, some pantomime baseball and my piano recital, and then sought out Itzel to see if I had to go through with the diving bit.

"No, I guess not," he said. "But cut down your act. We only wanted twelve minutes, and you ran twenty-five. We have to pay extra time for the movie projectionists when that happens. . . . But I do wish you'd take that dive in your last show. I'd like to advertise it."

I said, "You can bet I'll be drunk when I do it. If I gotta dive in that water, I don't want to know a thing about it."

Lottie Mayer's girls did their act in a big tank, making a spectacular "entrance" from under the water; at the end, each would high dive into the tank and disappear. I always wondered where they went after diving and how they got out of the tank. Anyhow, the last show of the week, after my act I gulped down half a pint of whiskey, and waited for the finish of the girls' routine. When there was only one more girl left, I strolled out and climbed the ladder, stewed to the ears.

I had on swim tights, big rubber boots, my tuxedo coat with tails, my battered old high hat, and carried an umbrella and I had a cigar in my mouth. I staggered out on the high board to the rhythm of light music. Then the drums began to roll. I opened my umbrella, moved toward the end of the springboard, and dropped into space. . . .

When I hit the water, the back row of the audience must have got splashed. They told me later I bobbed to the surface still with the umbrella in my hand and the cigar stuck in my mush, and I was white as a ghost. Next thing I knew, I was being pulled down by the feet. Then I heard a crash—it must have been the last girl making her dive. I heard the music and applause, and instinctively I went to take a bow—but all of a sudden I wasn't in the water any more. I was backstage, staring at a brick wall and ropes and props. And I still don't know for sure what in hell happened.

Within a couple of weeks, I had myself booked into the Capitol Theatre in Washington. The first thing I did when I hit town was look up Griffith. Finding him at his office, I barged in with a big smile and glad hand, saying, "Let me shake the hand of a rich man."

"What do you mean?"

"Why, you sold Cronin for a hundred and fifty G's, didn't you?" I said.

They sometimes call Griff "The Old Fox," and he sort of smiled like one right then. "I'll let you in on a secret," he said, lowering his voice. "It was more than a hundred and fifty thousand. . . . It was *two* hundred and fifty thousand."

"A quarter of a million!" I whistled. "And you didn't want to sell him!"

"I couldn't help myself," Griff said. "I met the Boston people at the Series, and they kept after me, raising the price every day. It would have been ridiculous to hold back any longer." (And to show you what kind of man Griff is, before he'd close the deal he got a guarantee that Cronin would get a five-year contract at thirty thousand dollars a year.)

Then he said to me: "You're in the deal too, Al."

"Me?"

"You're going to Boston with Cronin."

I was stunned. I hadn't heard about this before. I'd been with Washington and Griff for more than thirteen seasons all told . . . and now suddenly I'm out. It hits you. Finally I cracked, "What did they do, throw in a bag of peanuts to get me?"

"Joe wants you with him," Griff said. "Besides, they can pay you more in Boston than I can. But, Al, if you don't like it up there, you can always come back to this ball club. Remember that."

Everything seemed strange when I joined the Red Sox at Sarasota, Florida, the following spring. New training base, new teammates . . . The Sox were mostly a team of former big stars on their last legs, for whom owner Tom Yawkey had paid plenty of loot. No one knew if they could all pull together to bring a pennant to Boston. As for the club officials, they were swell people. But I felt ill at ease.

That season, the club hovered between fourth and fifth place, and my mind began to stray more and more toward giving up coaching to make straight clowning my full-time business. On off-days that year, I got bookings in minor league parks, where I entertained before the games for fees. My trial run seemed a whopping success, for I found I averaged around three hundred dollars an appearance. I started calculating how much I could make in a whole season of touring minor league towns, and decided that I'd make more money than I did as a coach.

So now I was on the edge, ready to make the leap. All I needed was some legitimate excuse to quit baseball, for I just couldn't up and walk out on so many people who'd been good to me.

Whenever I recall my time with the Red Sox, I can't help thinking of one of the odd characters of baseball, a catcher named Moe Berg. He is a graduate of Princeton, Columbia and the Sorbonne in Paris, France, and speaks about eight different languages. Moe, who was born in New York, broke into the majors around 1923 with Brooklyn, and joined Washington in 1932. In '34, he was sent to Cleveland, and now, in '35, he and I were teammates again at Boston.

I think I was first drawn to Moe one time when he was catching a game and the Washington pitcher and the opposing batter began to conduct a war of nerves, alternately stepping out of the pitcher's and batter's box. It was a hot, muggy day—Moe got disgusted waiting and said to the umpire, "When these two mental cases get ready to play ball, call me, I'm gonna take a bath," and went to the dugout and dumped a whole pail of water over his head.

In '35, Rick Ferrell was the Red Sox regular catcher, so Moe spent most of his time in the bullpen warming up pitchers. He'd made a trip around the world, and down in the bullpen he'd tell the boys about the different countries he'd been in. His favorite listener was Jack Wilson, one of our relief pitchers. Jack would say to me after a game, "You should have been down in the bullpen. Berg had us in China today." One day, our starting pitcher, Rube Walberg, was getting hit freely, and Cronin instructed me to bring in Wilson. I said to Joe, "I can't get him." Cronin snapped, "Why not? What's the gag?" I said, "You'll have to get Wilson a passport. Berg's probably got him in Russia by now."

Believe me, it's no fun being with a losing ball club. That's what the Sox were in 1935 and 1936. Yawkey had spent millions on his club, and it was going exactly nowhere. Still, the Boston fans stuck with us, even though disappointed that all the big names on the club were not delivering as expected. The trouble was, while most of our guys used to be great players, they all seemed to have slipped badly at the same time.

The climax for me came at Yankee Stadium, Labor Day, 1936. Between games of a doubleheader, I put on my burlesque prize fight, with Jack Dempsey acting as referee. During the act, I pulled a sudden switch and made a pass at the ref. Jack was surprised, and I guess instinctively threw out his straight left jab. It caught me solidly on the chin as I walked into it, and, off balance, I toppled to the ground. But instead of a relaxed fall, I landed hard on my left shoulder, and it hurt.

When the game began, I went to my third base coaching position. But I was getting shooting pains in my shoulder, until finally I called time and told Cronin I was going into the clubhouse and somebody should take my place. The club trainer looked me over and suggested I go to a hospital for X rays. The doctors examined the shoulder, X-rayed it and put my arm in a sling. The next day they reported the shoulder was dislocated. This is it, I said to myself. I immediately got in touch with Eddie Collins and asked if I could resign. He understood.

Out of baseball, after twenty-six years, I spent that winter planning for the next summer. I felt like I had a new lease on life.

chapter 17

The next five years were crammed with excitement, laughter, satisfaction and few—thank the Lord—disappointments. I don't think I'd been so happy since I was a kid playing ball in the sandlots. I was doing what I enjoyed most, entertaining people, trying to make them laugh, and able to do it through my first love, baseball. And getting paid well for it. They say too many people in this world are unhappy because they're laboring at jobs they don't really like. I guess I'm one of the lucky exceptions.

Of course, in my enthusiasm, I'd underestimated what a complicated and sometimes irritating operation I'd have to undertake in lining up dates for my clowning appearances. For example, I'd contact a minor league club through its business manager; say it was a class D club, which is as low as organized ball goes. Maybe that club would take in an average of about three hundred dollars per game during its season. I had to try to convince the business manager that I should get a hundred of it. Naturally, he'd never handled any proposition like mine before; he would doubt whether they could even afford my hundred-dollar guarantee. I had to convince him that I was an extra attraction who would draw extra fans to a ball game. Therefore my hundred dollars would not be a slice of the club's meager three hundred but a cut of the extra gravy my appearance would bring in.

I wore some of them down gradually, and a few bookings trickled in during the spring of '37. But the constant haggling wore me down too, and I got myself a professional booking agent, Christy Walsh, who'd had much success handling the affairs of such stars as Babe Ruth and Lou Gehrig.

That first season, I worked from May through Labor Day, though not steadily. There were many days, and sometimes weeks, when we hadn't been able to secure any dates.

The next summer it was different. I totaled 121 cities in 125 days, coast to coast. During one stretch, I worked in ball parks in eighty-nine different towns in eighty-nine days without a single layoff, and was never even rained out once. In fact, in all the years since, I've had the fantastic luck of rarely having an engagement postponed by the weather.

I drove wherever I went. Mileage never phased me. I'd average close to four hundred miles a day in my convertible. I might be in Jackson, Mississippi, one day and Charlotte, North Carolina, the next. Without exaggeration, I never saw a single ball game—my show always being before a game, as soon as I was through I'd dress, pick up my money at the box office and beat it.

Minor league games are usually at night, so I'd drive until midnight or 1 A.M., stop at a hotel, then start out again by 7 A.M. and drive all day, arriving at my next stopoff about 5 P.M. I'd nap for an hour, go to the ball park and do my stuff and scram. Starting in '38, I spent more time in my car than in my bed.

I wish I could remember every exciting or amusing thing that happened to me those first few wonderful years on the road. The going, going, going; and the new places and old, and strange situations and different people . . . and *strange* people. Like the two gentlemanly highwaymen I encountered in Oklahoma early one morning.

It was about 6 A.M., and I'd been driving for a couple of hours on my way from Tulsa, Oklahoma, to Lake Charles, Louisiana, when I pulled into a lonely filling station. It looked deserted at first—then, in the gray shadows of the dawn, I spied a pair of roughly-dressed guys loitering at the side of the building. A sleepy attendant shuffled out from inside the gas station, and I said, "Fill 'er up." The two characters kept eying me. I paid for the gas and was rolling slowly toward the road again when suddenly they jumped onto my running boards, and one growled, "Keep going, Mac!"

I kept going. The two young fellows, unshaven and ragged, climbed into my convertible from either side without a word. After about two miles, the leader ordered me to "Turn off up here." It was a dirt side road which disappeared into woods. A beautiful spot for a picnic—or a murder.

Deep in the woods, the talkative one added, "Stop . . . Git out. This is a holdup!"

My tongue was tied in knots. Finally, I stammered, "Look, fellas, you're making a big mistake (sounds like something out of a "Z" movie) . . ."

"Listen," the silent one spoke up, "we ain't et in two days. You look like you know where to get more cash in a hurry—we don't. Let's have your money."

I emptied my pockets of the eighty dollars I had with me, then asked, "Can you leave me something for gas? I still got a long way to drive."

"You just filled up, didn't you?" the first one demanded.

"Yeah, but I'm not sure I'll be able to make it all the way without stopping again."

"Well, how much do you want?"

I studied their haggard, grim faces and thought better of cracking wise at that point. "Oh, I guess a fin," I said meekly. And he handed me back a five-dollar bill.

"Okay, back in the car," the talker said. "Turn around and drive back to the main road." The two of them squeezed in the front seat with me. We might have been three chums going fishing early in the morning.

As it was, I was grateful they seemed to be letting me keep my car. And they didn't really seem such a bad sort. Relaxing, I kidded, "How's business?"

"This is our first job," the quiet boy said softly.

"Shuddup!" the other snapped.

They directed me back toward the filling station and told me to stop off the road alongside a battered Ford coupé, parked just beyond the station. They got out of my car, and the quiet one slid behind the wheel of the Ford.

"Okay, now get going," the spokesman said evenly, "and please keep your mouth shut." *Please?*

I've often hoped that those two scared young fellows made out all right—not as bandits, of course, but that they straightened out before they got in too deep. The rest of the way to Lake Charles, I didn't feel too bad at all about being robbed.

I had another experience with a sort of con man in Georgia—it could be called the Case of the Screwloose Promoter.

I was in Atlanta for an engagement, and was sitting reading a newspaper in the hotel lobby when along came this little fellow with the big grin and introduced himself to me. He was a hayseed from away back; the way he walked and talked and dressed, you could tell. Especially the grin. It was the kind of coy grin that seemed to say, I know babies don't grow on gooseberry bushes, but I ain't telling where they do come from, Yuk, Yuk.

He climbs all over me conversationally, and it comes out he wants me to perform at his home town, some place in Georgia named Tipton or Tippin or Griffin, or something like that. "Mistuh Schacht, that there town is jes' the greatest baseball town in the kentry, that's all. Why even sandlot games draws capacity crowds," he gushed.

"You got a team in some league?" I asked.

"Wal, no, but . . ."

"Then where will I put on my act? There's gotta be a game. You got a ball park?"

"Why sure," he said. "We got a nice ball park. Ah aim to git a shop to play . . . you know, a mill shop. There's lotsa mills around theah. Mistuh Schacht, ah don' wanna make no profit on this. Ah jes' knows ouah town folks would sure admiah watchin' you perfohm. Tell you what ah'll do. Ah'll give you 80 puh cent if you jes' say you'll come an' do your show fer us."

Eighty per cent of the take was too much to turn down even in No Name, Nevada. I told him my next available date was a Saturday afternoon about two weeks later, and that I'd have my New York office get in touch with him and send him plenty of publicity material, posters, feature stories for the newspapers, mats, etc.

"One thing is very important," I added. "You've got to advertise my appearance. We won't draw a crowd worth a damn unless you take pains to spread those posters around town and get the local newspaper to print stories about me. Lots of Ballyhoo."

"Don't you worry none," he grinned, "ah'll puhsonally put up them posters twenny miles outside o' town."

So, two weeks later, I drove into this town about Saturday noon, and on the way in I looked for the posters. There wasn't one to be seen. It was a sleepy little village and not even many people on the streets. I sent my man—I had a chauffeur at this particular stage—to have the car serviced at a filling station, telling him to find out where the local ball park was and to meet me at a lunchroom near the station. I was the only customer at the lunch counter. A young fellow ran it.

"You a baseball fan?" I asked him genially.

"I used to be a Brooklyn Dodger fan," he said, "but since I been down here I ain't seen any ball games. I come from Brooklyn."

"How long you been in Georgia?"

"About two years."

"Do you know of a game around here today?" I said.

He looked puzzled. "Gee, no, I don't know of any."

"Hmmm . . . Got a copy of the local newspaper?"

"Here's yesterday's," he said, handing me a folded paper from behind the counter. There was nothing in the paper about a ball game and especially nothing about me. I began to wonder if maybe I was in the wrong town. Then my chauffeur entered and said in my ear, "There's no ball park here."

"That's crazy," I said. "Let's call up the chamber of commerce." The counterman directed us to somebody in the town merchants' association who could give us information, and we called him up. This fellow said there used to be a ball park four or five miles outside of town but that it hadn't been used much in years. He didn't know of a game today, either.

We went looking. Driving about five miles, we still saw no ball park, so we stopped at a gas station to ask. This looked like Tobacco Road country.

"Yessuh, they's a old ball pahk aroun' heah . . . at least, they used to be. Ain't been no games theah fer some time. It's jes' ovuh thet bridge up ahead," he said, pointing half a mile up the road. "Somethin' goin' on today, stranger?"

"I'm wondering that myself," I said, getting back into the car.

Over the bridge, the road curved right, and there, down a dirt embankment, was our "ball park." It had no roof and only a few rotted boards were left of the fences. What looked like white bed sheets were strung up around the field so nobody could see the field itself from the road. There was no side road leading down to the park, so we pulled off the main road and drove the car right down the slope.

There was no one in sight outside the park. I stepped gingerly inside through the broken fence. An old man in an older tin lizzie was driving around what passed for an infield, dragging a battered doormat behind, obviously in an attempt to smooth out the infield. But there was no smoothing those rocks and boulders, boy, except with dynamite. In the outfield, the grass was two feet high if it was an inch.

Now this was getting funny. I walked out to the man in the jalopy. He was a grizzled old farmer, wearing overalls and a baseball cap.

"Who's playing today?" I asked.

"I dunno."

"Well, who's paying you to manicure the infield?"
"The comedian."
"What comedian?"
"I dunno," he said, clattering off in the jalopy. Now it wasn't so funny.

A few minutes later, an old sedan pulled up outside and eight young men piled out, all carrying bundles under their arms. They said they were a ball club. "How come there's only eight?" I asked.

"T'other fella don't get off 'til three-thirty," one drawled. "He's the pitchuh." They went off to get dressed—under a railroad trestle nearby—and came back on the field to begin practice. They were the raggedest crew I ever saw on a ball field; no two wore the same uniform. One had "Coca Cola" on his shirt front, another had "Kralnick's Bakery" or something. And they had only one beat-up baseball among them.

I was watching this, thinking many dark thoughts, when here came my promoter. He bounced up to me, still grinning, and he had a thick roll of tickets in his mitt. "How we doin', Mistuh Schacht," he cried cheerily.

"Are you okay in the head?" I growled. "Who the hell is gonna come see a ball game here?"

"Oh, you'd be suhprised," he grinned.

"You didn't advertise like I told you."

"Ah couldn't," he said. "Evuhbody would of wanted free passes."

"Cripes, you're cuckoo," I moaned, walking away in despair. But I was going to stick it out and see what happened. My chauffeur and I sat on the running board of the car. The Smiling Georgian went to an opening in the fence and stuck his roll of tickets on a nail, ready for business.

It was now near two-thirty, and the game was to start at three, but there was nobody to see it. Then a man and woman walked up, the gas station man I'd asked directions from and his wife, and they wanted to buy two tickets. He took out a five-dollar bill, and the promoter turned to me and said, "Mistuh Schacht, yo'all got change of a fahve?"

That was the last straw. Going to the couple, I said, "Don't buy any tickets, there's not gonna be any game here today. This guy is nuts. He's kidding all of us." They looked at each other, then at me and the promoter and back at each other, and turned around and silently walked away.

"You shouldna done thet, Mistuh Schacht," the character said, hurt. "How d'you expect to git a crowd iffen you tell folks to go away?"

"How the hell did *you* expect to draw a crowd when you didn't advertise?" I barked.

"Ah advuhtahsed," he muttered. "Ah made a speech in the mill shop."

"Great. How many people heard your speech?"

"'Bout three hunerd."

"Look, you nut, if you had a million people here today, what good would it do you?" I said. "You only got one team, and they only got eight men."

His eyes widened and he gaped at me for a second. "Don't you carry your own team with you, Mistuh Schacht?"

That's all. I hopped in my car and left before I went loony myself. At the top of the embankment, I stopped and looked back on that fantastic scene. He was still by the opening in the fence, chaperoning his roll of tickets, and as far as I could make out, he was still grinning.

Oh, I ran into some odd characters, all right. Odd animals, too. There was a dog in Jackson, Mississippi . . .

I was starting my feature stunt one day—my impersonation of a swell-headed pitcher who's getting his brains knocked out and refuses to believe it—when out onto the field wandered this mutt. On the mound, ready to go into my windup to pitch to the imaginary batter, I had to stop because the hound sat himself down between me and home plate. The crowd, thinking the dog was part of the act, got a great kick out of it.

Going along with the gag, I called to him, and to my surprise he got up and sat down alongside me in the pitcher's box. I went into the routine, and the dog watched me with big sad eyes and an expression that seemed to say, "So make me laugh."

When I stormed toward home plate to argue with the umpire who wasn't there, the mutt followed me. I ranted and raved, then turned to the dog to explain, with gestures, what a crumb the umpire was. I'll be damned if that dog didn't start yelping like his tail was caught in a screen door. The spectators ate it up.

I returned to the mound, the dog at my heels, and he mimicked every move I made. So help me. At the finish, when I slowly turned to watch an imaginary home run sail over the fence, the dog did likewise. Taking my bows, I headed for the clubhouse, Fido right behind me. The wheels were turning in my noodle. This dog could be a hell of an addition to my act. But when I turned around, he was gone. I raced about, trying to find him, but, strangely, no one had seen where he went. I even announced over the loudspeaker that I wanted to buy the dog and would the owner meet me to talk over a deal. But nobody stepped forward. I never saw that marvelous dog again. I believe to this day baseball fans in Jackson, Mississippi, still think that mutt was part of my act.

I had another strange experience with a dog some time later. Scheduled to perform at Lockport, New York, one night, when I arrived at the ball park the gateman said, "Al, you wanna see a great sight?"

"What's that?"

"You stand here a few minutes. Every night, about seven o'clock, there's a Dalmatian dog comes to the game all by herself . . . and she'll go under the turnstile and sit on the right field foul line and watch the game."

"I hope you're not kidding me," I said. "This I gotta see."

Sure enough, as the fans started arriving, here came this dog, promptly at seven. Minding its own business and paying no attention to any of the people, just as the gatekeeper had said, she strolled under the turnstile and trotted off along the right field foul line. I watched her sprawl comfortably near a small shed behind right field.

You know how sometimes you get fascinated by little, unimportant things? That's how it was with me and that Dalmatian. When I went out to do my act, I couldn't keep my eyes from straying to right field. She just lay there, watching everything that was going on. When I got through, I dressed hurriedly and returned to the field to see what the dog would do next. After the seventh inning, the dog got to her feet and nonchalantly trotted out the gate and was gone. It was the damnedest thing.

Later, I questioned the gateman about it. He said the dog used to belong to the park's groundskeeper. He'd take the dog with him to the game every night, and while he was busy in his tool shed down in right field, the dog would sit outside and watch the goings-on. Then the groundskeeper passed away—but his faithful companion kept coming out to the games alone. And she always left after the seventh inning.

"How does she know when it's the seventh inning?" I asked.

"Because the groundskeeper used to finish his work about the seventh and let his assistant take over . . . and then him and the dog would leave."

"Well," I said, "how does she know when there's a game?"

He explained, "This is a quiet part of town. That dog only lives down the road a ways. Soon as she sees the cars parking in front of the ball park, she knows . . ."

I went away marveling at what I'd seen—and wondering if that dog had liked my show.

Since I'm always mentioning "my show," I guess I should try to describe for those who've never seen me work what kind of shenanigans I go through. Generally, after being introduced I say a few words to the crowd, then vault into the grandstand and race around causing all kinds of havoc. I'll snatch girls and old ladies away from their escorts and show them to their seats personally . . . exchange different men's hats, finally getting them all mixed up . . . sneak up behind ladies and kiss them (on the foreheads—I haven't been slapped yet) . . . give away all a vendor's peanuts (which I pay for later) . . . bring a little boy and girl out on the field and "marry" them at home plate. In other words, all sorts of silly, crazy things, anything that comes into my head.

During the home team's infield practice, I'll "shadow" the third baseman, mimicking every move he makes. Then I relieve him at third and clown, letting ground balls knock me down or go through my legs, throwing two balls to the first baseman, catching the ball while lying on top of third base. Of course, you always add little gimmicks. Once, in Houston, Texas, I strained my side somehow clowning at third during infield practice and, finding I couldn't throw without some pain, I lit a cigar, grabbed a newspaper from someone in a box seat and sat down on the base, completely ignoring the baseballs that whizzed by me. Finally I reached out and snagged one ball, then called the batboy and had him run it over to the first baseman, who signed a receipt for it before relaying it back to home plate.

I wind up my show with a feature stunt, which may be my solo impersonations of the Swell-headed Pitcher, or the Nearsighted Pitcher, or, at other times, burlesque tennis or boxing. Lastly, I usually give my impressions of various famous hitters' styles, finishing with Babe Ruth's historic "called home run."

The big thing I learned about my trade was to keep things moving. If you let up for just a moment, you feel you're losing the audience. And if you don't get any laughs for a minute, it seems like an hour, all alone out on that wide field. In the beginning, I worried that maybe the fans wouldn't get my pantomime, which is most of the act. But I found it remarkable how well crowds everywhere did understand what I was doing. I think I enjoy working in small ball parks best, because it's easier to get around the stands for one thing, and the people feel closer to you and vice versa. But minor league or majors, people are all the same.

I have always done my utmost to keep my act perfectly clean. I've never thought much of any entertainer who has to resort to smut to get laughs. The way I feel, in baseball crowds you always have a lot of kids, and I'm proud to say I've never made one dirty gesture or remark in all my years clowning.

But the most important thing is, I have never walked onto a ball field and done my stuff without having more fun than anybody.

Which reminds me of the effect of my new profession on my mother. The family had never seen me perform, so Mom didn't really know what my work was all about, although she did know it had something to do with baseball. A rabbi used to visit the house now and then and sit and talk with my mother over tea. One day he inquired about me, and according to Esther, this is how she explained what I was doing:

"My son, he throws the ball and a fellow with a stick hits the ball and he runs . . . and somebody far out in the meadows chases this ball. . . . Then my son will throw the ball until nobody can hit it anymore. And it takes him three hours to stop the other fellows from hitting the ball. . . ."

The rabbi listened patiently, with a frown spreading on his face. When Mom finished, he sighed and said, "From that he makes a living?"

It was in Minneapolis that year, 1939, that I became one of the first non-medical men to find out what was wrong with Lou Gehrig.

I'd been in Florida that spring, and had worked out with the Yankees at St. Petersburg. One day, sitting on the bench watching batting practice, manager Joe McCarthy said to me, "Watch Gehrig. He hits the ball with everything he has and can hardly push it over the infield. He can't seem to get moving around first base either. Can it be he's slowed up that much since the end of last season?"

It was true, Lou looked terrible. He seemed logy and weak. Gehrig, the powerfully-built old "Iron Horse," one of the main cogs of the Yanks "Murderers Row"; who'd set an all-time major-league record by playing in 2,130 consecutive games—at thirty-six he seemed suddenly washed up.

As the season wore on, Lou got worse. He played in only about eight games, then McCarthy had to bench him. Nobody knew what was wrong with him, including Lou. Then, when I was in Minneapolis in midsummer, I read where Gehrig had decided to visit the world-famous Mayo Clinic at nearby Rochester, Minnesota, for a physical checkup. It so happened, a doctor from the Mayo Clinic asked me about that same time to give a talk at a doctors' luncheon in Rochester.

Sitting on the dais, I turned to a doctor next to me and said, "If it isn't too secret, do you know if they found anything wrong with Lou Gehrig, the ballplayer, who's here for a checkup?"

"Strange you should ask me," he replied. "I am one of those who examined Gehrig."

"Oh?"

"Unfortunately," he said grimly, "Lou has contracted a disease which gradually will paralyze him. . . ."

"Is—is it fatal?"

"I'm afraid so," he said.

A month or so later, I appeared at Yankee Stadium, and there was Lou, still in uniform—but at the sight of him my eyes filled. The big, strong hulk of a man I used to know, with his mighty shoulders and arms of a blacksmith, toddled about like an old man. He wasn't playing anymore, but he refused to give up that Yankee uniform, still in hopes of recovering from the strange weakness that shackled him. His spirit was great. I sat with him in the clubhouse and kidded him and clowned for him, and he still cracked that wide, heavy-dimpled grin of his.

Next time I saw Gehrig was at the World Series that fall, as the Yankees plastered the Cincinnati Reds. I'll never be able to forget the scene right after the last game of the Series in Cincinnati. The crowd was pouring down on the field and the Yankees were hurrying from their dugout to the clubhouse. Gehrig tried to run through the mob milling about, and the people, knowing he was so sick, separated and made a path for him, like a guard of honor, as he stumbled along.

That was Lou's last season—1939—and he only played in those eight games. He never came back again. But he never stopped thinking he'd get well. They had a "Day" for him before a huge crowd at Yankee Stadium, presenting him with many gifts. When Lou stepped to the microphone at home plate, he sobbed, "I'm the luckiest guy in the world!" He died in 1941 at the age of thirty-eight.

Shortly after Gehrig's death, I visited the greatest Yankee slugger of them all, Babe Ruth, at a hospital in New York, where he was recuperating from a busted knee. Although the story was that Gehrig and Ruth never had too much love between them, the Babe seemed broken up about Lou's passing. When Joe Williams, the sports columinist, and I found Ruth on the sun terrace outside his room, he had half a dozen bottles of beer lined up along the arms of his easy chair. He kept slugging away the beer as we talked, and finally I had to crack, "What are you here for, to fix your knee or drink beer?"

"This?" he said. "This ain't much beer. . . . Take a look in the bathtub."

I went inside and looked. The tub was piled high with bottles of beer and chunks of ice. "Don't you know there's a war on, and a labor shortage?" I said. "Why don't you move your hospital room to the brewery instead of bringing the whole brewery to the hospital?"

The Babe didn't laugh too much that visit. He said quietly that in the two weeks he'd been in that hospital, only three people had come to see him. This was the great national idol of only a few years before, the most famous man in the world. For a long time after, I couldn't wipe out the picture in my mind of the disappointment in his eyes. I kept thinking about him, and about Gehrig. And I wondered where the hell we're all going.

I was out touring in the summer of 1941 when I got a wire from my agent, who was now Murray Goodman, telling of an offer to appear at a "Little World Series" in Honolulu in October for fifteen hundred dollars plus expenses. It sounded great, especially as I'd often dreamed of going to Hawaii. I wired Goodman back my acceptance and told him not to book me for the World Series.

I finished my tour in Sacramento around the middle of September. But I hadn't heard any more about the trip to Hawaii. According to the plan I was to board a boat at Los Angeles on October 2, but I had no tickets, no idea where I should go in Honolulu, or even how many games they wanted me to work. For some reason, I hadn't received any mail from Murray Goodman in some time. Then I got a call from an official of the Matson Steamship Line which had traced my whereabouts through the newspapers. I told the man to forward the ticket to the Knickerbocker Hotel in Hollywood, where I planned to go next.

When I picked up the ticket there were two, and the envelope read, "Mr. & Mrs. Al Schacht." The next night, while I was out with Harry Ruby, Cary Grant, and several other people, I asked Cary how much it would cost to rent Hollywood Bowl.

"Hollywood Bowl!" he said, surprised. "Why?"

"I got these tickets on a ship to Hawaii, and they're supposed to be for me and my wife. But I'm not married . . . so I need a girl to go with me. If I put an ad in the paper, 'Girl wanted to accompany handsome fellow to Hawaii, All-Expense Cruise,' I'd need the Bowl to handle all the applicants."

"I'd love to go with you myself," Cary laughed.

"Why don't you?"

"No, it's a great idea . . . but I've made plans to go to Mexico in a few days." (And if my memory serves me right, Cary went to Mexico to meet Babs Hutton, whom he later married.)

When I finally boarded the boat, I was ushered into a big, beautiful stateroom—actually a suite. There was a gorgeous piano in the living room, and near it a horseshoe of flowers. On the mantelpiece were six bottles of wine. Turning to the steward, I said, "This is the wrong stateroom, isn't it?"

"No, Mr. Schacht, this is yours, all right," he said.

With that, the head purser entered and introduced himself. "Mr. Schacht," he said politely but firmly, "I have strict orders . . . you are not to put your hand in your pocket at any time on this voyage. If you pay for a single thing I'm liable to lose my job." Pointing to a button on the living room wall, he said, "If you need or desire anything, simply push this."

I was gulping for air by this time, my breath having been snatched away. I strolled around the room, noticing a tag on the horseshoe of flowers—it read, "Pleasant Trip, (signed) the Baldwins."

"Who are the Baldwins?" I asked.

"They are the people who are bringing you to the Islands," the purser said. "They're quite rich."

What next? I thought. "Are those bottles of champagne on the mantle?" I said.

"That is correct, sir."

"Then what are we waiting for?" I chortled, removing my jacket. Five minutes later, a steward carted in a tray of *hors d'œuvres* and the fun began.

You've heard of people going on diets. I went on a champagne diet for four days. I was a social butterfly, a gay blade. Champagne bubbles dribbled out my ears. The last night aboard, the captain even threw a party for me. It was a wing-ding, and nobody got to sleep. When the ship pulled into Honolulu about seven the next morning, I was stretched out across my bed fully dressed, and only semi-conscious. Vaguely I remember hearing Hawaiian music not too far off. I could barely move, I was so worn out and so saturated with wine, but I kept saying to myself "I hope somebody comes to get me. I don't know where the hell to go. . . ."

There was a knock on the door. I rolled off the bed and opened it. Three men came into the room; two of them had cameras. The other fellow smiled and said, "I'm Earl Vida. I represent the Baldwins. Did you have a good trip?" I could only groan.

The photographers took pictures of me wearing a Hawaiian *lei* and a sickly grin. Then Earl Vida took me in tow. We went into the city, and he dragged me around to meet all the big shots—the mayor, the district judge, and the famous old Hawaiian swimmer, Duke Kahanamoku, who happened to be the sheriff.

Finally I could barely keep my eyes open, much less keep smiling. "How about leading me to a hotel," I said to Vida, "where I can let the champagne settle a little."

"Oh, I'm sorry," he said, "but we have to go to the island of Maui."

"Why?"

"That's where the Baldwins live . . . they own the island. And it is where the 'Little World Series' will be played . . . We go by plane, private plane."

The islands certainly were some breathtaking sight from the sky. Even through my red-rimmed eyes. All you could see was blue-green ocean, and white beaches, big green splotches of trees, an occasional towering purple mountain. When we landed at the airfield on Maui, a young man stepped forward to greet me, Chew Baldwin, the son of the gent who owns the island. On the way over, Vida told me the Baldwins operated a giant sugar plantation, and had forty-five thousand workers.

"That's our house, up there," Chew Baldwin said, pointing to an honest-to-Pete castle perched on a hillside overlooking the sea. It looked bigger than all of the many apartment houses I grew up in combined. Chew then brought me to the main hotel on the island and checked me in, saying he'd come by and pick me up later to meet the rest of his family. I couldn't wait to get to my room and flop on the sack. But when I opened the door, another man was asleep in one of the twin beds.

I called the desk and asked what the deal was. "I'm terribly sorry, sir," the clerk said, "but this week the Maui fair opened and the hotel is so crowded it's impossible to keep track of everyone. . . . The gentleman in your room is checking out shortly. Please try to be patient."

I fell asleep, and when I awoke the man was gone. But there was another one. This happened once more that afternoon. Guys were coming and going like my room was the washroom. Hardly able to sleep, I called the Baldwins, and they sent a servant around to pick me up and take me to their "house." There I stayed the rest of the time on the island.

"We have a cocktail party arranged for you," was the first thing Mr. Baldwin said when we met. He was a hearty looking old gentleman, and I took to him right away. "I've been on a cocktail party for four days," I moaned. "I'd just like to sleep." He understood, saying, "Of course, forgive me. You'll have plenty of time for partying."

"Which reminds me," I said. "When is this 'Little World Series'?"

"Next Sunday." (This was only Monday.)

"Well, how many games will there be? And who's playing?"

"There's just one game," he smiled. "My team, the Filipinos, are playing the Japanese for the championship of the Hawaiian Islands."

"One game! . . ."

For the next five days all I did was swim, eat, sleep and attend gay parties. The Baldwins had me meet all the elite of the island. I could come and go as I pleased, and without being permitted to pay for anything with my own money. It was surely something like Paradise. And for this I was getting paid. Finally, Sunday, I went to work. There were maybe five thousand fans at the "World Series," a mixture of races the likes of which I never saw before—Chinese, Portuguese, Japanese, Filipinos and just plain Hawaiians, all of whom worked for the sugar mill.

That night, Mr. Baldwin threw a tremendous dinner in my honor. When it broke up afterward, he took me aside, handed me my fifteen-hundred-dollar check, then said: "You didn't get much chance to see the mainland, did you?"

"No," I said, embarrassed that he might think I was grumbling about anything.

"Well," he went on, "I've taken the liberty of arranging a two-week vacation for you at the Royal Hawaiian Hotel. You've heard of it?"

And here I'd been thinking I'd already had a grand time.

On the ship going home, it was the same mad merry-go-round —private suite, champagne, parties, no personal expense. I was a wreck when we docked at San Francisco. But what a way to die, huh?

A month or so later, the Japs bombed Pearl Harbor. I'm glad they waited.

When I went on the road in 1942, I found it tough going. The war was in full swing, and the gasoline, oil and tire shortages hit me hard. I bought an eighteen-gallon tank to fill up with extra gas, which I kept in my car trunk. I would have quit touring, or at least cut down a lot, except that now I started visiting Army camps to entertain the recruits.

I was scheduled to perform at the All-Star game at the Polo Grounds one evening in July, the first All-Star game to be played at night. I arrived in New York from Buffalo about 10 A.M. the morning of the game. Before going home to the Bronx, I stopped downtown to buy a couple of shirts, and walking along Madison Avenue I met Tom Farley, Jim's brother. When I told him of my gas and tire problems, he said, "What will you do next year? It'll probably get worse."

Kiddingly, I said, "Maybe I'll open a restaurant."

"You're crazy if you do," he said. "You don't know anything about restaurant business. Nearly every sports figure who opens a place winds up broke."

So we got into a discussion about restaurants. "Chances are," I said, "the guys who've gone broke were just fronting for somebody else, using their names. You need more than a name . . . people can't eat that. If I had a restaurant, I'd sell the best food I could get and take my chances."

"I still say you'd be crazy," he said.

Suddenly I said, "I'll tell you what. I'll bet you one hundred bucks right now that I open a restaurant inside of six months."

He studied my face. "All right," he said. "Good luck."

Later that afternoon, I was downtown again with my dear friend, Art Flynn, shopping for a restaurant. As we passed a little place on East Fifty-second Street, just east of Lexington Avenue, called the Filet Mignon, Art said, "Let's stop in here for a beer. I know the guy who owns this joint."

It was a musty little dive with a lot of dust and few customers. I heard the bartender tell another customer, "I'm going in the Army. I have to sell this joint."

"That's George, the young fellow who owns the place, with his mother," Art whispered to me.

"How much do you want for it, kid?" I called down the bar.

"Forty-five hundred," he said.

"What have you got?"

"Just what you can see," he said, moving toward us. I looked around. There were tables in the back and more up a short flight of stairs. What I saw I didn't like—but I wanted to win that $100 bet.

"How much liquor inventory you got?" I asked.

"Twenty-four hundred dollars' worth . . . sixteen hundred of it is gin." Gin was especially difficult to get then.

I said, "Well, I love dry martinis. Your place is sold. How much will you take down?"

"I'll take two thousand down and the rest . . . twenty-five hundred and twenty-four hundred for the booze, makes forty-nine hundred . . . when I leave."

"How soon can you leave?"

"How about August first?" he said.

"You're on." Turning to Flynn, I cracked, "Art, I'm a hundred bucks ahead already."

I gave George a check for two thousand dollars, then went to the telephone booth and called my brother Lou, an excellent designer and architect. "Lou," I said cheerily, "I just bought a restaurant."

"I don't believe you," he said. "Even you are not that crazy."

Telling him the story, I added, "I can't renege now. I gave this guy a check already. Come on down and look the place over."

When Lou walked in the door about twenty minutes later, he took one look around and gasped, "Phew! Do they have cockroach races on the bar?"

"Doesn't look so hot now, does it?" I laughed. "That's where you come in. I want you to remodel this joint with a lot of baseball stuff."

"Do you know what that'll cost you?" he snorted. "There's a war on, materials are hard to get. It will cost you at least thirty-five thousand dollars!"

"Look," I said, "here's a check for five thousand to start it rolling. I gotta get to the Polo Grounds now, then I'm off to Cleveland and the rest of my tour. I got no time to argue. Please, you take charge. You can tell me what a dope I am when I get back."

So, just like that, I'm in the restaurant business, without knowing a thing about it.

It rained that evening at the Polo Grounds—naturally, just *after* I finished my act. I was in the clubhouse ready to take a shower, when the rainstorm started. The clubhouse boy, looking out the window, said, "You could take your shower out on the field." Without hesitation, I got into my costume again, got a pair of hip boots from a groundskeeper, and I went back out and did my rowing and high diving bit off the pitching mound in the center of the tarpaulin.

The winning team in that All-Star game was to play another game in Cleveland the next night against an all-star service team, led by the Indians former ace pitcher, Bob Feller. I was to appear at that game too, so I drove to Cleveland right after my performance at the Polo Grounds.

The next night, I wound up my act just before game time, impersonating Feller's pitching movements at the same time Bob was warming up for the game. I was dressing in the clubhouse, and the game must have been on only about thirty minutes, when Feller trudged in. "What're you doing here so soon?" I said.

"You gave a great impersonation of me as a pitcher," he said, "but I just did a better one of *you* as a pitcher. They knocked me out in the second inning."

When I reached Indianapolis on my tour, a wire arrived from

Lou asking for more money. I sent him another check for five thousand dollars. As I went from city to city, there'd be more requests for money, and I kept sending it back to him. About twenty thousand dollars later, the place was nowhere near completed, and I was running very low in my savings. Then I remembered Sid Kramer.

Sid was a friend of mine in the garment industry who had long been after me to go into business with him. His idea, I'm sure, was to use my name "out front" to attract customers. I knew he was making good profits with the war on, so I called him and said, "You always wanted to get into a business with me. Here's your chance." I told him about the restaurant and added, "You put in say around seventeen thousand and we might really have something." He went for it on the spot. So now I've got a partner, although I still retained control of the enterprise.

I finished my tour the middle of September and returned to New York, only to find the restaurant still unfinished. So I pitched in myself. I designed a miniature baseball diamond on the floor of the upstairs section, then varnished the wooden ceilings. The place was shaping up. At least now it looked clean—no more cockroach races. Four days before our scheduled opening, I didn't have a single waiter or a chef or any help. In the next three days, on the advice of an experienced restaurant man friends had recommended to me, I hired twelve waiters, two bartenders, two captains, a chef, cook, salad man, dishwasher, porter, checkroom girl, doorman, three bookkeepers for the office, and Murray Goodman, who would handle business details for me—twenty-seven people.

We were ready for the great venture. I was excited, but nervous. Kramer was just excited and eager, so much so that I decided to settle something before we started.

"Sid, let's understand each other right away," I said the day before the grand opening. "This is *my* restaurant. You are a junior partner . . . very junior. I'd rather you didn't walk around here during business hours. I don't want anybody to get the idea I'm just a front man and you're really the boss. You look too much like a boss. You can come in every night, collect the money, if any, and deposit it in the bank. You can have your own bookkeeper if you want. You can sit in the office all day long. But I don't want you making any policy here. This is Al Schacht's big-league restaurant, and I want to run it in big-league style. . . . Under these conditions, we'll get along swell."

It wasn't until opening day that it struck me for the first time that my restaurant was located right between two funeral parlors. If the joint was going to die, I wouldn't have far to go to bury it.

Steaks and chops were the specialty, and we tried to buy nothing but the best cuts of meat. So what happened just a few days after we opened? Meat rationing. I had to institute Meatless Monday and Meatless Friday, and we closed Tuesdays. And steaks served only between 6 and 9 P.M. other days—except for servicemen, who could order steak any time.

The first month, we lost about five hundred dollars a week. Kramer was getting nervous. He started sticking his fingers in the pie, trying to cut down expenses by buying cheaper cuts of meat. And he was making more frequent appearances in the restaurant proper, fidgeting around and acting like the owner. I was beginning to dislike it.

The second month was hardly better than the first, and now Kramer was scared he'd invested in a turkey. We were in the office one day, leafing through a huge stack of bills, and I said, "Sid, I think we're each going to have to put in another thousand. We got to keep our credit good."

"Another thousand!" he wailed. "Do you think I'm made of money? Oh, this is terrible, terrible . . . we'll never get out from under . . ."

"What the hell are you crying about?" I snapped. "You can afford to lose this money a lot more than I can, but you're crying and I'm not. And come to think of it, I notice you roaming around downstairs quite a bit lately. I thought I told you I'm the only one to be seen down there?"

He was pacing the floor, eying that pile of unpaid bills and shaking his head, and frowning and mumbling to himself. "Oh, why did I ever want to go into the restaurant business?" he cried out at last.

"Okay, you're out of the restaurant business," I said sharply.

"What do you mean?"

"I'm gonna pay you back what you put in," I said. "All I want is for you to get out. You notify your lawyer, and I'll tell mine, and we'll set up a meeting. I'll see you don't lose a cent of your investment."

Maybe that was a brash statement, but I was getting cocky about the restaurant. We were losing only about $250 a week by now.

The very next day, Kramer and his lawyer met me and we all went to the office of my lawyer, Bill Weissman. Kramer's lawyer read a prepared statement of Sid's terms for giving up his share: he not only wanted his seventeen thousand dollars, but a six-thousand-dollar bonus for getting out!

"Six thousand bonus! The place is losing so much money, you ought to be tickled to get back what you put in," Weissman raged.

Kramer said, "That restaurant is liable to make forty thousand a year soon. . . ."

Then I spoke up: "He gets the six-thousand-dollar bonus."

Weissman almost fell over. "Are you nuts?"

"It's okay, it's my money," I said calmly. "Let's draw up the papers." I agreed to give Kramer twenty-three thousand dollars, payable in installments over eighteen months.

When they'd gone, Weissman said, "You haven't got a brain in your head. You let that guy get away with six grand, and you're losing your shirt."

"Listen, Bill," I said, "he don't know it, but he wasn't kidding about this place making forty thousand a year some day soon. What's more, I don't want him around any more, because he knows even less about the business than I do, and I know from nothing."

"All well and good," Bill said. "But how about that forty thousand a year . . . ?"

As fate would have it, that night, a Saturday, was the turning point. The most business we'd ever done in one night before was a five-hundred-dollar gross—believe it or not, that night we did twelve hundred dollars. And from then to the end of the year business picked up so well that we did take in forty thousand dollars, and I was able to pay Kramer off in a hurry and also my brother Lou.

236 my own particular screwball

I was on top of the world. I was not only lucky in business but I was in love.

chapter 18

I met her at a bowling alley. It was late summer, and I'd been asked to make an appearance at the opening of alleys financed by ballplayers Billy Jurges and Harry Danning, in Rego Park, Long Island. There was this redhead. Very pretty, and poised, and with the kind of warm, brilliant smile that you find it hard to turn away from. She laughed like she enjoyed herself, and enjoyed others, and even when she wasn't laughing her eyes were. We took a fancy to each other almost immediately.

Mabelle Russell was her name. She was a featured vocalist in a night club in New York, and, others told me, a really fine singer. One night shortly after, I went around to the club to hear her. As I walked in and got seated, Mabelle recognized me and changed her song to "I Cried For You," all the while looking toward me with that flashing smile and dancing eyes. I stayed for the next show, and then we sat and talked for a long time and I walked her home. If it sounds like simple boy-and-girl stuff, that's just the way it was.

It wasn't long before we both realized we were in love. I thought I'd been crazy about a few girls before, but next to her they were nothing. I'd sit sometimes and try to figure out how a person can feel this way about another. For a man, it's feeling at ease with someone, wanting to be with her more than with anyone, wanting to do things for her, yet seeking comfort from her. It's laughing at the same things, and liking the same and disliking the same. Possibly it was stranger for a guy like me—I was going on fifty, and all my life I'd been a loner and a mover, never tied down, never with any thought of needing anybody. But now I couldn't even fix in my mind anymore how it had been all those years without Mabelle.

I got to visiting her at the club practically every night after my place closed. Any doubts I might have had were surely banished when I found myself getting jealous of the men who leered at her in the club.

Thanksgiving, 1942, we had our first big date out. My place was closed, and we had dinner at another restaurant. I felt like a boy again, and even told Mabelle about the time Esther Levine and I had gone to dinner and I had to slip into the men's room to make sure I had enough dough. I ordered everything for us from soup to nuts and topped it off with a bottle of sparkling burgundy. Then I discovered I had no money with me, and she had to pay the check. And I didn't even have to go to the men's room to make the embarrassing discovery.

During the 1942-43 winter, and through the following spring and early summer, I divided my time between my restaurant, Mabelle and visiting Army hospitals and camps doing shows. I didn't make the circuit of the ball parks any more. Not only was it practically impossible under wartime restrictions, but I felt it would be almost unpatriotic to use up gas and oil and tires for my own profit.

In August, I ran into a Colonel Young, who brought up the idea of my going overseas to entertain the troops. I'd never thought of it before, and it hit me as a wonderful idea. Colonel Young said he'd fix me up.

A week later, I got a notice to report for inoculations. I took so many shots, I didn't think my body had room for one more puncture. Next, I was told to apply for a passport—and I still had no idea where I was going overseas.

One night, I was in the restaurant about eleven when an Army officer telephoned that a car would pick me up at five the next morning. I called Mabelle, and when she got through work we sat up all night drinking champagne. Here I was, with a new love and new business, and I was off to God-knows-where. We made the most of the farewells.

At 5 A.M. on the dot, the command car pulled up outside. I kissed Mabelle good-by and left on the great adventure.

We drove to La Guardia Field, where I was directed into a tiny room. An Air Force captain entered and said, "You're Al Schacht?"

"That's right."

"I'm Captain Cameron Robertson. I see I'm flying you to North Africa."

"How about that!" I said. "I don't know where I'm going, but you do."

He took me to another part of the building, where a lady behind a counter handed me official credentials. They were marked "VIP," with "No. 2 Priority." I'll have you know only generals got "No. 1 Priority." Then, just like the Army, we hung around until 8 A.M. before boarding the Air Transport plane.

When I got to Casablanca they put me in charge of Sidney Piermont, formerly a booking agent for Loew's Theatres, who was now a Special Services officer. We drove to Casablanca, and that Piermont really had me booked solid. He had me going all around Casablanca doing shows—on impromptu open stages, in theaters, off the backs of trucks, on decks of warships. We traveled into the surrounding hills and down into valleys in jeeps and trucks, and everywhere were our soldiers and sailors. I'd give a monologue, some pantomime baseball clowning and, wherever there was a beat-up piano, my recital. The best was ribbing back and forth with the G.I.s, and the bull sessions, mostly about baseball.

One of my greatest kicks while there was having lunch at a tiny villa just outside the city, where I ate at the same table that President Roosevelt and Churchill had eaten not long before. In town I stayed at a dirty little hotel just opposite the Arab open market. I never thought there could be so many smells all in any one place, and most of them foul.

After Casablanca, I went to Marrakech. Then, Oran. Then, Algiers. This was a bustling war city, General Eisenhower's headquarters. A Special Services officer, Colonel David, luckily got me a room in a hotel where only generals lived ordinarily. When I arrived at the hotel, I saw a pair of filthy, bedraggled men loitering outside, practically asleep standing against the wall. Glancing a second time, I recognized them as war correspondents, and one looked especially familiar. I looked again, and it was a good friend of mine, Quentin Reynolds. The other fellow turned out to be John Steinbeck, the author. They said they were looking for some place to stay but hadn't had any luck. When I told them I was staying in this exclusive joint, Reynolds' eyes sparkled and he said, "Only generals are allowed here, eh? . . . Every general has an aide . . . I'm your aide, General Schacht."

So Quent and I got a room with twin beds, and, with a little string-pulling, Steinbeck joined a couple of other correspondents who'd also finagled a room. It was funny the next morning to see Reynolds all rolled up in his bed's mosquito netting, looking like a trapped lion.

I moved from Algiers to Tunis, and, after a week, to Sicily. That's where the fun began.

Our C-47 landed in Sicily about 12 noon, in a broiling sun, and the pilot, copilot and I stood under the wing to get a little shade. I said, "Where the hell are we?" The pilot answered, "Catania."

The moment he said it the air raid alert sounded and German planes swooped out of the sky and proceeded to strafe the field. I felt like Schacht the pitcher again as those heavy slugs ripped the ground around us. The pilot slammed me to the ground, shouting, "Lie flat, but keep your head up!"

A minute or so later, the Jerries were gone. When the all-clear blew, the pilot, alongside me, got to his feet. I yelled up at him, "Should I get up?"

"Get up," he said, "and if you can still shiver you're okay."

I looked around. About half a dozen planes were afire, and ours was one of them. I had to grab at the wing for support. At last I said to my companions, "Either of you got a notebook?" The copilot pulled one out.

"Jot this down, will you," I said. "Catania, Sicily, September 2, 1943. . . . This war is officially on from now on as far as Schacht is concerned."

Catania was a shattered city. The Americans and British had chased the Germans from Catania, and the Germans had left little standing. The streets were almost deserted except for armed soldiers. The civilians had been driven to the hills and were just now trickling back down. For the first time I was struck by the horror of war, and it saddened me.

After doing my show in Catania, I hurried to Messina in a jeep, passing part of the British Fifth Army along the way heading in the same direction. I did my show before dusk, and that night slept in a pup tent outside Messina. Around daybreak I awoke to the most goshawful bombardment. It was the British invading the toe of Italy.

Back to Catania, then by plane to North Africa again, to Bizerte. The plane had to go a hundred miles off course, as the pilot expected we'd run into German planes. The harbor at Bizerte was stuffed with ships of all sizes, making ready for the invasion of Salerno, I heard later. They tell me Bizerte once was a beautiful seaport. When I got there it was a nightmare, not a building left standing. The city's inhabitants all were either dead or gone. I later visited many places that had been flattened in the war, but I don't think I saw anything as horrible as Bizerte.

The first night there, I did a show on the U.S. cruiser *Savannah*, one of those in the armada ready to go at Italy. Right after, as I was stepping into the Navy launch to return to shore, my Special Services aide, Lieutenant Bill McKeon, hollered, "There's the air raid signal. Let's get back fast. The Jerries'll be over any minute."

We chugged into the dock just as the German bombers came overhead. The racket was deafening, with the raiders dropping their heavy bombs and the ships all firing up at them. McKeon and I were right in the middle of it.

"Dive into that sewer!" he called, pointing to a wide sewer pipe under the street near the dock. It was open at both ends, and he crawled into one end and I the other.

I could see the whole show. The bombers would make their runs in single file, drop their loads and zoom up and away, to regroup and attack again. Tracer bullets from the ships in the harbor lit the sky like the Fourth of July. We lay there for three hours. Surprisingly, I was more thrilled than frightened.

After a particularly noisy barrage, I shouted to McKeon, but he didn't answer. I twisted around to see him, and he seemed to be lying still. I crawled through the pipe and shone my flashlight in his face. He was on his back, his eyes wide open but rolled up so only the whites showed; his mouth was open, quivering, like he wanted to speak but couldn't, and his tongue wagged helplessly.

I dragged him out of the sewer and, forgetting all about the raid, ran to find help. A couple of MP's helped me pull him to safety. When the shooting was over, they hurried him to 81st General Hospital about eight miles inland. Lieutenant McKeon had gone out of his mind. He'd been in the exhausting battle at Kasserine Pass and was one of the few survivors of his outfit, and had suffered a nervous breakdown and been put on limited service. Now he was mentally ill again. He was only around twenty-eight. The next day I happened to be doing a show in the very hospital they'd brought him to, and I saw him in the psychiatric ward. He didn't recognize me. When I went outside, I wept for the first time in many, many years.

From Bizerte I went to Constantine. But the Army was true to its word. They'd said my overseas tour would be for seven weeks, and almost on the nose I got my orders to return to the States. They flew me back to Algiers, where I was to transfer to another plane bound for Port Lyautey. At the Algiers air field, I dashed into a telephone booth, the only one in sight, and tried to contact the field Air Force transportation officer to make sure about the time of departure of my plane and see if my passage was all set. I had a little trouble getting through to the right man, and must have been monopolizing the phone for at least twenty minutes, when I noticed an Army captain pacing up and down outside. He looked on edge and kept sneaking glances my way, and I was suddenly chilled by the thought he might be a spy. So I lowered my voice to a mumble and cut off my conversation as soon as possible. But he'd stalked away by the time I came out of the booth.

A year later, I was in the Stork Club in New York with Mabelle one night when a tall fellow strode up to our table and said, almost angrily, "I know you!"

I said, "I'm Al Schacht. Who are you?"

"I could have shot you once in Algiers," he said.

"Why, was my show that lousy?"

"I was on the same plane with you coming into Algiers, and we had an hour stopover, remember? And I wanted to call a gal I knew, and you stayed in the goddam phone booth for half an hour and I never did get to talk to her. . . ."

The Spy. Mabelle was grinning at me. I shifted uncomfortably and murmured, "It's a small world, isn't it?" Then he laughed and clapped me on the shoulder, and we all had a drink on it.

New York looked like a fairyland to me after seven tough weeks away. My only thought was, however, did I still have a business? At no place overseas had my mail caught up with me, and I knew nothing about any developments either at home or with the restaurant. I walked into the restaurant and stood in the doorway and drank the joint in for a moment. Then I dropped my bags easily, like I just came from the Bronx, and yelled, "Drinks on the house for everybody!" (If there'd been more than twenty customers on the bar I wouldn't have said it. Not so loud, anyhow.)

The restaurant was prospering nicely now, and I began to feel like a full-fledged businessman, even though I didn't spend much time at it. That winter I visited quite a few hospitals throughout the country. The following summer, I managed to work a ball park now and then, but my regular tour was *kaput*. In September 1944, I was getting inoculated again for overseas. This time it would be the Pacific, although, as usual, I had no idea where exactly.

I did a couple of shows at the air field in steaming heat, then was flown to Oro Bay and from there to Guadalcanal and Bougainville for quickie shows. In Hollandia, I wore my baseball uniform for the first time in the blistering South Pacific, entertaining before the "world series" ball game (of New Guinea) between the 32d and 24th Divisions. I can't recall now every ex-big league star who played in that game, but there were several, including catcher Ken Sylvestri and pitcher Hugh Mulcahy. There must have been twenty thousand G.I.s looking on; it seemed every outfit in New Guinea had some representation at this big game, and the betting was terrific, and you could sense the rivalry and tension, just like a real World Series.

When I got home again several weeks later I found myself gripped in a kind of horror. About my hearing. It was almost gone. The two trips overseas had left me nearly completely deaf.

chapter 19

I was thinking I'd have to get a hearing aid. Then one night a Mrs. Smith, one of my regular customers, came into the restaurant with a bandage over one ear. Mrs. Smith had been hard of hearing, but this night she seemed to hear wonderfully. She told me joyfully she'd recently undergone an amazing operation which had cured her deafness. This hit me like a ton, because I'd often been told that no doctor alive could ever cure an organic hearing disorder. She said her doctor's name was Julius Lempert and I went to see him that week.

After examining my right ear, he said, "I think I can restore your hearing." He said it calmly, confidently, and immediately I felt I could put my trust in him.

That was a Monday. On Wednesday, I entered his clinic to be operated on. Before the operation, I turned on a small radio on a table to the right of the bed, and told the nurse, "Please leave it on." Usually, in order to hear a radio, I'd have to turn it up full blast. This time I tuned it low, thinking if I could hear it later, I'd know the operation was a success.

The way I understand it, there's a tiny hole in a bone in your ear, through which you hear. That's probably simplifying it greatly, but it works something like that. With me, the bone had hardened and closed this important opening. Dr. Lempert built what he called a new "window" in my ear by drilling a hole in the bone and lining it with gold to keep it open. When I awoke I thought a violinist was playing right in my ear. It was the radio, still playing softly.

I returned to my business, after twelve days in Dr. Lempert's clinic. In the restaurant now, it seemed like everybody was shouting at the tops of their voices when they were only talking normally.

The clatter of dishes and glass was thunderous to me in my new world. But I soon realized the disadvantage I now was under—I could hear all the baloney, *too* clearly.

Several months later the U.S. had won the war and I had another crisis on my hands. My landlord, who owned one of the funeral parlors next door, bluntly informed me I'd have to pack up my restaurant and get out. He said he wanted to enlarge his funeral parlor. So there I was with a successful restaurant and no place to put it. I started looking around for property, either to buy or lease.

One night I got into a conversation with a gentleman at the bar named Mavis, who said he was a former opera singer. He was also a Giant fan. "I've passed this place a number of times," he said, "and saw your name outside, but I never realized until tonight that you were the baseball man. You've got an attractive place here."

"Take a good look while you're here," I said sadly. "Next time you come by this may be a funeral parlor." I told him my problem.

"I happen to have some property for sale," he said.

"Whereabouts?"

"Just a block from here . . . Fifty-second Street, just east of Park Avenue. I've got two twenty-foot frontage adjacent buildings."

"I'd like to look at it," I said. We walked up the street, and the property looked good. Two three-story apartment buildings. The location was great, too. "How much do you want?" I asked.

"A hundred and ten thousand dollars . . . seventy thousand cash down."

"Let's go back and have another martini," I said.

We drank and talked some more, then I said, "Mr. Mavis, you got a deal. I'll bring my agent around tomorrow."

When he'd gone, I called up Lou. "Brother, I bought two buildings." There was silence on the other end, then a long sigh. Lou knew me; we were off again. The next day he and I went to look at the property, and when I told him the terms, he said, "You got a steal. But what on earth are you going to do with these buildings? You'll have to tear them down and rebuild, and that will take an awful lot of money. Which you haven't got, my friend."

He was right. If I liquidated everything I had—bonds, insurance, savings—I could manage $120,000, tops. And Lou estimated it would take maybe three times that much to complete this venture. But I figured I'd cross that bridge when I came to it. First, before actually completing the sale with Mavis, I went to the Liquor Control Board to make sure about my license, because there was a small building next door to my new property where a group of Catholic nuns lived, and I wanted to know if that would restrict me from transferring my liquor license. The board, after an inspection, said that while it was a Sisters' home, it was not a place of worship and so I was in the clear.

Next, I had to try to buy out the tenants of the two buildings. I offered them cash settlements—about $250 average—and tried to find other apartments for those who didn't know of any vacancies. All but one of the fourteen families made it easy for me. That one, an elderly woman, refused to leave. Everything was set to begin demolition, but we waited four months on her. She wanted three thousand dollars cash to get out, which was ridiculous. Finally we went ahead tearing the buildings down right around her. But of course, it had to reach a point where, if she called my bluff, we'd have to stop. At last she settled for one thousand dollars and moved out. When we'd finished demolishing, all that was left were three brick walls.

With my total finances already invested, I still needed fifty thousand dollars to start building, so work was suspended while I made the rounds of banks to see if I could borrow the money. But I got nowhere. The banks said they didn't want to get into the restaurant business; and I really couldn't blame them. A couple of weeks went by and all there was of my new restaurant was the original ruins, and I put a huge photo of myself in costume snoozing on a gigantic baseball glove where the front window should be—the caption on the picture was: "When this place opens, wake me up."

One afternoon, returning from another unsuccessful visit to a bank, I found Lou with the plumber going over our contract.

"I want copper piping plumbing," I butted in.

"Without money, lead piping is good enough," Lou cried.

I said, "If this fella don't know yet that I got no money, he's wasting a lot of time here."

"We'll work something out," the plumber smiled.

On the last page of items, he said, "What kind of toilet seats do you want in the ladies' room . . . what color?"

"There's a hell of a problem," I laughed.

Just then, a well-dressed young fellow with a big package under his arm tiptoed across the narrow board catwalk from the street toward us. "Who's Mr. Schacht?" he asked pleasantly.

"I'm Al Schacht," I said, "the guy who's financing this mess without a dime . . . this is my brother Lou, who's building it, and he's got less than me . . . and this is the plumber, who wants thirty-thousand smackers without even copper piping . . . and what's worrying all of us is the color of toilet seats. What're you selling?"

"Toilet seats." With that he opened his package and pulled out a sample, and it was one of those violet ray sanitary type seats. "I'd like to give you a demonstration," he said.

"Standing or sitting?"

"Have you got an electric outlet?" he asked, ignoring me. Lou showed him one, and he plugged it in and the seat lit up and slowly lifted.

"How much are they?" I said.

"A hundred dollars apiece."

I turned to the plumber. "How much are yours?"

"Twenty-three dollars for the regular and twenty-six for the colored."

"How many do we need, Lou?"

"Eight," he said. "There'll be two powder rooms and two men's rooms . . . two in each."

"Lou," I announced, "we're getting the violet ray seats."

He slapped his hands to his head and began walking around in a circle. "You're crazy . . . you're crazy! Where are you getting all this money?"

"Listen, Lou," I said quietly, "I want to tell you something. When we were kids going to school, I carried a pitcher's finger mitt along with my bologna sandwiches, and I wanted to be a big-league pitcher. And I made it. . . . I wanted to be a clown, and I did that. . . . I opened one restaurant on a prayer just because of a lousy hundred-dollar bet, and it's done all right. . . . Now according to your designs and blueprints, this new restaurant will be a real big-league joint. . . . If I want to owe money, I want to do it in a big-league way—I want to owe a *lot* of money."

I don't know if I convinced Lou, but I wasn't kidding myself—I was getting worried. Then, that very night, Fate smiled on me again. My dear friend Joe Laurie, Jr., the actor and writer—he's gone now, God bless him—walked into the old restaurant, pulled me away from the crowd at the bar and said, "Come into the office (the men's room), I want to tell you something."

Inside, Joe continued: "I hear you're scraping the bottom of the barrel for dough." Handing me a folded slip of paper, he said, "Put this in your pocket. If you ever get rich, you can give it back to me." It wasn't for an hour or two that I thought to glance at what he'd stuck in my paw—a check for five thousand dollars.

The next night, another friend, Harold Reiner, came in and gave me the same line and another check for five thousand dollars. Lloyd Clayton came through with still another five thousand dollars. Joe Smith bowled me over with a check for ten thousand dollars. Each of my pals seemed to be passing the word along. I was thunderstruck. Within ten days, my friends had lent me forty-five thousand dollars, which was what I needed to start building. Mabelle and I sat up alone in the restaurant until the small hours one morning and just held hands and talked about wonderful people.

Where with the first restaurant I'd had to hire twenty-seven employees, this time it was sixty. Lou did a tremendous job designing the place with a modern baseball decor, and even laid out an apartment for me on the third floor of the building. As for the great sums of money I owed Lou, I disposed of him in a hurry—I gave him a one-third interest in the place. He's a terrific guy. Without his strength and wisdom to back me, I probably wouldn't have had the guts to follow through. As it was, when we opened in December of 1947 I not only had what I now think is one of the finest restaurants in New York, but it was big-league—I owed only $260,000 on it.

About ten days before the big opening, I got a scare. Having long since checked with the Liquor Control Board about my license, as regards the nuns' home next door, I'd taken it for granted everything was okay. But the restaurant was practically set to open, and I realized I still didn't have the license. So I went to the board again to find out what was happening.

"You're in a tough spot," a commissioner told me. "While the law does specify that the sisters' residence is not a house of worship, if the Church doesn't want you as a neighbor they can stop your license."

"Well, this is a fine time to tell me!" I exploded. "I've put nearly four hundred thousand dollars into this business!"

He said, "If you can get a letter from the Mother Superior, saying she doesn't oppose your restaurant as a neighbor, I'll grant your license on the spot."

This was better. I'd been to see the good nuns several times already. The first time was when we'd started to build; I wanted to meet them and tell them my place would not be any all-night club but just a good eating place. The nuns had gathered around as I spoke to Mother Superior, and, naturally, sensing an audience, I'd told them some stories, and they seemed to get a kick out of it. Then, at Thanksgiving, Mabelle and I had brought them some turkeys, and we had a pleasant time chatting all around.

I told Mother Anita the story, and she said, "You sit down, young man. I'll just be five minutes." When she returned, she handed me a sealed envelope and said to give it to the liquor board. I hurried right down to the Commissioner's office and turned the letter over to him, not having opened it myself. He read it and smiled warmly. "This is one of the most beautiful letters I ever read," he said, handing it to me. It said, in part:

". . . Not only do the sisters not oppose Mr. Schacht as a neighbor, but we have been praying for the success of his new restaurant . . ."

I got my license. And when I went back to thank Mother Anita, what did she do but present me with a pair of beaded bags which the sisters had made for my sister and mother.

Opening night of the new restaurant, it was jammed, mostly with my special friends. Joe Laurie, Jr., took me aside and said, "I know this is difficult on your opening night, but I promised a parish priest you'd say a few words at a church bazaar for underprivileged kids. It's only at Ninety-third Street and Third Avenue . . . it'll take about fifteen minutes. What d'you say we hustle over there now?"

I thought, Lord, I shouldn't leave here tonight of all nights, but Joe looked so earnest I said, "Joe, I can't turn you down. But I want to get back here no later than a half hour." So we got into a friend's car and drove up to Ninety-third Street. But there was no church.

"Maybe it's Eighty-third," Joe said. Nothing there either.

By now, a half hour had passed, and I was restless about Mabelle having to entertain all those first-night customers and well-wishers. "I'm sorry, Joe," I said, "but I got to get back to my business."

When we walked into the restaurant, most of the people were gathered around a white sheet hung over a section of the wall near the bar. "What's going on?" I called. Somebody pulled the sheet away, and there was a beautifully done oil painting of me. Joe was grinning at me. I was so moved, I had to wipe my eyes with a handkerchief. The same guys who'd loaned me the money to get started had chipped in fifteen hundred dollars for this painting. This, of course, was why the imaginary church routine.

I was tremendously proud of my new enterprise. After all the work I'd done for so many years, all my traveling, I felt a sense of security at last. Except I still owed $260,000. But I had complete faith in the success of the place, even though nobody probably ever started in a business with less knowledge about what he was doing. But I was smart enough to hire the best help, and serve the best food, and I knew we couldn't miss. I also made up my mind I'd never have a place catering only to celebrities. Everybody who walks in my front door is a celebrity to me. I figured my best publicity would not come from items in Broadway columns but word-of-mouth from people who ate my food. If they liked it, they'd tell their friends about it. You can't eat celebrities.

chapter 20

The next summer I went out touring the ball parks again, although no longer booking myself so heavily as before. I was a restaurant man first now, and the clowning had to be more or less a sideline, just because I love doing it. However, I'll admit this particular summer I did have notions about picking up some extra dough. I still owed a bundle of cash, and with business naturally slipping in the summertime, I thought I could take up some slack by touring. But I limited myself to thirty engagements, plus the All-Star Game and the World Series. And every time I took a fall for laughs, I'd say to myself, This is for the joint.

The summer of 1949, I got an urgent call from my sister Esther in Carmel, New York. I'd bought a small country place for my mother, and she and Esther were spending the summer there.

Esther's voice was strained. "Al, it's Mama!"

"What is it, Esther?" I asked.

"It's bad, Al. . . . Mama . . . it's bad . . ."

"Are you at the place?"

"No, the hospital. . . . Can you come right away? Hurry, Al . . ."

I drove like a demon. Up the Bronx River Parkway into Westchester, right on Route 22 at the Kensico Dam circle . . . I thought about her. A wonderful, strong, sensitive woman, the strength of the Schachts. Her quiet, wise humor. I couldn't help go far back to when I was a kid crazy about playing ball in the lots, and how she screamed I was turning into a bum. I remembered how tolerant she'd become of my baseball when it finally started paying off both for me personally and for the family. And later, how proud.

There was the time a year or so before when I called the country place to ask how everybody was. Esther mentioned a road worker had stopped by for a drink of water and asked about the "Schacht" on the mail box, if they were related to Al Schacht, the baseball comedian, who was appearing at Peekskill a few days later.

I said to Esther, "That gives me an idea. You and Ma never saw me. How about if I pick you both up and take you to Peekskill on my way there?" Esther was thrilled. So, a couple of days later, I stopped by and picked up Esther, Mom, and my brother Mike and his wife, and when we got to the Peekskill ball park I sat them in the center of the grandstand right behind home plate. Now, after all those years, my mother was seeing me at my work—but I think I was more nervous about it than she. The stands were full.

Stepping to the field microphone at home plate, and looking straight at Mom, I announced, "Ladies and gentlemen, I'm very happy to be in Peekskill today for two reasons. First, judging by the size of this crowd, it looks like Schacht will do all right with the loot. . . . And, most important, there's a lady here today who's very dear to me who's never seen me perform, either as a pitcher or a clown. I been in baseball thirty-six years, and I appeared at Yankee Stadium in New York many times. And this lady lived two blocks from the Stadium for years, but she never saw me perform. In fact, she never before was even inside a ball park. But she had more to do with me being here, or any place, than anyone in the world. . . . Ladies and gentlemen, I want you to meet my mother!"

Mom rose and took the first bows of her life as the people cheered. But when the applause died down, she kept bowing, and they kept applauding. The crowd was waiting for her to stop bowing, and she was waiting for them to quit applauding. It was a stalemate. I was doubled over laughing. Finally I called over the loudspeaker, "All right, Mama, they've seen you. Sit down and stop hogging the act."

When I finally reached Carmel that afternoon, all the family was at the hospital, waiting. Mom was on the critical list. She'd been stricken with a vicious kidney attack, something called Bright's disease. At her age—about eighty-two—her chances were slim. Especially because for the past few years she'd been undergoing treatment for hardening of the arteries. It seemed impossible her heart could stand this latest load.

We sat, and paced, and smoked and prayed most of the day. The doctors were noncommittal. The old lady was fading. But by nightfall, her condition had "stabilized," as a doctor said. My eyes burning, I drove back to New York. The next morning, I drove up to Carmel again.

Esther looked exhausted, but she was smiling a little when I reached the hospital. "They think she's coming out of it," she said softly. Mom was battling. She rallied. And within a day or so, the brave little old woman was out of danger.

We thanked God—and Dr. Murray Israel. He was the third great doctor who had influenced my life. Dr. Israel had not fought for Mom's life after the kidney attack, but it was he who had treated her arteries, which had saved her heart.

Today Mom is an old lady whose eyesight is going and who doesn't hear too well any more, but whose mind still is as bright and keen as a razor blade. The fact is, when I mention at times how old my mother is, I'm guessing. We have it down pretty close, but none of us kids really know her exact age—maybe she doesn't either. One day not long ago, I decided to try to find out. Snuggling up alongside her easy chair and planting a few smooches on her ear, I asked lovingly, "Ma, how old are you?"

Without hesitation she snorted, "Ha! Did I ever ask you how old you are?" What's the use?

As for me, here I am—a Jewboy who was born on Catharine Street on the East Side of New York of an orthodox Jewish family . . . a boy who wanted to be a big-league pitcher but whose folks were very much against it . . . a boy who studied to be a rabbi, sang in a Jewish choir, and wound up with a chew of tobacco in his mouth, striking out Babe Ruth with the bases loaded. You might say I'm successful now . . . though I guess it's all in how you look at it.

Since I've opened up my restaurant, I've done a lot of traveling. I've been to France, Germany, Austria, the Philippines, twice to Japan, and once to Korea during the Korean War. Also I've made numerous visits to hospitals all over this country.

The past summer, 1954, as usual appearing in ball parks only because I still get a kick out of it, I was asked to perform at a benefit ball game for a hospital in Walton, New York, the town where I'd begun my professional baseball career in 1910.

The day before my appearance, I drove from New York to Walton, knowing I'd again pass through some of the towns whose teams I'd played against way back then. I noticed signs and posters on trees and in store windows, which read, "AL SCHACHT DAY . . . Walton vs. Delhi . . . for benefit Walton Hospital." And believe me, I couldn't help choking up a little. I stopped at the hotel in Delhi because—I have to say it—Delhi always had a better hotel than Walton. That evening I stopped in a diner in town for a snack, and the owner recognized me. "I bet on Delhi against you in 1910," he said. I won the game he was referring to, and maybe his losses that day might have prevented him from becoming a bigger restaurateur.

The next morning I drove into Walton. It was practically the same town, hardly changing at all. The stores and streets looked the same. So did the people. In front of the hotel ten of the fifteen original directors of the 1910 team waited to greet me. I looked at them. These were mostly the same fellows who weren't impressed with me when I first reported to Walton and wanted to fire me. And now here they were laying out the red carpet. Among them were Jerome Farrell, the former president of the ball club; Mr. Guild, the banker; Mr. McLean, the drugstore man; and young Austin, the son of the former mayor of the town. I told Austin that his father had once bet four hundred dollars on me and promised to give me fifty dollars of it if I won the game.

"Does anybody remember," I said, "why I didn't collect that fifty dollars?"

The one who nodded was McLean, so I said, "Mac won't mind if I repeat this story. We were playing Oneonta, and I was after my eighteenth victory in a row. We got to the ninth inning and were ahead two to one. There were two out, but Oneonta had a base runner (a guy named Reg Nash, who later became a famous coach up in Massachusetts). Reg's brother Ken (later a well-known Massachusetts judge) was at bat, and he hit a soft, looping liner over shortstop into left center field. I forgot to say that this baseball field was usually used as a cow pasture, and therefore when I tell you the baseball suddenly disappeared, you'll know what happened.

"My left fielder, who was running closest to the ball, came to a screeching halt. The center fielder ran over and also pulled up sharply. Both runners scored while they were trying to figure out a way of retrieving that ball." McLean laughed and said that's the way he remembered it too. That noon I went to lunch with the Peck family, whose parents had run the boardinghouse which I used to stay at; the Peck daughter is now married to the gent who runs the Walton paper.

After lunch I dressed at the hotel. When I got to the ball field, I saw it was the same Fairgrounds where I'd used to pitch. Same pitcher's mound. I was introduced to the crowd, which was standing all around the field because there was no grandstand; it had burned down. Listening to the introduction, I glanced around, and behind home plate, standing near my auto, was Margaret Guild, the girl I'd fallen out of the hammock with. I really felt misty.

Here I'd come into town driving an eighty-six-hundred-dollar Cadillac and that afternoon when I was getting ready for my appearance, I looked in the mirror and saw the battered top hat, the tail coat, and the baseball pants. As I drove to the ball park, I was still thinking how queer it was to be back here after forty-four years in this crazy costume, driving a car which I wouldn't have dreamed of owning even as a big-league pitcher.

"Ladies and gentlemen," I began hoarsely over the loudspeaker. "I'm sure glad to be back in Walton after . . . oh, a few days' lapse. Forty-four years ago yesterday, right off this same pitcher's mound, I pitched and won my first professional game. And I was getting four dollars a week and board. To show what a wonderful country we live in, if a guy just has enough ambition to take advantage of opportunities that knock on your door like they did for me, I come back here forty-four years later, and instead of getting four dollars a week, I'm not getting a damned dime!"

WITHDRAWN

myownparticulars00scha
myownparticulars00scha

myownparticulars00scha

Boston Public Library

COPLEY SQUARE
GENERAL LIBRARY

GV865
.S35A32

86818803-01

The Date Due Card in the pocket indicates the date on or before which this book should be returned to the Library.

Please do not remove cards from this pocket.

The 1955 Mutual Baseball Almanac

EDITED BY ROGER KAHN AND PAUL LAPOLLA

Here is a completely revised and enlarged edition of the popular baseball source book. For bleacher statisticians there is an original, ready-reference summary by Allan Roth that includes the batting, fielding, and pitching averages of 650 major and minor leaguers, grouped logically according to league and team within a compact, easy-to-read format. Other new features include a chapter on "What Makes an All-Star," plus the 1955 MUTUAL BASEBALL ALMANAC All-Star Team. This team includes such diamond greats as Stan Musial, Duke Snider, Willie Mays, Yogi Berra, and Bob Lemon, and each member of the team makes his own analysis of what makes an All-Star player. There is a section on the Little League, the greatest little big thing in baseball, and one telling in detail what scouts look for that even includes actual scouting reports. Another new feature is a simplified summary of the Rules of Baseball and the Rules of Scoring.

If you love baseball—and who doesn't?—you'll find this complete and up-to-date ALMANAC is a book you just can't get along without.

PRINTED IN THE U.S.A.

Printed in the USA
CPSIA information can be obtained
at www.ICGtesting.com
LVHW011511311023
762493LV00009BB/1205

9 781014 345936